Library of
Davidson College

The Essential Chaim Weizmann

The Essential Chaim Weizmann

The Man, the Statesman, the Scientist

Compiled and edited by
Barnet Litvinoff

Holmes & Meier Publishers, Inc.

First published in the United States of America 1982 by
Holmes & Meier Publishers, Inc.
IUB Building
30 Irving Place
New York, N. Y. 10003

Copyright © 1982 by Barnet Litvinoff
All rights reserved.

Library of Congress Cataloging in Publication Data
Main entry under title:

ISBN 0–8419–0823–0

Printed in Great Britain

Contents

Acknowledgments	VII
Introduction	IX
A Weizmann Chronology	1

1 The Road to Nationhood

The Arab Question	11
The Scheme for Jewish Settlement in East Africa	25
The Russian Revolution of 1905	36
The Russian Revolution of 1917	42
On Jewish Strength and Weakness	45
The Revival of Jerusalem	59
The Boundaries of Palestine	74
The British Connection	86
America and the Americans	94
The Hebrew University	108
The Jewish Situation between the Wars	116
The Jews and the Second World War	125
On Jewish Terrorism	143
Zionism and Judaism	150

2 Among his Contemporaries — **155**

3 The Leader Observed — **177**

4 Steps to the Balfour Declaration — **191**

5 As Chronicler of his Age — **203**

6 Advocate of his People: *Negotiations with*

Arthur James Balfour	217
David Lloyd George	218
Prince Faisal of Hedjaz	220
Jan C. Smuts	221
Winston Churchill	222
Woodrow Wilson	224

Léon Blum	226
Benito Mussolini	227
Franklin D. Roosevelt	228
King Ibn Saud	229
Harry S. Truman	230

7 Weizmann and the Zionist Congresses — 236

8 The Scientist — 243

Appendices

A The Weizmann Family	249
B The Basle Programme	250
C The Balfour Declaration	251
D The Faisal–Weizmann Agreement	252
E The Mandate for Palestine	254
F The MacDonald White Paper	263
G The Proclamation of Israel's Independence	273

Glossary	*276*
Bibliography	*278*
Index	*281*

Acknowledgments

Listed in the Bibliography are the many sources to which I feel indebted. I would particularly express appreciation to the Trustees of the Weizmann Archives in Rehovot, the Central Zionist Archives and Government State Archives in Jerusalem, the Public Record Office in London and the Zionist Archives and Library in New York.

I record my special thanks to the Beaverbrook Foundation for the passage quoted from *The War Memoirs of David Lloyd George*.

Introduction

While many nations have produced statesmen who were Jews, Chaim Weizmann was the only truly Jewish statesman of the twentieth century. His great forerunner in Zionism, Theodor Herzl, did not live to see the movement he founded grow beyond its beginnings as a minority interest group largely ignored by most of Jewry. His successor, David Ben-Gurion, led a new nation and spoke specifically as an Israeli, even questioning the validity of the international Zionist Organization once his independent state was created.

Weizmann bridged the two eras. For fully a half century he concerned himself with the needs, aspirations and limitations of his people. He decided how the Jewish world should organize behind Zionism after the First World War, and for thirty years he gave the desire for Jewish national rebirth its direction and emphasis. Perhaps this could have been done more effectively by another leader, but there was no one else of sufficient stature available for the task.

He was born an East European ghetto Jew in 1874, when spoken Hebrew was a rare and wondrous medium. The homeland was a concept floating between a dream of a golden future and the memory of a distant past, to be kept alive only by the force of religious practice. He died the President of a Jewish State which had been formed in 1948 through the intervention of the two superpowers in Palestine's affairs and as the result of a genocidal tragedy, and because the Jews successfully resisted a determined military effort to frustrate the state's birth.

In the interval he travelled the world, goading and cajoling his people like a prophet of old. He pleaded their cause among governments, shaped the pattern of the infant Jewish community in the Holy Land and wrestled against the inadequacies of his political apparatus, all the while conducting himself as a Prime Minister in exile.

Nationhood for Israel could not spring into life as it did with subject peoples released within their own terrain from long and alien servitude. The Jews had to be brought there; the land was already occupied by another race; the morality, as well as the practicality, of Zionism was vigorously disputed, among the Jews as much as the Gentiles. Weizmann won what he wanted, though he died before his vision of Arab–Jewish confraternity could be brought to realization in the Middle East. That goal is not yet attained. Perhaps it is unattainable, but Weizmann ennobled his cause by his striving for it.

The calibre of Jewish leadership on the international plane suffered in the present century because those most qualified for the role did not aspire to it. Zionism had the world's only concentric Jewish organization, and to lead it one had to subordinate sentiments of natural patriotism to the urge to be part of another nation. Louis D. Brandeis, for example, wished to remain and be remembered as an American, Léon Blum a Frenchman, Herbert Samuel an Englishman, Albert Einstein an internationalist. All of them were moved as Jews to assist the cause, but from a distance. Almost always those who contested Weizmann's fitness to lead, or who desired to replace him, were lesser men. Twice, in 1931 and 1946, the members of the Zionist Organization thought to dispense with him. On both occasions he had to be recalled to service.

Weizmann's greatest triumph was his success in linking Great Britain to the Zionist ideal with the Balfour Declaration of 1917. His greatest defeat was the MacDonald White Paper of 1939, which virtually barred the gates of Palestine to refugee Jews – again Britain. Weizmann nevertheless clung to the British connection. While his colleagues on the Jewish Agency Executive in Palestine regarded the Mandatory Power as their enemy, he saw it as their ally. A gulf thus opened between the 'reasonable' policies adopted by Weizmann and the 'activist' policies advocated by Ben-Gurion. The old leader spoke for the straggling international movement and with it the Jews as such, who were a vague quantity of uneven dedication to the ideal. Ben-Gurion personified the emerging, compact nation-in-miniature. After the Second World War it was time for the younger man to take over. As in Biblical days, when the Children of Israel wished no longer to be led by a prophet and demanded a king, so the leader bred from the debating chamber was eclipsed by the commander in the field.

For a true understanding of the nature of contemporary Jewish history it is important to recognize that the legend of Chaim Weizmann died in his own lifetime. The independent Jewish nation he did so much to create became as it were the burial-ground of his fame. The new Israel judged Jewish achievement by a catalogue of values different from those by which he lived. When Weizmann was the dominant personality in his people's story the community in Palestine remained a segment of the whole. Once Israel came into existence the situation was reversed. Israel made the far more numerous Jewish Diaspora the segment, and itself the whole.

Not that the Jews outside wished it otherwise. In many respects they regarded the transfer of their co-ordinated activities and responsibilities to this little country in the Eastern Mediterranean with relief, if not joy. They now craved for a more heroic stance, which only statehood could provide, because for centuries they had seen themselves as limbless, a collective nonentity. They felt they were the victims of history, not participants in it.

Though ranking with the world's statesmen, Weizmann had to struggle merely to obtain a hearing for the Jewish cause. The organization for which he spoke existed more on paper than in reality. He had no regular parliament to give him daily reassurance, or to reflect the wishes of an electorate as this is normally understood. He could not negotiate from strength when his only instrument was the force of his argument. But when Israel became a fact, with its own army, the Jews obtained in a few swift strokes of the sword all that Weizmann's rhetoric had failed to achieve in thirty years of diplomacy. Ben-Gurion had all along been convinced that some day the Arab relationship with the Jews would have to be settled by armed conflict. Weizmann on the other hand worked throughout his life to prevent such a conflict. In the circumstances, he retired as a figure-head President of Israel to the home and scientific institute he had built at Rehovot. Before long he was dead; not much longer, and he was forgotten.

It is history's quality to grant a perspective and restore the truth which immediacy distorts. The State of Israel has of late lost some of the enchantment it held for those who, in its earlier days, regarded Weizmann as a latter Patriarch. Problems with the Arabs have taken a new, more urgent form. Questions remain of national cohesion and the religious function within a state drawing its *raison d'être* from the Bible. The necessity has grown to look again at Weizmann's ideas on these pressing matters. The present volume acknowledges his exceptional role in giving Zionism its character as an undying Jewish instinct for cultural and physical self-preservation. We attempt to recapture his ideas exactly in the style he uttered them, together with his own idiosyncrasies of grammar and spelling.

He will be seen as a man with a profound sense of mission, but also one who perforce was daily engaged in the cut and thrust of political disputation. Weizmann the prophet was also Weizmann the tactician, a complex personality of human dimension. With all of this, there was a grandeur about his intervention in the Jewish destiny.

A Weizmann Chronology

1874 *27 November*	Born at Motol, village in White Russia, the third of Ozer and Rachel-Leah Weizmann's twelve children. Ozer was a timber merchant.
1885	Enters secondary school at Pinsk, where family settle some ten years later.
1892	Enrols as student of chemistry at Darmstadt Polytechnic, residing at a Jewish school in Pfungstadt where he teaches Russian and Hebrew.
1893	Enrols at Charlottenburg Polytechnic, Berlin, and joins Russian-Jewish Academic Society, forming lifelong friendships among its members.
1896	Meets Ahad Ha'am (Asher Z. Ginzberg), Hebrew essayist and protagonist of national renaissance, who becomes his mentor.
1897	Enrols at Fribourg University, Switzerland.
1898 *August*	Attends Second Zionist Congress, Basle, and is elected to Standing (Steering) Committee. About this time becomes engaged to Sophia Getzova of Minsk, medical student at Berne University, but breaks with her in 1902.
1899 *January*	PhD, Fribourg, *magna cum laude*. Appointed lecturer (*Privatdozent*) in Organic Chemistry at Geneva, his specialization being dye-stuffs.
1900 *August*	First visit to London, for Fourth Zionist Congress. Meets Vera Khatzman of Rostov-on-Don, medical student at Geneva, whom he was later to marry.
1901 *April*	Presides at conference of (mainly Russian) Zionist youth in Munich, to formulate a cultural programme as counterweight to Theodor Herzl's concentration on political aims.

December	Democratic Fraction, first separate party within Zionist Organization, is formed in Basle, prior to opening of Fifth Zionist Congress. Weizmann heads its Geneva Bureau, which also becomes headquarters of campaign for a Jewish University.
1902 *March*	Inaugurates University project as a main activity of Democratic Fraction. His closest associates are Berthold Feiwel and Martin Buber.
September–October	Undertakes propaganda and fund-raising tour for University project in Russia. Attends All-Russian Zionist Conference at Minsk.
1903 *April*	Police disperse a Zionist meeting being addressed by Weizmann at Minsk, but he escapes arrest. Kishinev pogrom diverts funds promised for University to victims' relief, halting activities of Geneva Bureau.
August	Democratic Fraction fails to make impact on Sixth Zionist Congress and peters out. Weizmann ranges with opposition against East Africa ('Uganda') scheme, and is elected to East Africa Commission (not the survey expedition). Decides to settle in England.
October	Visits London, discusses East Africa scheme with Earl Percy and Sir Clement Hill of Foreign Office, and with prominent Zionists. Prepares material for use by anti-Ugandist faction, which is led from Russia by Menaham Ussishkin.
1904 *July*	Death of Herzl leaves Zionist Organization in disarray. Weizmann settles in Manchester as research student in University's Chemistry Department. Meets Charles Dreyfus, prominent figure in local Conservative Party and President of Manchester Zionist Association, of which Weizmann joins committee.
1905 *January*	Appointed Research Fellow at Manchester University, with part-time employment in Clayton Aniline Company, of which Dreyfus is head. Brief meeting with Arthur J. Balfour, Prime Minister and MP for East Manchester. Elected Vice-President of Manchester Zionist Association.
July	Elected to Greater Actions Committee (also known as Zionist General Council) at Seventh Zionist Congress, where East Africa proposal is rejected.

December	Fall of Balfour Government. Winston Churchill, a junior minister in Liberal caretaker government, campaigns for election in Manchester constituency which includes Jewish district of Cheetham. Churchill speaks, with Moses Gaster and Weizmann, at protest meeting against Russian pogroms. Weizmann receives request from Churchill's election agent to use his influence among Jews, but passes this to David Wolffsohn, who has succeeded as President of Zionist Organization.
1906 *January*	Historic discussion with Balfour on Zionism, East Africa, etc. Meeting with Churchill.
June	Receives MSc degree from Manchester.
August	Marries Vera Khatzman at Zoppot, near Danzig.
1907 *February*	Elected Provincial Vice-President of English Zionist Federation, of which Gaster is elected President, thus marking victory of 'Practical' over 'Political' Zionists.
June	Birth of first son, Benjamin.
July	Receives DSc degree and appointed senior lecturer.
September	First visit to Palestine, to investigate prospects for agricultural industry there.
1908 *January*	Together with his Zionist intimates, Harry Sacher and Leon Simon, forms close association with Ahad Ha'am, who has settled in London.
1909 *March*	Begins vacation work in research at Pasteur Institute, Paris.
December	Elected to key position of chairman of Standing Committee at Ninth Zionist Congress (and Tenth Congress, 1911, and Eleventh Congress, 1913).
1910 *November*	Naturalized as British subject.
December	Applies for membership (FRS) of Royal Society, but this not achieved.
1911 *February*	After three years out of office, is again elected Vice-President of English Zionist Federation, which has been in state of disintegration since 1907. Joseph Cowen is elected EZF President.
1912 *January*	Proposes a Chemistry Department, with himself as Director, for projected Haifa Technical College.
1913 *March*	Nominated to direct renewed campaign for Hebrew University, to which he devotes all Zionist activity until outbreak of war.

May	Is passed over for professorship at Manchester, and appointed Reader in Biochemistry.
1914 January	First meeting with Baron Edmond de Rothschild, patron of Hebrew University project.
August	Outbreak of First World War finds him on holiday in Europe.
September	Meets C. P. Scott, editor of *Manchester Guardian*, who is a confidant of David Lloyd George.
November	Following entry of Turkey in war, decides that Zionism must be linked to Britain's cause, though this not policy of Zionist Organization. With this object reinforces contact with Scott, and meets Herbert Samuel, Jewish member of British Cabinet who has similar intention.
December	First meeting with Balfour since 1906.
1915 January	First meeting with Lloyd George, then Chancellor of Exchequer.
February	His acetone fermentation process inspected by representative of Nobel's Explosives Co.
June	Discusses Britain's shortage of explosives with Lloyd George, now Minister of Munitions in Coalition Cabinet, in which Balfour is First Lord of Admiralty.
July	Removes to London as chemical adviser on acetone supplies, Admiralty and Ministry of Munitions.
1916 April	Appointed Superintendent of Admiralty laboratories at Lister Institute.
November	Birth of second son, Michael.
1917 February	Participates in meeting of leading Zionists with Sir Mark Sykes, Middle East expert in Cabinet Secretariat. Becomes President of English Zionist Federation in uncontested election.
May	Makes public announcement that Britain supported creation of Jewish Commonwealth in Palestine.
July	Sent by Foreign Office to Gibraltar to dissuade Henry Morgenthau Sr from pursuing a plan for a separate peace with Turkey.
2 November	Balfour Declaration issued. Sends Aaron Aaronsohn to USA to stimulate recruitment in Jewish regiment of British Army.
December	Appeals to Russian Jewish merchants, now that Russia is discussing separate peace, to prevent food and other supplies reaching Central Powers from Black Sea ports.

A WEIZMANN CHRONOLOGY

1918
March — Received by King George V.
April — Arrives in Palestine at head of Zionist Commission, remaining till September.
June — Visits Prince Faisal at Arab HQ at Waheida, near Ma'an.
July — Presides at dedication of Hebrew University site on Mount Scopus.

1919
January — Weizmann–Faisal Agreement on future Arab–Jewish co-operation signed in London. Meeting in Paris with President Woodrow Wilson. Is formally co-opted to Zionist Executive.
February — With Nahum Sokolow, presents Zionist case to Council of Ten at Paris Peace Conference.
June — First meeting with Louis D. Brandeis.

1920
April — Present with Sokolow and Samuel at San Remo Allied Conference, where Palestine Mandate is awarded to Britain and Samuel appointed High Commissioner.
July — Elected unopposed as President of World Zionist Organization, with Sokolow as chairman of Executive. Rift between Weizmann and Brandeis.

1921
April — First visit to USA (accompanied by Albert Einstein and others) to launch *Keren Hayesod* fund-raising campaign. Received by President Warren Harding.
June — Pro-Brandeis faction withdraws from Zionist Organization of America following Cleveland Conference. Contracts with Commercial Solvents Corporation of Terre Haute, Indiana, for industrial application of his patents.

1922
June — Formally accepts Churchill White Paper on behalf of Zionist Executive, following which (July) League of Nations ratifies Palestine Mandate.
October–November — Is target of virulent anti-Zionist campaign in British Press. Begins discussions towards forming expanded Jewish Agency by inclusion of non-Zionist elements.

1923
January — First meeting with Benito Mussolini.
December — Presents plan for Jewish Agency to meeting of Jewish leaders convened by Louis Marshall in New York.

1924
September–October — First visit to Palestine in two years, for comprehensive tour of country under impact of vastly increased immigration resulting from American restrictions on East European immigration.

1925 April	Participates with Balfour at inauguration of Hebrew University.
September	Elected with Einstein Joint President of Hebrew University Board.
1926 March	Wins High Court action against pre-war scientific colleagues for infringement of his fermentation patent.
November	Received by President Calvin Coolidge.
1927 September	With economic crisis and unemployment in Palestine, initiates appointment by Zionist Congress of non-party triumvirate as Palestine Executive with plenary powers.
1928 January	Clashes with Judah Magnes over latter's administration of Hebrew University.
March–May	Faces storm of criticism in USA, led by Stephen Wise, over conduct of Zionist affairs.
1929 August	Inaugurates enlarged Jewish Agency at Zurich, with himself as President, Edmond de Rothschild as Hon. President. Serious Arab rioting in Palestine results in 250 Jewish and Arab dead. Accuses British Administration of hostility towards Jewish National Home policy.
1930 October	Resigns Presidency of Jewish Agency and Zionist Organization in protest against Passfield White Paper.
November	Prime Minister Ramsay MacDonald assures Weizmann of his goodwill and authorizes Cabinet sub-committee to negotiate a revised statement with Zionists.
1931 February	Receives MacDonald Letter, vindicating Zionist activities.
July	His reported statement that 'Jewish majority not necessary' causes furore at Zionist Congress, and he is not re-elected to Presidency. Succeeded by Sokolow.
1932 February–May	In South Africa on fund-raising mission.
June	Is refused facilities for chemistry research at Hebrew University, and decides to open his own institute elsewhere in Palestine.
1933 March	With endowment from family of Israel Sieff, plans Daniel Sieff Research Institute at Rehovot.
April	Together with Magnes, invites Einstein, who due to Hitler has renounced German citizenship, to work at Hebrew University (offer is declined).

July	Given spectacular reception at Chicago's World Fair, to raise funds for German Jewry.
August	Nominated in his absence by Zionist Congress to head Jewish Agency Department for Settlement of German Refugees.
1934 *April*	Inaugurates Daniel Sieff Research Institute.
1935 *August*	Reconciliation with Stephen Wise and re-election to Presidency at Zionist Congress, with David Ben-Gurion as chairman of Executive. Revisionists, led by Vladimir Jabotinsky, leave Zionist Organization.
1936 *April*	Arab rebellion in Palestine.
June	Begins discussions with Nuri es-Said of Iraq and other non-Palestinian Arabs as likely mediators to effect peace.
November–December	Gives evidence before Royal (Peel) Commission on Palestine.
1937 *January*	Informally told of partition plan for Palestine, which he accepts in principle. Visits Prime Minister Léon Blum in Paris to win his support.
August	Is empowered by Zionist Congress to negotiate with Britain on basis of partition, which Arabs have rejected.
1938 *January*	Agitates for speedy action on partition as government indicates reluctance to implement this solution.
March	Contracts with American publisher for his memoirs.
November	Visits Turkey, bringing proposal for Jewish help in developing Turkish industry. Hopes also to win Turkish goodwill to influence Arabs, and to assess Turkish intentions in event of war between Britain and Germany.
1939 *February*	Heads Jewish delegation to St James's Conference, which ends in failure, with MacDonald White Paper rendering Jews a permanent minority in an eventual independent State of Palestine.
May	Enlists support of British public figures, including Archbishop of Canterbury and Churchill, for debates in Lords and Commons on government's Palestine policy, which in consequence is approved with much diminished majority.
August	As war appears inevitable, offers Prime Minister Neville Chamberlain full Jewish co-operation in struggle against Hitler.

September	Proposes Jewish Division under own flag. Pleads for suspension of White Paper regulations for duration of emergency.
October	Enters into discussions with Harry St John Philby for co-operation in Middle East with King Ibn Saud.
1940 *February*	First interview with President Franklin D. Roosevelt.
May	Is charged by Ben-Gurion with weakness vis-à-vis Britain, marking beginning of long conflict.
July	Appointed Hon. Chemical Adviser to Ministry of Supply. Jewish Division sanctioned in principle.
1941 *March*	Notified of postponement for six months of Jewish military formation, on grounds of lack of equipment.
November	With continued procrastination in implementing plan for Jewish force, he makes negotiations public in major speech.
1942 *January*	Publishes article in *Foreign Affairs* advocating Jewish State in Palestine.
February	Younger son Michael lost on RAF mission over Bay of Biscay.
May	Zionist Conference in New York, with Weizmann and Ben-Gurion as main speakers, demands Palestine as Jewish Commonwealth.
August–November	Activities restricted through severe breakdown of health.
1943 *January*	Seeks to create pro-Zionist lobby in Washington from among Roosevelt's immediate advisers. Initiates efforts to form united front in American Jewry to consolidate Zionist action.
April	Submits memorandum to Anglo-American Bermuda Conference on refugees, relating to Palestine's preparedness for refugee absorption.
June	Third and final meeting with Roosevelt.
July	Returns to London after fifteen months in the USA.
1944 *March*	Renews demand for Jewish formation, to participate in liberation of Europe.
July	Accompanied by Moshe Shertok (Sharett) meets Anthony Eden, Foreign Secretary, to request positive response to Brand mission, relating to exchange of Jews for supplies to Germany, and to bomb extermination centres.

August	Informed of approval for creation of Jewish Brigade Group.
November	At meeting with Churchill learns of possible solution of Palestine problem by partition. Assassination of Lord Moyne, which leads Churchill to abandon any contemplated action. Arrives in Palestine for first visit in five years, and is acclaimed on his seventieth birthday.
1945 August	At first post-war World Zionist Conference Weizmann is at odds with Ben-Gurion and Abba Hillel Silver, American leader, who advocate active resistance in Palestine because of government's refusal to grant immediate immigration to 100,000 European survivors. Operations are undertaken by *Haganah* in association with *Irgun Zvai Leumi* and Stern Group, without Weizmann's sanction. British security forces and Jews in open conflict.
1946 March	Gives evidence in Jerusalem to Anglo-American Committee of Enquiry.
June	Sends ultimatum to Jewish Agency activists to stop anti-British outrages, or he would resign. The Agency reverts to diplomatic struggle, though *Irgun* and Stern continue terrorist activities.
December	Fails to gain re-election as President at Zionist Congress. The office is left vacant, Ben-Gurion and Silver being joint chairmen.
1947 July	Gives evidence, in his private capacity, to UN Special Committee on Palestine. Awarded honorary doctorate by Hebrew University.
October	Addresses UN Ad Hoc Committee in New York, and remains to strengthen Jewish Agency efforts among delegations for an affirmative vote in partition proposal.
November	Visits President Harry S. Truman to persuade him of importance of retaining Negev in contemplated Jewish State. General Assembly votes for partition, with necessary two-thirds majority.
1948 February	Returns to America in response to plea by Agency leaders, who fear American *volte-face* on statehood.
March	Intercedes personally with Truman again.
May	Advises Jewish leaders in Palestine to proclaim independence. Elected President, Provisional State Council of Israel.

1949 *February*	After General Election in Israel, is sworn in as President. Publication of *Trial and Error*.
November	Formal inauguration of Weizmann Institute of Science at Rehovot. General Smuts is principal speaker at London banquet to commemorate seventy-fifth birthday of Weizmann and inauguration of Weizmann Forest in Israel. Physical weakness, and near-blindness, keeps him at his home in Rehovot for the rest of his life.
1951 *November*	Takes second oath of office from his sick-bed on re-election as President.
1952 *9 November*	Dies at Rehovot.

I
The Road to Nationhood

The Arab Question

Weizmann's attitude towards the Arabs evolved from early assumptions, typical of European thinking prior to the First World War, that colonization by Europeans need take no account of the susceptibilities of native peoples. He later came to realize that Arab national feeling could not be ignored. He then began to work for a Zionist policy that would allay Arab fears and make for harmonious co-existence.

Arab labour in the early Jewish colonies
The colonies are slowly progressing, and the colonists are learning to be self-reliant, and they are laying the foundations of the coming Jewish State. However, the welfare of the colonies is seriously affected by the Arab labour question. Sixty to 80 per cent of the labourers are Arabs; in Petach Tikvah 800 out of 1,000 labourers, while in Zichron Ya'acov 400 Arab labourers live in the colony. This involves two issues: a) Arabs are being civilized at the expense of their Jewish neighbours, and b) it places the prosperity of the Jewish colonies too much in the hands of the Arab population. The Arab retains his primitive attachment to the land, the soil-instinct is strong in him, and by being continuously employed on it there is a danger that he might feel himself indispensable to it, with a moral right to it.

The colonies cannot be regarded as really Jewish so long as Arabs form so powerful a part of the labour force.
From a speech in Manchester, October 1907, following his first visit to Palestine.

Stirrings of Arab nationalism
There is alarming news from Syria about the Arab national movement. With the weakening of central authority in Constantinople, the periphery of Asia Minor is beginning to totter. And the Arabs are beginning to organize, though in a very primitive manner. They consider Palestine their own and have embarked on an intensive

propaganda campaign in their semi-national, semi-Christian and 'semi-antisemitic' – an expression that can hardly apply to the Arabs – Press against the selling of land to 'Zionists', the enemies of Turkey and the usurpers of Palestine. We shall soon face a serious enemy.
From a letter to his wife. Manchester, 23 February 1913.

Address to Arab communal leaders in Jerusalem
It is with a sense of grave responsibility that I rise to speak on this momentous occasion. I wish to speak of peace, harmony and co-operation between the communities represented here. It is true that we are still surrounded by dire and dismal realities. It is true we can still hear the thunder of guns within a few miles from us, and destructive weapons still pass over this roof, but one cannot help feeling, as I am sure you all must, there is something mystical and great, almost supernatural, presiding over our meeting.

Here my forefathers stood 2,000 years ago. Here they taught. From here they sent forth the great message. They sent it forth to the world almost like bread cast upon the waters, and now the waters have brought this bread back to us, their descendants, and here we are tonight united under the wing of the mightiest of the world's Powers, which is fighting for the great ideals rooted in the lore of the old Prophets of Palestine. Here our seers and poets proclaimed the universal ideals of justice and peace, ideals which our legislators translated into realities, and here we are the guests of the representative of the greatest of the Bible-loving nations. This great nation has told us that our work, which was accomplished in this country centuries ago, has not been forgotten, and that our long devotion to this country has found recognition. Truly it is not all accident – it is destiny.

I am not a stranger to this country, although born and bred in the remote north. Neither is anyone of my scattered brethren a stranger to it. By mighty efforts, wars, and revolutions, did our forefathers heroically defend their inviolable right to this sacred place, and only after having been overwhelmed by a fate more sanguinary and more cruel than even the present fate of Belgium and Armenia, they lost their physical hold upon Palestine. But our ancestors did not relinquish their claims to it. Instead of a political Palestine they set up a moral and intellectual Palestine, which triumphantly resisted the onslaughts of every conceivable destructive force.

We therefore do not come to Palestine: we return to it. We return in order to link up our glorious ancient traditions of the past with the future, in order to create once more a great moral and intellectual centre from which perhaps a new world will come forth to a sorely-tried world. That is for us the innermost meaning of a National Home. But a centre like that, in order to be real, must lean on real props. It must have roots in the earth, it must derive its strength from the soil of Palestine. We desire therefore to create conditions under which the material and moral development of those of our people who have chosen freely to come here will be rendered possible; and we are convinced that it will, it must be, made possible, not to the detriment of any of the great communities already established in this country, but on the contrary to their advantage. There is land enough and room enough in Palestine, and this I have been told by many of your own leading people, to sustain a population many times larger than the present one. And all the fears which have been expressed openly and secretly by the Arabs, that they are to be ousted from their present position, are due either to a fundamental misconception of our aims and intentions or to the malicious activities of our common enemies. Both morally and materially it is to our interest to live in friendship and peace. It is only under such conditions that the great development of this country is possible.

Our pioneers here have shown that even under the deadening Turkish regime they were capable of transforming the desert into flourishing villages. How much more could an industrious, diligent and intelligent population achieve under civilized conditions, under a just and strong government! They could readily transform Palestine once more into a land flowing with milk and honey, and the benefits of this transformation will be enjoyed equally by all the inhabitants of the country. That is a sincere expression of our aims, and I solemnly warn you against all misinterpretations or false allegations. Do not believe those who insinuate that we intend to take supreme political power of this country into our hands at the end of the war. We know too well the burdens and responsibilities of a government, and I think that Jews and Arabs alike have carefully watched the fate of Albania and the fate of Russia. These two severe lessons teach us the great truth that self-government in modern times is a complicated science, and that people cannot be educated to it in one day. It needs a long and hard apprenticeship under well-trained and trustworthy teachers, and we Zionists declare that we desire the supreme political authority in this country to be vested in one of the civilized democratic Powers, which should be selected for this purpose by the League of Nations. We desire this Power to hold Palestine in trust until the population becomes capable of self-government.

It is not for me to say at the present stage which Power it should be, but Jewry before long will make up its mind, and I think that when the happy day of peace arrives, it will raise its voice and speak its opinion, and will demand to be heard on this all-important point, with which it is vitally concerned. But let me say only, at the present stage, that we do not believe that the internationalization of Palestine, or any partition, or any form of dual or multiple control, can benefit this country. Palestine in its integrity must have one just and fair guardian, and only one. We watch with deepest sympathy and profound interest the struggle for freedom which the ancient Arab race is now waging. We see the scattered Arab forces being cemented and united under the sympathies of the Entente and freedom-loving Powers, and new and mighty political possibilities shine through the thick fog created by the war. Once more we see rising a strong and regenerated Arab political organism, which will revive the glorious traditions of Arab science, and literature, so much akin to our own. This kinship found its most glorious expression in the Spanish period of Judeo-Arab development, when the best of our writers wrote and taught in the Arab tongue as freely as they did in Hebrew.

To the north, further away beyond the mountain range, the Armenian nation, which at present is paying the bloodiest toll to a cruel enemy, will in the end rise triumphantly and proudly claim justice and the right to live in peace on the soil which is being drenched with the blood of the best of its sons, and it will obtain this right. To this nation our hearts go out, and we feel that these three nations, Arabs, Jews and Armenians, who have suffered the most in the world, have perhaps the highest claim to a life of their own – to a life of freedom and peaceful development. Destiny has chosen these three nations to guard the classical gate into the ancient world, to guard it against the Turanian hordes which, armed by the deadliest of modern weapons, are being organized by their taskmasters in the steppes of the Urals and Turkestan. We Jews are already beginning to feel the effects of this new menace; our communities in that part of the world are being ruthlessly destroyed. The Armenian massacres in the Caucasus, the Jewish massacres in Turkestan, should serve as a warning to all of us. They should teach us that we must stand united in order to resist the forces of darkness which threaten to overwhelm the civilized world. If this guard of freedom stands firm, Palestine may look confidently to a future as great as its past. It will become a link between East and West, interpreting the one to the other and harmonizing their different but not opposing conceptions of life. I think that our people are eminently fitted to perform this honourable task. We ask only for the opportunity of free national development in Palestine, and in justice it cannot be refused. We want to cultivate the long-neglected land by modern methods, and under a just economic system, avoiding the evils from which the advanced countries of Europe are only now beginning to free themselves. We want also – and here I mention what will perhaps be regarded in future as the coping-stone of our present work – to help to make Palestine once more a fountain of knowledge and idealism through the creation of a Hebrew University, a great intellectual centre open to every man, in which the ancient truths of our Prophets will obtain expression in a modern form. In all this work, whether agricultural or intellectual, we shall not be injuring our neighbours in Palestine. On the contrary, we shall be helping them towards a fuller and richer life. I would ask you not to underrate the measure of our help. Though we are but few as yet in Palestine, the eyes of our scattered people in every corner of the globe are fixed on what we are doing here, and the Jewish communities of the west are not without their influence in the councils of the nations.

This city of Jerusalem, in which I speak tonight, is for us Jews a holy shrine. For that reason we are able to respect the sentiments of others for whom Jerusalem is sacred. We wish to interfere in no way with the Holy Places to which the hearts of Moslems or of Christians turn with reverence. We wish to live at peace with all, on the basis of mutual regard and mutual respect. A message of goodwill going forth from Jerusalem will do much to allay fears and suspicions, to bring to the stricken masses of our fellow-men the hope of a new and better world. The hand of God rests now on the peoples of Europe. Let us unite in a prayer that it may rest lightly.

Speech delivered in English, 27 April 1918, and translated by Sir Ronald Storrs, Military Governor of Jerusalem, who presided.

First meeting with Emir Faisal
Minutes of discussion lasting three-quarters of an hour:
1. After a cordial exchange of greetings Dr Weizmann pointed out that he had been sent by the British Government to enquire into the development of the Jewish interests in Palestine and amongst other instructions the most important one was for him to get into touch with Arab leaders and try and co-operate with them.
2. At this point Shereef Faisal expressed his opinion of the necessity for co-operation between Jews and Arabs. He referred to the historical tradition of both races, and at the present time the need of close co-operation was necessary to both.
3. About any definite political arrangements Shereef Faisal was unwilling to express an opinion, pointing out that in questions of politics he was acting merely as his father's agent and not in a position

to discuss. As regards the future he considered the interests of both Jews and Arabs must be closely allied together.

4. Dr Weizmann pointed out that the formation of the existence of a Jewish Palestine would be helpful to the development of an Arab Kingdom and the development of an Arab Kingdom would receive Jewish support.

5. Dr Weizmann pointed out that the Jews do not propose setting up a Jewish Government but would like to work under British protection with a view to colonizing and developing the country without in any way encroaching on anybody's legitimate interests.

6. Shereef Faisal declared that as an Arab he could not discuss the future of Palestine either as a Jewish colony or a country under British protection. These questions were already the subject of much German and Turkish propaganda and would undoubtedly be misinterpreted by the uneducated Bedouin if openly discussed. Later on when Arab affairs were more consolidated these questions could be brought up. Shereef Faisal personally accepted the possibility of future claims to territory in Palestine which Dr Weizmann emphasized, but could not discuss them publicly officially as he was in no way representing the Arab Government and was greatly afraid of the dangers of enemy propaganda. He again emphasized the necessity for close co-operation between Jews and Arabs for the mutual benefit of both.

7. Dr Weizmann explained that he was proceeding shortly to America and that the influence of the Jews both in that country and elsewhere would be . . . Wilson . . . and the sincerity . . . and would use the Jewish influence . . . in that country and elsewhere in favour of the Arab movement and the formation of an Arab Kingdom. This statement of Dr Weizmann's afforded Shereef Faisal great satisfaction.

The interview ended with mutual cordial expressions of entente and an invitation from Shereef Faisal that the meeting might be renewed after Dr Weizmann's visit to America.

Meeting at Faisal's camp, Waheida, near Ma'an, 4 June 1918. Minutes by Colonel P. C. Joyce, British Army.

'Palestine must be a Jewish country'
The Prime Minister had found it necessary to ask me to go out to Palestine, the irony being that I should go out to Palestine to quieten the Jews. It is the Arabs who threaten us with massacre and therefore it is just the reverse – the Arabs have to be quieted down and not the Jews. I am quite ready to go out and I think I shall go. I am charged with the mission of making peace between the Arabs and the Jews. The only way to make peace between the Arabs and the Jews is to get the Jews to

start work, and show that we do not want to take away the Arabs' land. I repeat what I said at the beginning: whether Jewish blood is going to be spilt in Palestine or whether it is spilt in Pinsk or anywhere else, we are quite blasé in these matters. We have decided to go, and we shall go, to Palestine. . . . My hope . . . is that Palestine will be a Jewish country. I make no bones about it. The question is only 'When?'
From minutes of meeting of Zionist Advisory Committee with British Middle East experts attached to British Delegation to Paris Peace Conference. London, 10 May 1919.

'There is room for both of us'
The Arabs are not strangers, they have lived in the country for centuries. They are a primitive people, and they do not wish to leave Palestine as we enter Palestine. We say: 'There is room both for you and for us; you will benefit by our coming in, and we shall benefit by friendly relations between you and us.' . . . We cannot go into the country like Junkers: we cannot afford to drive out other people. We who have been driven out ourselves cannot drive out others. We shall be the last people to drive off the *fellah* from his land; we shall establish normal relations between us and them. The Arabs will live among us, they won't suffer. They will live among us as the Jews do here in England. That is our attitude towards the Arabs. Any other attitude is criminal, childish, impolitic, stupid.
From an address to English Zionists. London, 21 September 1919.

Arab attacks upon the Jews first occurred in 1920: in Upper Galilee, where they were mistaken for French colonists, and in Jerusalem. Far more serious were the May Day riots of 1921, mainly in Jaffa, where forty-seven Jews and forty-eight Arabs died.

'The Arab movement is anti-European'
It is difficult to understand how one can build on Arab loyalty so near the vital communications across the isthmus of Suez. All one has seen and heard of the Arab movement leads one to believe that it is anti-European.
From a draft letter, never despatched, to Winston Churchill, Secretary of State for Colonies. London, November 1921.

'The Arabs now a factor'
Nowhere in Herzl's writings, and not in his newly published diaries, is there a word about the question which today is almost the central problem of our movement, the Arab question. In Herzl's time, the Arabs did not exist politically. Today they are there. There lives a people in Palestine that does not wish the Jewish people to gain ground

there. This is wrong, but it is a fact which you, we and the British statesmen have daily to take into consideration.
From an address to the Annual Zionist Conference. Carlsbad, 25 August 1922.

Buying Arab goodwill
Those Arabs who will choose constructive, constitutional methods and who will co-operate with the government, and possibly with us, are bound in the long run to win the day, more particularly as the *fellaheen* are beginning to feel tired of political excitement, which costs them money and which is partly responsible for the economic crisis prevailing in the country.

All these causes, which we have examined carefully on the spot together with your Representatives and with those Palestinians who know something about the Arab movement, have brought us to the conclusion that concerted and systematic action should begin immediately, this action to have the following objects in view.

A. To help in the organization of moderate opinion contrary to the practice prevailing hitherto. Definitely to abstain from giving sums of money to individual Arabs without asking them for a specific equivalent in form of work. We shall still maintain the Moslem Societies formed by Mr Kalvarisky but we have distinctly pointed out to the people concerned that we do not propose to pay vast sums, and we have reduced their budgets to about one-third of the original size. In Jerusalem, for instance, where about £360 a month was being spent, we have reduced the cost to £100 a month. This applies also to Tiberias and Haifa. At the same time we have demanded from the people public action in favour of co-operation, on the basis of the Mandate, between all sections of the population. The last letter received from Colonel Kisch confirms me in this point of view, and although at the time there was an outcry by the Arabs because we were depriving them of their subsidy, nevertheless they will be glad in the end to receive this small sum and they will respect us more if we demand some results for it.

B. The Moslem-Christian Societies, which are losing ground in the country, must be further obstructed, and this can be done by dealing separately with the Moslems and Christians. We intend to start two small reviews, one run in Palestine by Christian-Arabs and the other run in Egypt by Palestinian-Moslems. These reviews would group round them the most intelligent people of the Moslem-Christian Societies, and they will influence opinion from both sides in favour of co-operation.

C. We shall advance to Sheikhs in the villages small sums on definite security but on long term. It is a mistake to advance vast sums, but with small loans distributed in important centres one obtains more effect than with a large sum thrown into the lap of a single *Effendi*. I am aware of the fact that probably half of this money will never be recovered but it is, I think, well spent in view of the situation.

We have drawn up a detailed budget of which a copy will be presented to you after I have received it in its final form from Palestine. This budget covers the following heads. The Reviews – maintenance of National Moslem Societies – a certain amount of propaganda literature – the loans – maintenance of a small office dealing with all these questions. For this we should need a sum of about £15,000 to £20,000 a year. This budget will be covered partly by the Zionist Organization, which is contributing about £9,000 a year, partly by the Egyptian Jewish community which is particularly interested in this work.

From a letter to Gaston Wormser, aide to Baron Edmond de Rothschild. London, February 1923.

Palestine not empty

Palestine is not an empty country. It contains today about 600,000 non-Jews, the overwhelming majority Moslems, a small minority of Christians and another small minority of Jews. Roughly, there are 500,000 Moslems, 100,000 Christians and 100,000 Jews. We recognize that since the war, and even earlier, there has been a striving on the part of the Arab people for a revival; and being anxious for the revival of the scattered Jewish people, we treat with respect and reverence any attempt of revival amongst other people. We are the last, and should be the last, to look down on other people and say: 'You cannot do it.' We shall assume that Arab culture will blossom again as it had in Spain, as it had when Europe was completely in darkness, for it was the Arab people together with the Jews who were the bearers of the torch and the preservers of civilization, who prepared and paved the way for the great renaissance which followed. We recognize today that between us and the Arabs in the Near East, and particularly in Palestine, stand many forces – perhaps destructive forces – which try to emphasize this estrangement which has taken place between two races which are akin to each other. But we also see at present in Palestine that the tendency which was so marked three or four years ago, the tendency of two entrenched camps watching each other with suspicion, is gradually declining. We are trying to co-operate with them. We work with them. We are looked upon with a certain amount of suspicion. We are looked upon with suspicion particularly because to the Eastern races we represent the West, and the West is looked upon with suspicion at present in the Near East. The various tribulations through which

Europe and the East is passing today, Bolshevism, Kemalism, the unsettlement of European affairs, the fact that no conference of European Powers comes to any definite issue, all this reflects on the fancy of an Oriental people. Every rumour in the Press is exaggerated. Every vibration in the political world is reflected and exaggerated in Palestine.

Palestine is a peculiar country. There is no other country in the world where the distance between the sublime and the ridiculous is so small. One stands constantly with one foot in the sublime, for eighteen generations gaze down. Palestine is like a sounding-board. Every noise is blazoned forth over the world. If a Jew is killed in Piccadilly, in the Ukraine, or run over by a motor-car on Broadway, it is an ordinary affair. If something of this kind happens in the Holy Land, it becomes an act of state, an act of violence, two races clashing with each other. All these factors, the unsettlement in Europe, the tribulations of Europe, mental and moral strife, contribute to make life in Palestine much more difficult than elsewhere.

From a speech to Jewish journalists. New York, 13 March 1923.

'Palestine is not Rhodesia'

I admit that by a political impression, by an effective speech or demonstration, some minister or official may be influenced, but that is only for the moment. Once the moment has passed there comes the reaction for which one has permanently to pay. I will not conceal from Jabotinsky, and certainly I am making no personal attack (it is hardly necessary to say that our personal relations remain those that are customary among gentlemen): I helped you against the will of my friends according to the measure of my powers at the time of the raising of the Legion, because at that time I could go along with you. I would, however, regard such a demand today not only as useless but even as harmful. The key to the situation lies in another direction. Not in the 900,000 dunams which the government can or cannot give us. Not in the *Machlul* lands, not on the hills of Judea, the cultivation of which costs perhaps twenty times as much as the government has to be paid for rent. The key lies in opening up the Near East to Jewish initiative in real friendship and co-operation with the Arabs. Palestine must be built up without disturbing a hair of the legitimate interests of the Arabs. The Zionist Congress must not confine itself to platonic formulae. It must recognize the fact that Palestine is not Rhodesia, but that 600,000 Arabs are there who, from the point of view of international justice, have just as much right to their life in Palestine as we have to our National Home.

So long as we fail to make this idea part of ourselves, you will seek artificial narcotics and wax enthusiastic for things of the future – and our Jews, who are suffering, are very prone to do this – but you will see the future in a false light. Only if we refrain from that sort of thing and work in this direction have we any prospect of obtaining the credit that we need in order to secure for our natural biological expansion the empty places of the earth. It is a difficult road, a road that the best of us follow with great effort. What the Syrians and the Romans in Palestine, what the Germans in Poland, failed to do, the British Government in Palestine will also not be able to do. It will not dislodge the *fellaheen* in favour of the Jews. We must take Palestine as it is, with the sand dunes and the rocks, with the Arabs and the Jews as they come. That is our work. Everything else is make-believe.
From an address to the Fourteenth Zionist Congress. Vienna, 23 August 1925.

The Jewish Agency, which brought non-Zionists into partnership with the Zionist Organization for the development of Jewish Palestine, was formed on 11 August 1929. Later that month Arabs made a concerted assault upon Jews in Jerusalem, Hebron, Safed and elsewhere. The toll was 133 Jews and 116 Arabs killed, the latter mainly by British security forces pacifying the country.

Terms for Arab–Jewish peace
I believe that negotiations with the Arabs are only possible on one condition, namely if the government were to make clear to the Arabs that they firmly intend to carry out the Mandate. If they do not do so, the Arabs will believe – and rightly so – that we have been abandoned by Britain and they will not then have much interest in linking themselves with us. They do not yet understand or do not want to understand what we are bringing them, and what real friendship between us could mean to the world as well. They are too primitive for that and too much under the influence of factors such as Bolshevik, Catholic agitation. The Arab people have not yet spoken; the spokesmen of the people today are corrupt Levantines, such as the Mufti and the like. I have explained to Ramsay MacDonald, and have also given it to him in writing, that we are prepared to sit round a table with the Arabs, but that he – MacDonald – must make it clear to them that the Mandate, National Home, etc., are *choses jugées*. If they accept this, we will also accept a Palestinian parliament, but it must be of a kind that is not a dagger in our back. There are only two alternatives: either we can go to Palestine as of right or we are foreigners who slip in through good manners and through money. If the world does not recognize our proper right, that is an error on the world's part and a

misfortune for us, and I know the world has misunderstood us for two thousand years. We have no desire to rule over anybody, but we also do not want to bow down before anybody or be ruled by anybody – enough of that! Little Palestine was the one place on earth where we stood upright. . . .

I have never been a firebrand, as you know from the whole of my past. I have always preached most unpopular realities to the Zionists, have always been attacked most bitterly. I too believe in an agreement with the Arabs; it is necessary for us, for the Arabs and for the English, but all three parties must assist and – give and take. So far we have done all the giving, have already explained to the Arabs what we are prepared to do, and that over the fresh graves of our brethren. The Arabs have not even once expressed regret for what has occurred.
From a letter to Albert Einstein. London, 30 November 1929.

'We should be content with a bi-national State'
The declaration in favour of the Jewish National Home in Palestine was naturally coupled with a guarantee for the 'civil and religious rights' of the non-Jews in the country; there was to be absolute equality of individual rights between Jews and Arabs. Still, as far as political 'group rights' were concerned, there can be no doubt that the picture in the minds of those who drafted the Balfour Declaration and the Mandate was that of a Jewish Commonwealth in Palestine. Palestine was to be a Jewish State in which the Arabs would enjoy the fullest civil and cultural rights; but for the expression of their own national individuality in terms of statehood they were to turn to the surrounding Arab countries – Syria, Iraq, Hedjaz, etc. – a position shared by fragments of even the most powerful and highly civilized European nations. . . .

Now we should be content with a bi-national State, provided it was truly bi-national.
From a letter to James Marshall. London, 17 January 1930.

Zionism and statehood not identical
I come to a proposition regarding which I can make myself very unpopular: the Jewish State and Zionism are identical. This is not true. It is incorrect that the Basle Programme and the Balfour Declaration imply a Jewish State. Anyone short of an argument in a fight with the Executive drags Herzl from his grave and waves his pamphlet with the title 'The Jewish State'. In my view the essence of Zionism is to create a number of material foundations upon which a national-Jewish commonwealth can develop. This surely is not a Jewish State, and most certainly not a Jewish State in the sense of the old Prussian State. It is

untrue that the Palestine Mandate has underwritten a Jewish State. Perhaps it is true that Lord Balfour and Lord Robert Cecil thought originally in terms of a Jewish State. So did I. But the Mandate was formulated as the mists of war conditions dispersed, and we came down to reality: not a Jewish State, or Palestine as a Jewish National Home, but a Jewish National Home in Palestine. . . .

I too believed at one time that Palestine could be as Jewish as England is English. After a difficult struggle I persuaded myself that this could not now be. . . . The awakening of the Orient has progressed more quickly than we considered possible. . . . Certainly, we have rights in Palestine. But the Arabs too have a claim on the land. Of course, we are a state-forming element in Palestine, but so are they. We shall endeavour to bring the maximum number of people to Palestine, and when we become the majority there we shall not dominate the Arabs, just as we would not allow ourselves to be dominated while we are the minority.

From his reply to a discussion at the Zionist General Council. Berlin, 27 August 1930.

'Jews do not need to be a majority in Palestine'

I have no sympathy or understanding for the demand for a Jewish majority. A majority does not necessarily guarantee security. We may have a majority and still be insecure. A majority is not required for the development of Jewish civilization and culture. The world will construe this demand only in one sense, that we want to acquire a majority in order to drive out the Arabs.

From an interview with the Jewish Telegraphic Agency. Basle, 3 July 1931.

Wants Arabic inscription on Rehovot Research Institute plaque

With regard to the inscription on the tablet, I am afraid I have to differ from you. You seem to have caught the Palestinian spirit very soon. I do assure you that it is essential to have the inscription in English as well as Hebrew; if I have my way, we shall also have it in Arabic. We shall be an official Institute; there are three official languages in Palestine, whether we like it or not; we have accepted this state of affairs in the Mandate, and I should be the last man to attempt petty evasions.

From a letter to E. David Bergmann, his Scientific Director at the newly built Daniel Sieff Research Institute. London, 12 January 1934.

With the deteriorating Jewish condition in Europe, some 62,000 immigrants arrived in Palestine during 1935. An Arab rebellion, with a general strike, was proclaimed on 19 April 1936. The Arab Higher Committee demanded prohibition of further Jewish immigration and the establishment of an independent government.

The country remained in a state of unrest until the outbreak of war in September 1939.

Rights of Arabs and Jews
There is an Arab nation with a glorious past. To that nation we have stretched out our hand, and do so even now – but on one condition. Just as we wish them to overcome their crisis and revert to the great tradition of a mighty and civilized Arab people, so must they know that we have the right to build our home in *Eretz Israel*, harming no one, helping all.
From an address to the Twentieth Zionist Congress. Zurich, 4 August 1937.

'Line of least injustice'
I recognize fully that what I ask for will meet with considerable opposition on the part of the Arabs, and I know there may be Arabs present, opponents or friends or whatever they are – I think probably opponents. But there is no counsel of perfection in this world, and there is no absolute justice in this world. What you are trying to perform, and what we are all trying to do in our small way, is just rough human justice. I think the decision which I should like this committee to take, if I dare to say this, would be to move on the line of least injustice. Injustice there is going to be, but if you weigh up on the one hand how the Arabs have emerged out of this war – I do not begrudge it them – they have emerged with so many kingdoms, at any rate two kingdoms, four republics; they will have six seats in the UNO, one seat in the Security Council. To speak quite frankly, which may be forgiven – for at my age it may be permitted to be frank – I do not know if it is commensurate, what the Arabs have gained during this war. What is the number of their casualties? Have they suffered so much? If you compare it with our sufferings, with our casualties, with our contribution – you will find a great deal about this in the memorandum of the Jewish Agency. I say there may be some slight injustice politically if Palestine is made a Jewish State, but individually the Arabs will not suffer.
Extract from evidence to the Anglo-American Committee of Enquiry. Jerusalem, 8 March 1946.

'A dignified relationship'
As for the Arabs, the establishment of a Jewish State offers inducements of which we believe many of their most thoughtful representatives are keenly aware. It offers them finality. It will establish the possibility of an equal and dignified relationship between Arabs and

Jews, whose states should find it to their interest to co-operate in the execution of joint development schemes and in the achievement of greater economic security.
From an address to the Twenty-Second Zionist Congress. Basle, 9 December 1946.

'Where an Arab builds, a Jew cannot build'
There are a million Arabs in Palestine. Where an Arab builds a house a Jew cannot build; where an Arab plants a tree a Jew cannot plant, unless he uproots that tree. And those who think they can are making a mistake. No one has said it here specifically, but it is implied when one says 'We will assume authority over a million or a million and a quarter Arabs and tell them that they are to have equal rights.' The Arabs can well say: 'Why not the other way around? Are you afraid of what might happen to you in an Arab country? You will enjoy equality with us.' Just as we do not wish to be a minority in Palestine, neither do the Arabs. What is right for us is right for them. Do you think all this can be sidetracked by grandiloquent eloquence?
Replying to debate at the Twenty-Second Zionist Congress. Basle, 16 December 1946.

How the world will judge the Jewish State
There must not be one law for the Jews and another for the Arabs. We must stand by the ancient principle enunciated in our Torah: 'One law and one manner shall be for you and for the stranger that sojourneth with you. . . .' I am certain that the world will judge the Jewish State by what it will do with the Arabs.
From Trial and Error, *published 1949.*

The Scheme for Jewish Settlement in East Africa ('Uganda')

Joseph Chamberlain, the British Colonial Secretary in the government of Arthur J. Balfour, offered Herzl a colonization project in the British Protectorate of East Africa, then known as Uganda but falling within the territory of Kenya. This was in April 1903. The Englishman agreed to the Zionists sending a fact-finding mission to the region. It was shortly after the Kishinev pogrom, which had resulted in the loss of forty-nine Jewish lives in the Russian city.

Herzl announced the proposal to the Zionist Congress at Basle on 23

August 1903. To his consternation there was widespread opposition, particularly from Russian delegates, but the Congress agreed to the despatch of a fact-finding mission by a vote of 295 (the 'Yea-sayers') against 178 (the 'Nay-sayers'). Although, to assuage the opposition, a group was nominated also to study possibilities within Palestine itself, this led to a split in the movement between those favouring further investigation of the project, subsequently known as 'Politicals', and those against it on any terms, the 'Zion-Zionists' or 'Practicals'. Weizmann was elected to a sub-committee, the East Africa Commission, comprising supporters of both sides, to oversee the progress of the investigation. The proposal awakened his realization of the importance of England in the future of Zionism. He decided to go to London, via Brussels and Paris, to test opinion and consult experts in African colonization, simultaneously making arrangements for his own future in Britain.

Impact on the Congress of Herzl's announcement

Herzl opened his address with a vivid picture of the situation of the Jews, which we, the Russian Jews, knew only too well. He deduced from it only one thing: the urgent necessity of bringing immediate, large-scale relief by emigration to the stricken people. Emergency measures were needed. He did not relinquish the idea of Palestine as the Jewish homeland. On the contrary, he intimated that von Plehve's promises to bring Russian pressure to bear on Turkey had improved our prospects in Palestine. But as far as the immediate problem was concerned, something new, something of great significance had developed. The British Government had made us the offer of a territory in British East Africa. Admittedly British East Africa was not Zion, and never would be. It was only an auxiliary activity – but on a national or state foundation.

It was an extraordinary speech, carefully prepared – too carefully in fact, for its cautious, balanced paragraphs betrayed the essential contradictions of the situation. Herzl had already encountered deep opposition in the closed session of the Actions Committee. But he had obtained a majority, and had enforced the unit rule, so that he could present the British offer in the name of the Actions Committee. Knowing, then, that he would encounter similar opposition on the floor of Congress, he did not submit the proposition that the British offer be accepted; he cushioned the proposal by suggesting that the Congress send a commission of investigation to the territory in question, to report on its suitability.

The effect on the Congress was a curious one. The delegates were

electrified by the news. This was the first time in the exilic history of Jewry that a great government had officially negotiated with the elected representatives of the Jewish people. The identity, the legal personality of the Jewish people, had been re-established. So much, then, had been achieved by our movement; and it meant much. But as soon as the substance of the offer, and Herzl's manner of announcing it, sank home, a spirit of disquiet, dejection and anxiety spread through the Congress. It was clear that Herzl's faith in von Plehve's support of our hopes in Palestine was more or less put on. And again, it was all very well to talk of Uganda as an auxiliary and a temporary measure, but the deflection of our energies to a purely relief effort would mean, whatever Herzl's intentions were, the practical dismantling of the Zionist Organization in so far as it had to do with Zion.
From Trial and Error.

Rallying the opposition
You and some of our other comrades in Russia are now, more than ever, called upon to stand at the head of our cause without as yet demolishing the idols of our own making. Of course, 178 Nay-sayers do not all of them represent reliable forces able to remain with honour at an exacting post. Nonetheless, they are a nucleus, a force of some size. I do not know how the majority of Zionists in Russia will react to *Ost-Afrika*. I do not know whether they will be seized by the same African fever that struck their representatives in Basle. It is essential to mark time, but one thing is clear: we must come armed, and with an integrated view regarding the future of the cause – above all, the Palestine cause. Otherwise we shall find ourselves overboard at the VII Congress.

Unfortunately, our cause has hitherto developed in such a way that the party has failed to produce specific cadres, fully-defined groups on whom it might be possible to rely in critical times. The Fraction is not as yet something definable, complete; it cannot represent a determinable force, although its various elements have rallied; the programme of work has become clearer, and I hope that it will now become active. I shall send you the Fraction's first Circular, from which you will see what kind of work we have mapped out for ourselves. Indisputably, it is no longer possible for the Fraction to continue in the shape in which it has so far existed, or as it became reflected in the minds of the people or the so-called 'Fractionists' themselves. It would be a blessing if young intelligent elements of our movement were to form an *Arbeitsgemeinschaft* and try, particularly at this moment, to work for a pure Zionism, a national Zionism, and devote all their efforts to the study of Palestine.

On this subject, a few more words. A committee consisting of Oppenheimer, Warburg and Soskin was elected at the Congress. With the exception of the last-named, the committee includes no national Zionists. I do not know, moreover, whether these gentlemen will be given the 15,000 francs assigned. In brief, I do not believe in Warburg and Oppenheimer and in their wish to deal intensively with Palestine affairs. On his own, Soskin will not be able to do anything. Furthermore, I have grave doubts whether they will be given the money to start their work *immediately*. If we do not come to the Congress with a defined programme concerning work in Palestine, and if we are not able to answer these questions, now arisen in all their acuteness:
1. *Die Colonisation und Industrialisierung Palästinas und der Nachbarländer*
2. *Ankauf von Boden in Palästina und den Nachbarländern*
3. *Kulturelle Arbeit in Palästina und unter den Juden des Orients*

then we shall not be able to have even the 178 *Neinsager* that we had, and we shall be powerless in the face of the solid block of *Mizrachi* and western Zionists who, in the name of 'the Jewish people', will say that Palestine cannot be had, that the people are starving, and therefore we must grab Africa! But if we are able to counter all these clamours not just with goodwill but also with a practical programme (it doesn't matter if at the beginning the programme did not cover the entire question), then we shall achieve power!

From a letter to Menahem Ussishkin, Russian Zionist leader, who had not attended the Congress. St Gingolph, 16 September 1903.

The practical aspects

During this present journey, I had an opportunity to form a picture of the possibility of creating a Jewish settlement in British East Africa. Even now, without waiting for the report of the expedition, it may be stated unequivocally that a significant mass colonization of whites is out of the question in East Africa. Some excellent reports about the country exist, exhaustive studies with good maps by very competent writers. I hardly believe that any conceivable expedition of ours will tell more than these studies, made by men who have travelled more than once in the territory, have lived there and administered it for years. Sir Harry Johnston was the Special Commissioner of the British Government in Uganda. He has written a two-volume study of Uganda, and every other writer refers to Johnston as the most widely recognized expert on African problems. I possess all the relevant material, I have personally talked at length with Johnston, and in Brussels I visited the best-known geographer of modern times: Élisée Reclus.

They all came out with a blunt negative against the plan. These objective considerations require a separate paper, and while indeed I reserve the right to produce one, I wish at this moment only to report on the discussions with Johnston and Reclus. I put the following questions to Johnston: Why do you consider the project impractical? 2) Is it possible to create a white settlement in Uganda? 3) How many people can be settled there under the most ideal conditions? 4) What is the attitude of the government and the High Commissioner of Uganda towards the plan? 5) English public opinion? 6) Why did Chamberlain make this offer? 7) Why are you in favour of colonization in Palestine? 8) What will be the attitude of the British Government and of English public opinion towards our aspirations in Palestine? Our discussion lasted more than an hour. On the basis of all the maps, Sir [Harry] Johnston produced his explanations. Earlier, the government had considered ceding the Nandi Plateau, the best part of the entire Protectorate and eminently suitable for colonization, to the Zionists. However, this is now out of the question, because many concessions have already been allocated in this region to Englishmen, natives and English companies. Furthermore, it would be unjust to award the only good portion of land to outsiders, with the British taxpayer being left with nothing. There remain only two other portions for possible colonization, on the highlands in the north and south of the Eastern Province of the colony – a total area consisting of 12,000 sq. km. However, a strong, warlike population, capable of becoming civilized, lives there. It is not liable to disintegrate on contact with modern culture, but on the contrary is invigorated, as, e.g., in the Cape, where blacks already sit in Parliament. It was otherwise in Australia, to take one example, where the natives have died out. Everything else in the Uganda region is unsuitable for white settlement. The cost of settlement amounts to at least 300 pounds per person. In the circumstances described, a homogeneous, white settlement is unthinkable; perhaps after long years of enormous difficulties and expenditure, a settlement of up to 10,000 families could be dispersed in individual colonies incapable of maintaining a cohesion.

The government, according to Johnston, is in a delicate situation; what it can offer the Zionists is an irony in respect of the Jewish people (his words) but it is committed nevertheless. According to my information the government is opposed to sending an expedition, and has proposed that negotiations take place with the High Commissioner first. Sir Charles Eliot, the High Commissioner, does not seem to be favourably disposed to the plan. When we came to speak of Chamberlain, Johnston characterized him in words that reminded me of what we have sometimes said of our own leaders: *C'est un homme qui saute sur les idées sans les connaître.* This description incidentally coincides fully with the one recently given by Rosebery.

Élisée Reclus demonstrated the impracticability of an agricultural settlement in East Africa. He spoke of a plantation-type colonization in which white entrepreneurs would employ blacks, a form of colonization that would render the settlement of only a few people possible, and therefore valueless to us. Regretfully, he interposed this remark: *Ce M. Herzl a bien trompé le congrès de Bâle.* This is the opinion of one of the most significant personalities in Europe.

When Johnston came to talk about Palestine he became quite enthusiastic. He declared himself ready, in association with political friends, to use every influence to induce the British Government to assist us in Palestine. In his opinion England would have to do this because she could never permit another nation to exert influence in Palestine. But England cannot get Palestine for herself. Further, the English are the people of the Bible and the Zionists will do themselves a great deal of harm if they allow themselves to be diverted from Palestine. That we have already forfeited considerable sympathy was confirmed to me through other sources. Johnston, who is very influential in English political circles, gave me an undertaking that he would come out against Africa and in favour of Palestine at a public meeting. He, together with other Members of Parliament, has asked for a statement on Zionism, and assured us of an opportunity to give a lecture at the Royal Asiatic Society, frequented by the élite of London's political world. The lecture will be delivered by Gaster. The statement is in preparation and will, I hope, be a good one; it will be delivered in fourteen days. I learned from Johnston, incidentally, that he has discussed El Arish with Colonel Goldsmid and together they agreed that this territory is capable of colonization. The water problem can be easily solved and opposition of the Egyptian Government headed by Lord Cromer will not be an insurmountable difficulty. In any event, it clearly follows from this experience that:
a) Colonization in East Africa is impossible.
b) The East Africa idea has caused us harm among the better sectors of public opinion.
c) An opportunity exists for activity in Palestine.
From a letter to Menahem Ussishkin and others. Geneva, 20 October 1903.

East Africa and the cultural question
Seven years of Zionist activity have finally taught us that we have sought in vain to construct a unity out of heterogeneous elements. Diverging views already revealed themselves within the Zionists'

following at earlier Congresses. The wretched cultural issue, prowling unsolved like a ghost from one Congress to the next, was in essence the psychological evidence of what has now, of course, emerged into the open more drastically through the Africa issue. It is definitely no coincidence that the most embittered opponents of Zionist cultural activities were the strongest adherents of the Africa project.
From a letter to Menahem Ussishkin and others. Geneva, 26 October 1903.

Zionism and an 'overnight shelter'

Let us examine more closely the arguments advanced in favour of the scheme. Not one of its supporters dreamt even for a single moment of surrendering Palestine; they were merely taking the present situation of the Jews into account, and the interest of the people, which brooks no delay. In order to avoid 'more Kishinevs' Zionism must put up an 'overnight shelter'. In this opposing of the two concepts, 'Zionist party' and 'Jewish people', we already have a glimpse of the destruction of a fundamental principle of Zionism. The strength of the movement lay in Zionism's regarding itself – and itself alone – as the real Jewish people, the people on the way, the people in the process of creation. The Zionists broke radically with all the *Galut* traditions and all the *Galut* ways of solving the Jewish question, and inscribed on their standard the device: The Jews will either be Zionists all, or they will cease to be. Whatever is outside the Zionists in the people, the whole periphery, is an unorganized mass, still inwardly enslaved, who have first to be turned into full, true national Jews, have first to be made Zionist. We therefore refrained from contrasts between the Zionist party and the periphery, from speaking of the interests of the Zionists and the interests of the people as though these are two different things.

But should Zionism concern itself with putting up 'overnight shelters'? The moment this question is answered by the movement in the affirmative, Zionism loses its radical character and betakes itself to a sphere of activity to which all non-national or anti-national Jewish bodies have adhered: dispersing Jewry and extending *Galut* rather than assembling and concentrating Jewish forces on the national soil. Here Zionism is doing the work of ICA, the work of those Jews and non-Jews who fear the drive of the Jewish masses towards the centres of Western Europe and America. Here Zionism does its work not out of positive national-Jewish motives but out of purely negative motives, out of Jewish distress. It degrades its activity to pure philanthropy, and thereby sinks to the level of an aid society. But we are told, the overnight shelter is to be of an altogether special kind. It is to be a national-Jewish training ground. It is to be a school of citizenship.

This conception of the East Africa scheme needs to be most energetically and fundamentally repudiated, since it mostly leads to misunderstandings, and it will continue to do so.

If a Jewish settlement in a country other than Palestine is to become a model Jewish community, a training ground, with a national content, then the colonists of the new country must constantly regard themselves as true, full citizens there, and must work for their new country as their fatherland. Only on this hypothesis can they make the great sacrifices inseparable from colonizing an uncivilized region, and overcome the tremendous difficulties in the way of creating a new communal existence. Thus, if it were indeed possible to found a normal Jewish community on African soil, then the work and sacrifices of generations of settlers, stored up in the institutions of the new country, would establish in its soil the necessary tie between the land and the population, and produce a patriotic attitude and thereby transform the new land into their fatherland. The section of the Jewish people living there could no longer regard Palestine as their fatherland: it would forget it, indeed it would have to forget it in order to be able to take root in the new soil. The new colony is thus an overnight shelter no longer, but a permanent homeland.

After these objections of pure principle, a whole range of objections of a practical nature can be brought forward. To those who oppose the Africa scheme on pure principle the practical objections are of no account. But since so much has been said of the necessity and the possibility of giving help to the Jews in their need by means of this new scheme, you will permit me a few remarks. No single territorial scheme is capable of diverting the existing current of immigration, which is constantly rising, away from those countries to which it is directed at present. Under the lash of need, a stream of humanity is pouring into America, Canada, South Africa, to find a haven from the deprivation of rights under which they have suffered so sorely in the lands of their birth. It is not the need for autonomy, but the need for air and bread, for immediate satisfaction, that drives these masses of people out into the world in search of better economic and cultural circumstances. The stream of Jewish emigration pours into the great industrial cities, where alone will it find the possibility of immediately selling its labour to earn its daily bread. In this way the Jew avails himself of the institutions already established in the country; he regards the new country only as a country of refuge, and thus he carries the *Galut* along with him, yes, develops it further. Emigration moves steadily from places with a lower culture to places with a higher culture. For Uganda to take a large immigration, tremendous preliminary work has first to proceed over many long years. But if one looks somewhat further into the history of the development of colonies, one sees that even those communities that had the best circumstances in which to develop needed a long time in order to be capable of absorbing any significant mass of people. Indeed, it is part of the necessary presuppositions, if a colony is to thrive, that its population should only increase slowly, little by little.

The country offers not the slightest possibility of settling millions, as many people in their excessive zeal have already hastened to declare. In Uganda one would have to begin with colonization on a small scale, and decades would have to elapse until an 'overnight shelter' of any significance could exist there. 'We are not giving the signal to strike camp' – so said the President of Congress. But the propagandists could not do enough to sing the praises of the land full of promise, and the New Judea was already pictured by Zangwill in the rosiest of colours for the hungry imagination of the Jewish people. People who make so much of their own political cleverness and accuse others of lacking '*sehel*' should really be more careful when they deliver their momentous political speeches.
From a lecture to the Berne Academic Zionist Society. 8 November 1903.

Russian reactions
An unbelievable confusion bordering on anarchy prevails here. In truth the Zionist Organization has ceased to exist, except for the ruins occupied with their feuds. Uganda has been driven into the movement like a wedge, and the unhealthy agitation with which 'the project' was promoted has roused in the heads of immature and semi-educated supporters a number of adventurous theories that sound almost like lunacy. The *Poalei–Zion* movement, good though it was as a first stage in enlisting support from among the ranks of workers infected by the 'Bund', is now off the track and split. Zionism has been supplanted by territorialism. I always placed the greatest hope in that part of Russian Jewry which is courageous, aware, honest and productive. Now these people have been literally driven out of Zionism. All our youth, our hope, our future, has gone astray!
From a letter to Moses Gaster. Pinsk, 11 April 1904.

The House of Commons debated the project on 20 June 1904. A government spokesman pointed out that land would be leased, not transferred, to the Jews. There was no great demand by Europeans for land in this region, where the priority of British settlers for the best land was recognized. He added that feelings of sympathy for the Jews, besides the need to develop East Africa, had inspired the offer.

'Just earth for the grave'
It is clear from these debates (I received a shorthand account today) that the government is not even thinking of offering the Jews autonomy. All it will give, if it gives anything at all, is earth for the grave.
From a letter to his fiancée Vera Khatzman. Geneva, 25 June 1904.

Theodor Herzl died on 3 July 1904, throwing the Zionist Organization into further confusion.

The British attitude
My conversation with his Excellency Earl Percy: The first question I ventured to put to his Excellency concerned the project, approved by the English Government and submitted by the late Dr Herzl to the VI Zionist Congress in Basle, for Jewish colonization in East Africa. I requested HE to enlighten me, if possible, on the boundaries of the territory in question, and in the first place to specify the political conditions under which such colonization would take effect. With the head of the Zionist movement unfortunately dead, it was absolutely necessary to know the true position of the Zionist party vis-à-vis the English Government.

HE then replied that the main conditions had already been stated in Lord Lansdowne's letter addressed to the Congress and signed by Sir Clement Hill. I raised the objection that the details had not been precisely expressed, and so Lord Lansdowne's letter had been interpreted in different ways, and it was only after the answer given by HE during the recent debate in Parliament that many details were clarified. For example, the question of autonomy, etc., still remains obscure. To this HE replied that there could be no question of Jewish autonomy, but at the most a 'local government'. Regarding the details, and the publication of documents, it will be absolutely necessary to await the report of the expedition. As the split produced among the Zionists in consequence of the Africa project was raised during the conversation, I allowed myself an explanation of its reasons for the benefit of HE. I had the honour to declare that all Zionists, without distinction of opinion, were profoundly grateful to the English Government for having sustained the idea of a Jewish colonization project under august English protection. But in this particular case the majority of Zionists considered the movement one of national regeneration of the people of Israel, and it could not therefore take place anywhere but in the Holy Land. Such regeneration would take place in Palestine or it would never occur at all.

HE expressed the opinion that the English Government certainly had the best intentions of doing something for the persecuted Jews, but it considered colonization in Africa to be an undertaking having but little to do with the Zionist idea and the national aspirations of Israel. Furthermore, in view of the objections raised by the native populations, as well as the energetic protestations in England itself, against the establishment of a Jewish colony in Africa, the government feared that the Africa project might give cause to a hostile movement against the Jews, which would be most regrettable. As for the other particulars, HE recommended me to Sir Cl. Hill of the Foreign Office.

My conversation with Sir Clement Hill: On being introduced by HE Earl Percy to Sir Cl. Hill for the purpose of obtaining detailed information about the Africa project, Sir Clement was kind enough to show me on the map of the Protectorate the position of the territory marked for the establishment of the Jewish colony, as mentioned in the letter addressed by Sir Cl. Hill to Mr J. L. Greenberg and read out to the Congress in Basle. The territory in question, not far from the Nandi Plateau, is located at the remote end of the railway, by which all necessary transportation for the colonization would, at very high cost, have to be effected. Colonization would be very expensive, and its final success most doubtful. Furthermore, it must be stated that the English Government accepts no responsibility for the protection of the settlers against the natives, who – Sir Clement observed – would all be against you. All these points were fully agreed upon between the English Government and the Zionist Agent. In my opinion, said Sir Clement, Jewish colonization only of a type similar to that in Argentina could result from it. Thus the actual project differs profoundly from the interpretations given it in Zionist circles. If I were Jewish, added Sir Clement, I would oppose such a project absolutely. For a Zionist there is nothing to look for in Africa.

From a letter to his fiancée. Manchester, 1 August 1904.

'Herzl died in time'

Africa can now without doubt be regarded as finished. There is a whole sea of intrigues. I am staying here till tomorrow evening, and will soon leave, my sweet, with a very nasty feeling that we are standing amidst the ruins of the cause, and that the deceased himself contributed quite a bit to it. Herzl, *for his own sake*, died in time.

From a letter to his fiancée, written during the Annual Zionist Conference. Vienna, 18 August 1904.

In May 1905 the fact-finding mission reported unfavourably on the East Africa scheme. The Zionist Congress, meeting that year, therefore rejected the proposal, and Israel Zangwill led a secession movement out of the Zionist Organization.

'Perilous adventures'

There is a mighty confusion of mind here. It is rumoured that the Dutch intend offering Jews Surinam, Dutch Guiana, a place for the deportation of criminals. I have heard that Zangwill is now in Holland. Can there possibly be people who envisage such perilous adventures? This is real wickedness, and more frightening the more one thinks about it.

From a letter to his fiancée. Manchester, 7 September 1905.

'Like mushrooms'

I also saw Zangwill. He has been very ill, is aging, exhausted, apparently disillusioned. He interrogated me about the possibility of receiving a concession from the Russian Government for a stretch of land in Siberia – for the Jews; the most bizarre, most fantastic projects appear and vanish like mushrooms. But against the background of Whitechapel's hell all this demoralization in Zionism has an overall dreadful effect on one. I was glad to leave London, with the intention of not returning there on Zionist business for a long time.

From a letter to his fiancée. Manchester, 5 March 1906.

Balfour and Uganda

Suddenly I said: 'Mr Balfour, supposing I were to offer you Paris instead of London, would you take it?'

He sat up, looked at me, and answered: 'But Dr Weizmann, we have London.'

'That is true,' I said. 'But we had Jerusalem when London was a marsh.'

From Trial and Error, *recalling a discussion with Balfour, 9 January 1906.*

The Russian Revolution of 1905

Calamitous defeats in the Russo–Japanese War, beginning February 1904, exposed the incompetence and cynicism of Russia's rulers and roused both peasants and factory workers to open demonstrations of their discontents. Disorders spread from St Petersburg when, on 22 January 1905, a procession of workers and their families was fired on by the police, causing hundreds of deaths. Thus began the 1905 revolution, characterized by riots, strikes and mutiny among the armed forces. In October 1905 a general strike forced Tzar Nicholas II to promise a parliament, the Imperial Duma, based on popular suffrage, with full civil rights for Russians of all religions and races. It met in May 1906, to a background of further disorders and loss of life. Jews were prominently represented in the ranks of the revolutionaries, and the period gave rein to violence by extremist nationalist-monarchist groups known as the Black Hundreds, which made the Jews, who had organized self-defence squads, their principal targets.

The prelude
This decision to communicate with you is reinforced by the impressions I received while in Russia. I have been there twice during the past six months, and had occasion to visit the most important Jewish centres in north and south Russia. It is not my wish to detain you with a report on the economic situation of the Jews in Russia, though I am convinced that a realistic Jewish picture cannot be obtained from even the most ideal of theories – not that we have any ideal ones. The events in Kishinev have shed a glaring light upon the fate of *one* city. In my travels I made the alarming discovery that distress has grown to a frightening degree. As a consequence of the present crisis, the destitute in some Lithuanian towns have increased by 30 per cent. This could be verified in various ways, such as in the distribution of corn money before Easter. More terrible still is the all-pervading sense of helplessness and perplexity resulting from legal restrictions that grow more severe daily, and are to be intensified to a point beyond endurance in the near future. These restrictions are said to be an answer to the growing Jewish revolutionary movement. But the Jewish revolution is the product of unlimited political and economic disabilities. This vicious circle, constantly opening and then closing again, can be broken in both senses only by Zionism. . . . In Western Europe it is generally believed that the large majority of Jewish youth in Russia is in the Zionist camp. Unfortunately, the opposite is true. The larger part of the contemporary younger generation is anti-Zionist, not from a desire to assimilate as in Western Europe, but through revolutionary conviction.

It is impossible to calculate the number of victims, or describe their character, that are annually, indeed daily, sacrificed because of their identification with Jewish Social Democracy in Russia. Hundreds of thousands of very young boys and girls are held in Russian prisons, or are being spiritually and physically destroyed in Siberia. More than 5,000 are now under police surveillance, which means the deprivation of their freedom. Almost all those now being victimized in the entire Social Democratic movement are Jews, and their number grows every day. They are not necessarily young people of proletarian origin; they also come from well-to-do families, and incidentally not infrequently from Zionist families. Almost all students belong to the revolutionary camp; hardly any of them escape its ultimate fate. We cannot enter here into the many factors, political, social and economic, that continuously nourish the Jewish revolutionary movement; suffice to say that the movement has already captured masses of young people who can only be described as children.

Thus, during my stay in Minsk, they arrested 200 Jewish Social Democrats, not one of whom was more than seventeen years old. It is a fearful spectacle, and one that obviously escapes West European Zionists, to observe the major part of our youth – and no one would describe them as the worst part – offering themselves for sacrifice as though seized by a fever. We refrain from touching on the terrible effect this mass-sacrifice has upon the families and communities concerned, and upon the state of Jewish political affairs in general. Saddest and most lamentable is the fact that although this movement consumes much Jewish energy and heroism and is located within the Jewish fold, the attitude it evidences towards Jewish nationalism is one of antipathy, swelling at times to fanatical hatred. Children are in open revolt against their parents. The elders are confined within tradition and Orthodox inflexibility, the young make their first step a search for freedom from everything Jewish. In one small town near Pinsk, for example, youngsters tore the Torah Scrolls to shreds.
From a letter to Theodor Herzl. Geneva, 6 May 1903.

What strikes the eye is the difference between the mood last year and this year, the outcome of course of the oppressive and exceedingly fresh recollection of Kishinev and Homel, a recollection that turns into pain and trepidation now, on the eve of Easter week. Most alarming rumours are circulating, but there is no need of course to give them that acute character that they assume on superficial observation. In the south the fear is great; the incitement in the Russian Press is rather strong. It is my conviction that there is no danger at all in the large Jewish centres, but that great danger exists in the small district towns, especially where troops are stationed. Shabbiness and the impoverishment of the masses are on the increase. The war and the accompanying crisis in all walks of life are ruining even those few families that were considered 'well-to-do'. Bankruptcies are so numerous that they are now being regarded as a matter of course.

Literally everywhere, the situation of the Jews is the only topic of conversation. This struck me as characteristic as soon as I entered

Russia. Whichever circle of society you happen to be in, discussions revolve round this one and only theme. People talk wildly, working out the most bizarre and unheard-of projects about a total exodus from the Pale, about various Ugandas, Canadas, Paraguays, Uruguays. Some preach constant and persistent action upon the ruling circles by means of deputations, memoranda, etc., etc. Others advance ideas no less fantastic of a quite different nature, and in everything one can discern utter helplessness, and all manner of *Ghetto-Ideen* have never attained such a frenzy as now!
From a letter to Zvi Aberson and Rosa Grinblatt. Pinsk, 3 April 1904.

My dearest, melancholy comes through my letters because the life one sees around one is so very oppressive, and weighs down one's spirits terribly. Somehow everything seems to be drifting rudderless, without sail. There is nothing in the present, there is not a glimmer of light ahead; awful impoverishment and helplessness are a separating factor, while unifying bonds become weaker. One is influenced despite oneself by everything one sees around. Pinsk has another special feature besides. Next to terrible poverty there exists a caste of people here exceedingly rich and arrogant who, in their cardboard grandeur and ignorance, consider themselves City Fathers. The local Jewish rich have combined in themselves the arrogant attitude of West European financial wizards towards 'their poor brethren' with the lack of culture of the Pale. All this is very unpleasant, and you can understand the ferment in the minds of the youth. But I have no hopes that this fermenting youth will give something positively Jewish. It is destructive, and great in its destructive self-sacrifice, but it is not creative and does not know how to be so; for it is not led by anyone, it has no teachers, it feeds spiritually on whatever comes along, it suffocates from lack of air and light.
From a letter to his fiancée. Pinsk, 11 April 1904.

I am absolutely shattered by the news from Russia and have to write about it before my own affairs. As I read the newspapers tears filled my eyes – it is really terrible. *Il sonne comme l'histoire*. Blood-stained pages of Russian history; that is, not only Russian but also world history and, partly, our own Jewish history too. . . . I am horror-stricken by the realization that this conflagration which broke out in Petersburg and cannot be quelled by streams of blood will spread to the provinces, and that torrents of Jewish blood will also flow. This mixing of the two streams of blood, the Russian and the Jewish, fills me with fear. All day yesterday, and today, I felt as if I were going out of my mind and God only knows to what degree my nervous system has broken down! I myself cannot understand what came over me then.

There is a terrific, unprecedented excitement among the English, more so than at the time of the Hull incident. Perkin arrived from London today and reports that he has never seen such excitement in London. It goes without saying that all sympathy is totally with the masses. Even the conservative and pro-Russian newspapers refer to the Tzar and the army as bandits; all Europe has become aware of the lies and turpitude of the Tzarist Government, and so forth.

Newspapers publish extra editions that are snatched up. The faces of the readers betray feelings deeper than mere curiosity. What is going to happen? Events are developing at a breathtaking pace. We are fated to live in a difficult but eventful era. For the Jewish people and particularly for our cause the consequences will be crucial. To describe the mood here I must add that both here and in London the evening papers came out even on Sunday, which happened only once before, at a critical moment of the Boer War.
From a letter to his fiancée. Manchester, 23 January 1905.

Hopes dashed
The Russian 'revolution' is over for the time being, although the quiet described in the newspapers is none too assured. Lives were not sacrificed in vain – the blood of those killed demands revenge, and the vengeance will be terrible. In any case, the Geneva meeting will not influence the course of events. The present need is for heroes who will not allow the Russian people to relapse into sleep. What a vile people! Statements of abject loyalty are already pouring in – though it may well be that they are fabricated at the 3rd Bureau of the Criminal Investigation Department. I put my faith in Kuroki and Togo [the Japanese commanders].
From a letter to his fiancée. Manchester, 30 January 1905.

In that accursed Russia another outburst of the Kishinev drama, this time under the title Zhitomir. According to the papers, the Jews defended themselves with glory and courage. This is the only consolation, if consolation is indeed possible.
From a letter to his fiancée. Manchester, 12 May 1905.

The period of Russian revival will be written into Russian history in Jewish blood. The Russian spring is for us a time of bloodshed. The projected reforms will exclude Jewish participation in the 'new' life. And how about our youth?! Thousands of victims are sacrificed on the

altar of Russian freedom, while the ranks of Zionism reveal flabbiness.
From a letter to his fiancée. London, 15 June 1905.

Of course I have read no word of a declaration of Jewish rights. The revolutionaries don't mention them in their demands, yet it is the Jews who are making the sacrifices for the revolution. The Jews have given the Russians freedom, but there is nothing as yet for the Jews themselves.
From a letter to his fiancée. Manchester, 4 November 1905.

I wish you wouldn't ask how English Jewry is reacting to all this. They are petrified. They are committing a second pogrom. They have given money *on condition* that their unfortunate Russian brethren do not emigrate to England.
From a letter to his fiancée. Manchester, 13 November 1905.

The aftermath

The Bund is a purely social-democratic Jewish organization. It even has a national programme, such as the demand for autonomy for the Jews in Russia: this national element is sheer inconsistency, a mask forced upon them by the power of the Jewish national movement so as to go down better with the Jewish masses. In practice it is anti-national, anti-Zionist – this goes without saying – and destructive in the Jewish cultural sense, and as a revolutionary party it has naturally been playing a large part just now. But where it comes to something constructive in Russia it has lost its basis; for its positive Jewish programme = o, and it dissolves in the general social-democratic mass. It has no connection with the liberal elements of the bourgeoisie. It is strictly Marxist and a proletarian party (it numbers no more than 10,000 organized workers). But every young Jew in Russia calls himself a Bundist now: the thousands of dentists who have no practice, the thousands of students or candidates for admission to universities who cannot get in because of the discriminatory laws. Thus, in addition to the organized, purely proletarian element (in the West European sense), the Bund also contains hordes of semi-intellectuals, a vast petty-bourgeois element, intellectual *'sansculottes'*, and *déclassés* who only talk socialism without living it, good cannon fodder for the revolution but who will now desert the party.
From a letter to Moses Gaster, who had requested information on this Jewish party, referred to in the Press as having sent agents to foment revolutionary activity in Odessa. Manchester, 27 November 1905.

It is vital that eminent Russian Jews also raise their voice against the

infamous indifference of the radical parties in Russia.
From a letter to Nahum Sokolow. Manchester, 28 November 1905.

It is a great pity that there isn't a single outstanding Jew in the Duma to speak with the tongue of the Prophets, to pronounce *j'accuse* from the tribune of the Duma against all of Russian society.
From a letter to his fiancée. Manchester, 13 May 1906.

My hatred of the Russian regime grew as I contrasted life in Russia with life in England, where freedom of speech and thought were things taken for granted, like the air one breathed. The hopes which were born of the impending defeat of Russia made it harder than ever for me to bear with my self-imposed exile from public affairs. A great struggle was going on over there; the will of the Russian people was beginning to manifest itself, a desperate and tottering bureaucracy was striking back with the last remnants of its forces. The people emerged with a partial victory. A parliament (with very limited powers, it is true, but still a parliament) was brought into being, and if its legislative actions were cancelled by imperial ukases, at least a tribune had been created from which the Russian people could address the world. We naturally hoped that, in the fundamental changes which were taking place, Jewry, which had given its full share to the toll of victims in the struggle, would also receive its share of the benefits. Perhaps the era of savage oppressions was over, perhaps the intolerable laws which hedged in the life of the Jewish community would be rescinded. All these hopes were doomed to disappointment. A few Jewish deputies were elected to the Duma, and there they had the opportunity of speaking up on behalf of the inarticulate millions which they represented. But the Russian Imperial Government had already chosen the path which was to lead, a decade later, to its irretrievable ruin. The Revolution was liquidated amid Jewish pogroms; the Duma was repressed, the ancient tyranny returned.
From Trial and Error.

The Russian Revolution of 1917

This is taken as beginning with the nomination of Prince Lvov in March (Gregorian calendar) as Prime Minister and the abdication of Tzar Nicholas II, continuing to the Bolshevik *coup d'état* in November.

Greeting a new dawn

Special Conference of English Zionist Federation assembled in London this day cordially welcomes the liberation of the great Russian nation. The Zionists of England as of the whole British Empire recognizing the noble emancipation of our Russian fellow-Jews, confident in the sense of liberty and justice towards all nationalities animating the Russian democracy and realizing that the destinies of a large part of the Jewish people are indissolubly united with it, offer sincere good wishes for Russia's glorious future.

Telegram to Georgi Lvov. London, 20 May 1917.

The Revolution and Zionism

For Zionism a free Russia means full liberty for the public propagation of its ideals and opens out new and far-reaching possibilities of progress and development. Hitherto propaganda has had of necessity to be carried on in secret by various and devious methods in order to circumvent an autocratic government, whose main function was to deprive human beings of elementary rights and of preventing a propaganda which denoted freedom for the Jewish soul and liberty for the Jewish people. It is possible that some of those who have based their Zionism on the persecution of the Jews will fall away from the movement, now that freedom is at hand. If so, we shall lose a little in quantity, but Zionism will gain qualitatively. As the choice of free men Zionism will be a nobler, healthier and more intensive movement than as an economic panacea for a people bound in chains of misfortune. It has never been claimed that Zionism could solve the Jewish economic question. Economic questions which cannot be solved exist in the most powerful and wealthy of states. To base Zionism on persecution is totally to misunderstand and misinterpret the spirit of the movement.

One effect of the Revolution will probably be to diminish emigration from Russia, which was primarily economic in its origin. Thus the Revolution will cut off at its source that invigorating stream of immigration into the countries of Western Europe and America which has contributed so largely to keeping Judaism alive in those countries.

Assimilation amongst the Jews in the western Diaspora has reached serious proportions, and had these countries not been fed by the constant flow of Jewish emigrants from Russia, it is certain that their Judaism would have been so emasculated by its 'liberal' progress as to be non-existent. Judaism in these countries was and is dependent on outside factors for its persistence. So far as the history of political emancipation of the Jews in these countries is concerned, it has meant a period of hyphenation, in which the Jew tends to approach the predominant type of the country in which he lives. In Russia it may be assumed that a similar development will take place, and that many will attempt to eradicate their distinguishing characteristics and become 'real' Russians, in the same way as Jews in England have sought to become Englishmen, Jews in France Frenchmen, and so on. If there were no corrective to this development we should then logically arrive in time at a point at which Jews would belong to every nation except the Jewish nation.

Zionism will provide the necessary corrective, will create that bond of unity which is lacking, and will be the common agreement to which Jews of all lands can appeal. Political emancipation concerns the Jews as individuals, whereas Zionism is concerned with the Jews as a people, with their restoration to a national centre of their own, where Judaism as an influence in the civilization of the world may be preserved and where a free and liberal Jewish spirit can develop.

From an article in Zionist Review. *London, May 1917.*

Need for a British statement of Zionist support

I quite understand that everybody is preoccupied now with the grave situation in Russia, but I am afraid there is very little hope that the reasons for this preoccupation will cease in the near future; it seems to me that things have gone out of bounds there and I am afraid that even if Kerensky succeeds now in establishing a semblance of order it will only be of a very short duration. The real trouble lies in the fact that the Soviets are the real government and possess executive power without responsibility. The elements constituting the Soviets are not constructive, they are narrow-minded and fanatical. The misfortune of Russia is that it possesses a small group of intellectuals inexperienced in statecraft and a huge mass of inert peasants who can be swayed by political demagogues. Instead of teaching the peasants the elements of constitutionalism and of grammar they are told by the Soviets that they are called upon now to establish a millennium in Russia and build up ad hoc a society which will be far advanced in comparison with the bourgeois West. They have destroyed all the elements of discipline and order without being able to create a substitute for it. The so-called Maximalist tendencies have demoralized not only Russia but threaten to undermine the state of things even outside Russia. I felt that in a minor degree in my own organization. Being constituted as it is chiefly of Russian Jews they began to introduce Soviet tactics into the Zionist movement and my only answer to that was that not desiring to take the responsibility for the consequences I would leave them to continue the work if they can. This has had the effect of sobering them down and

hence the rumours of my resignation. My hands would be very much strengthened if the declaration of which I spoke in my last letter could be obtained as soon as possible. It would be of very great value not only here but in Russia and in America, and therefore I think that it is of importance not to postpone it if possible.
From a letter to C. P. Scott. London, 13 September 1917.

After the Balfour Declaration
Your sacred duty now to strengthen pro-British sympathies in Russian Jewry and counteract powerfully all adverse influences. Remember providential coincidence of British and Jewish interests. We rely on your doing your utmost this critical and solemn hour. Wire steps you propose to take. Jabotinsky who now co-operates with us could go Russia help you.
From a telegram to Israel Rosov. London, 23(?) November 1917.

On Jewish Strength and Weakness

Absence of Jewish intelligentsia in Britain
I used to be concerned exclusively with scholars and students, people untouched by life. I saw the 'real world' only when I was on the road, conducting propaganda, and even then I saw it merely as a pageant. All is changed now. Everything I see around me is 'real', and so dreary as to be devoid of the faintest poetical haze. There is none of that poetical tone perceptible in Russian Jewry, the poetry compounded of deep, centuries-old suffering that can be detected even in everyday life. Materialist, commercial England has succeeded in burning out everything exalted in our Jews, so that the creation of a Jewish intelligentsia here has become an impossible task.
From a letter to his fiancée. Manchester, 14 April 1905.

Maccabean force
Zionism is becoming estranged, shallow and insensitive, descending from its democratic eminence to the baize-green table of plutocratic philanthropists, and perhaps as low as to the back-door of the elements dead to Judaism. Brussels [conference to protest against the Russian pogroms] was a sterile attempt to travel together with those people in a great and distressing issue. Nothing practical came out of it, and this is just as well, for any practical step *with* those people would inevitably have brought discredit upon Zionism.

Don't call me a fanatic, or a narrow-minded man. Zionism exercises its Maccabean force of attraction and its greatness as a freedom movement so long as it solves the Jewish question radically, or strives to do so. The moment it chases after transient successes at the expense of Jewish distress the gates are opened wide for the politics of the ghetto.
From a letter to Judah L. Magnes. Manchester, 13 February 1906.

Abnormal situation

Zionism is often briefly defined as a solution, or rather *the* solution, of the Jewish question. The Jewish question consists in the endeavour to bring about an adjustment of the Jews to their environment, and Zionism maintains that the only effective adjustment can be achieved by a restoration of the Jewish people to their ancestral country. Whatever country we examine in which Jews are settled in large numbers, we find the position abnormal. In Russia and Galicia there are compact masses of Jewry who live a life of their own, preserving the culture of ancient times, and producing a literature of their own at the present day. But the confinement of the Jews to the Russian Pale and their voluntary seclusion from the national life in Galicia are both abnormal phenomena.

Russia is frank in its hatred of the Jews, and tries its best to crush them out of existence. As for the Jews of Galicia, the mere fact that they pursue their own national life in an alien environment and upon alien soil inevitably produces something unnatural in their character. In Western Europe, Jews participate very freely and largely in the life of their respective countries, socially and politically. Nevertheless they find it necessary constantly to emphasize that they are Frenchmen, or Germans, and so forth. In France, the great majority of Jews are differentiated in very few respects from ordinary Frenchmen; in appearance, habits, views and prejudices, they are very much alike. And yet the Jews in France feel compelled every now and again to assert their French citizenship, as though fearing they might be suspected of disloyalty. This tendency of Jews towards chauvinism can be observed in every country in Western Europe, and to a certain extent it is evident even in Eastern Europe.

From this it may be gathered the Jews never feel rooted in the country of their residence. However comfortably they might be established, they can hardly be animated by the same sentiments and traditions that fill the hearts and minds of their fellow-citizens. The reason has nothing to do with patriotism. It is simply a question of history. The Jew, with his long, glorious and chequered history, and thousands of years, cannot help feeling somewhat apart in relation to the modern country in which he lives – a country which, even upon the most liberal reckoning, began to have a continuous history only some hundreds of years after the downfall of the Jewish State. As for the culture of his native country, the Jew feels he is above it; in other words, his own life has grown up from a different moist soil. The Jew might even contribute to the culture of his country, to its science, its learning, its general advancement; but the Jewish people obtain no profit from this. The persecution in an Eastern country would not be less because Jews had contributed to the improvement of Western countries. Surely such a position must seem unfair and unjust to all who consider the Jewish people as a whole. So much energy is put forth in producing for others, so much energy expended in the mere effort of self-preservation, and yet if only the same amount of energy were applied in a positive direction in a Jewish land it would be productive of such great national benefits.

It should also be noted that the Jew is very adaptable, no matter in what country he settles; but the culture he picks up in each successive place is superficial. He remains a Jew after all. Zionism contends that the abnormal position involved by the dispersion of the Jews should be brought to an end, and that this can be accomplished only by a national rehabilitation on a territory of our own. There are some who say that any territory will do. But as a Zionist I maintain that only one territory can answer the desired purpose – the land of Palestine. I shall not enter into questions of climate, soil and politics. I would simply remind you of the long history and the innumerable traditions that bind the soul of the Jew to Palastine. To cut the future of the Jewish people off from that country would damage its moral development; it would produce a new type, which would not be a natural and normal development from the past. We have only to remember how, throughout our dispersion, we planted a moral Palestine in our communities. That will bring home to you how intimately the Jewish soul is knit with the idea of a return to that country. To be a Zionist it is only necessary to be convinced of the necessity of rebuilding the Jewish nation in the Holy Land. It is not necessary, in the first place, to be convinced that the idea can be carried out. But those who are convinced of the ideal will surely be animated by sufficient enthusiasm to do everything in their power, to the extent of personal sacrifice, to translate the ideal into reality.
From a lecture to London University Zionist Society. 21 March 1909.

Swinging between extremes
The Jews are strong enough not to disappear completely and too weak to be able to lead an independent existence. So in every relationship,

both economic and spiritual, Jewish life consists of the swing between extremes, between what is German and what is Jewish, between what is Czech and what is Jewish, between what is French and what is Jewish. And every Jew is a mixture of different elements – not a synthesis of the Jewish part with the surrounding milieu, but a direct mixture, with sometimes the one thing more apparent, sometimes the other. This situation provokes friction in every sphere of human activity. When one is so fractured, when there are as many lines in one's moral spectrum as there are in the Jewish spectrum, then it is impossible to stand with feet firmly on the ground. The host countries are not the cause of this situation, for it repeats itself in every historical epoch, in all lands, under totally different external conditions: the Jewish character always remains the same. The bearer of the Jewish problem is in fact the Jew himself. The problem lies first and foremost in an ineradicable national feeling in the Jews, much blurred at times, but existing nevertheless, sometimes in latent form and sometimes openly.

This is why I do not believe in assimilation and do not see a national danger in it. Individual Jews may split off, even a community here and there, but the core will always remain. A process of assimilation like today's was known in many historical epochs: there was Greek assimilation, which bit much deeper than the German, but even that did not touch the national core. There is a certain stiff-necked obstinacy that saves Jewry from complete disappearance.
From a lecture to Bar-Kochba Student Society. Prague, 27 March 1912.

Where genius flourishes
The charge that Jews are only copyists, incapable of producing an original genius, is partially true. But it is applicable only to Jews living in non-Jewish surroundings. It is totally untrue of Jews in their native environment, be this their own land or the ghetto. An example is Mesopotamia, the cradle of civilization, where the Semitic Accadians invented cuneiform.
From a lecture in Manchester. 21 June 1912.

A Monaco with a university
We are a nation in as much as we resist all influences making for the destruction of our race, and not a nation because we assimilate ourselves superficially, and are always ready to attach ourselves quickly to surroundings. That is the reason why we are so widely misunderstood. We are a people without a status, and if in normal times such a position is tolerated, in times of crisis it becomes dangerous. If the Jews had at present a place where they formed the

important part of the population, and led a life of their own, however small this place might be, for example, something like Monaco, with a university instead of a gambling hall, nobody would doubt the existence of the Jewish nation, all the fatal misunderstandings would disappear, we should have a definite passport, and we should therefore not be suspected.
From a report to Zionist Executive. London/Manchester, 7 January 1915.

A sub-national life
The persistence of the Jewish people through 2,000 years of dispersion is due to its capacity for organizing a group-life of its own, under whatever external conditions, on the basis of a spiritual idea – the idea of the eternity of Israel as bound up with the eternity and universality of the God of Israel. This idea, carrying with it as a corollary the belief in a future restoration of the people to its homeland, has been at the root of the Jewish attitude to life, and has supplied in the Jewish struggle for existence the place of the more concrete expressions of nationality. The people of Israel, the God of Israel, the land of Israel – these are the indestructible kernel around which has grown an outer shell, of belief, tradition, religious observance, and social custom. So in Babylon, in Spain, in North Africa, in France and Germany, and later in Poland, large groups of Jews were able to create and carry on a distinctive life of their own, borrowing always from their surroundings – particularly in the matter of language – but remaining always completely conscious of a separate identity. The history of the Jewish people in exile is the history of the growth and decay of these successive centres of Jewish national life, or – if we may coin a term to indicate the absence of complete nationhood – *sub-national* life.
From his introduction to Zionism and the Jewish Future, *edited by Harry Sacher. London, August 1916.*

'Assimilation, disintegration, dissolution'
My only 'intolerance' consisted in the statement that I don't care what will happen to the Jewish community here or in France. I stand by it and this is my reason. The highest ideal for which this community is striving is assimilation, disintegration, dissolution. They will achieve that, they are on the road of achieving it and the sooner they do it the better. I have only reiterated their own fervent wish!
From a letter to James de Rothschild. London, 15 October 1916.

The Hebrew educationalist
I am a teacher myself, and have spent the best half of my life in teaching science in various countries to all sorts of students, and I must say in

some respects the achievements of the Jewish teacher in Palestine are certainly magnificent. Most of them came into the country fifteen years ago and have found there a complete chaos and demoralization. There was practically no trace of Hebrew teaching, but on the contrary there existed French, English, German schools (run by Jews); there also existed the missionary schools which had a hold over the Jewish community. Our teachers began their work in the teeth of a suspicious Turkish Government, which viewed Zionism and Jewish schools with disfavour (please don't forget that all the other above-mentioned schools leaned on their respective governments and, as they were run by our opponents like the *Alliance*, the Anglo-Jewish [Association], the *Hilfsverein*, say nothing of the missions, they helped to combat us), without money, without the elementary necessities of the most modest educational requirements. There were no books, no maps, no dictionaries in Hebrew. I saw the first beginnings of the Jaffa Gymnasium fourteen years ago, and shall never forget that Mr and Mrs Mossinson, Mr and Mrs Bograchov, were teaching in daytime, and in the evening they were scrubbing the floors of the three school rooms they had, because they could not afford to get a servant. They struggled like that for years and became eminently successful. Nine years after the above-described events there was in Jaffa a fine school building with something like 700 young Jewish children from all parts of the globe. Hebrew began to be heard in the streets of Palestinian towns and villages. Text books, newspapers in Hebrew began to appear. And now we have 14,000 Jewish children in our schools out of 16,000. Such a gigantic achievement is due entirely to the unbounded devotion, love and enthusiasm of the teachers who have performed this pioneering work heroically.

But certainly the schools at present suffer from many fundamental faults, namely: (1) The teachers are not *à la hauteur*, all of them. The very fact, perhaps, which has made them into excellent pioneers is militating against them *now* when you require good, ordinary, perhaps commonplace teachers, sound, steady men and not heroes. Moreover, the type of teacher we have in Palestine is in most cases a man who has made his way straight from the *Yeshiva* into the university. He lacks the ordinary elementary and secondary school education. He is therefore in many cases not acquainted with a good many elementary facts. They lack poise, they lack steadiness, and sometimes sorely lack manners. But whereas other nations have seminaries, institutes where they train their teachers, our teachers had to grope in the dark, gain their experience in their own way, had to break new ground without anybody to guide or to help them. They had – what is the most difficult of all – to 'hebraize' methods and values which they had picked up in foreign universities and to assimilate knowledge they have acquired in strange languages. All that grew rapidly, perhaps too rapidly, and no wonder that the whole system of Palestinian education lacks stability, lacks tradition, savours of a sort of *parvenu* atmosphere, does not draw on the ancient Jewish tradition. There is no bridge between the Russian Jewish *Cheder* or *Talmud Torah* and a French or Swiss university, and many a young man after he has come from the *Cheder* into a university tries to forget or divorce himself from the tradition of the *Cheder*. Only the rare few succeed in achieving the harmonious synthesis between the traditional and the modern.

(2) Most of the teachers come from Russia, where Jewish life is in a sense not real, where it is never attached to the daily requirements of the country. The Jew in Russia is cut off from the great stream of real facts which make up the life of a normal community. The Russian Jew strives to become a university professor because the career of a chimney sweep is closed to him. That state of existence, combined with the unbroken tradition of learning, has produced in the Russian Jew this semi-sterile intellectuality which is so characteristic of our present generation in Russia. He lives in a world of thoughts and sentiments, which revolve round himself. The Jew reproduces himself always, and creates values out of his own inner existence detached from nature surrounding him. He becomes self-centred and learns to consider the world outside as a medium averse to the existence of the Jew. This produces an intellectual type who is as *weltfremd*, as devoid of a sense of reality, as was the type of the old Jew who lived only within the walls of the moral and material ghetto which was constructed round him. Such a psychology of the teacher left an impress on the teaching, which is not in all cases adapted to Palestine, and therefore must work for export. But one must not forget that Palestinian life was and is as yet very small, very poor, very limited, and in many instances very artificial. It cannot offer much enrichment to the soul of a teacher and the teacher must always be a poet or a prophet in order to derive inspiration constantly, daily inspiration, from the stones and grass, from the bare hills and sandy valleys, and always picture to himself the glorious past or the beautiful future in face of a miserable present. Think what life offers to a teacher and to a pupil in a modern European city, and what it does to our Palestinian child.

One of the greatest faults of our educational system in Palestine is the lack of a proper understanding of the religious elements in education. I need not labour this point at great length. This also can be explained by the natural history of the Russian Jew. He has broken with the religious

tradition of the ghetto of which he preserved only bitter memories. The religious tradition became a handicap and not a help or a comfort in the moment when he succeeded to tear himself away from the ghetto. Here again you have the lack of gradual transition which is so necessary for the production of steady progress. We fall from one extreme into another, from bondage into freedom, and sometimes this freedom becomes licence.
From a letter to Abraham Tulin. Chamonix, 22 August 1920.

Stalking through history
The question has frequently been raised: How can we be Jews, and as a group, make our contribution to America, or to Italy, or to England, where we happen to live as a group? It seems to me that such commentators sound like Zionists without Zion, like Zionists frightened of a long-distance journey, perhaps of seasickness.

I myself have lived through this search for a divinity sufficiently flexible to answer these two demands. I have experienced the attempt to reconcile service to the culture in which we live as a group, while at the same time maintaining a group consciousness in a positive, aggressive, creative way.

There have been such movements in the past; the Bund, for instance. The Bund tried to make its contribution to the life of Russia while maintaining a Jewish entity, a Jewish programme. The search of the Bund differed somewhat from the present search in that the Bund had the enormous pathos of suffering and tragedy. It had been sanctified by the terrible sufferings of the Jews amidst the Russian people. Out of a community of suffering, we dragged a common programme.

But even despite this creative and fructifying pathos of a great suffering, what was the result of the Bund? As a Jewish group, the Bund disappeared in the stream of Russia. And I think as a Jewish creative, positive, aggressive group, any similar group must dissolve in the stream of American creative life. It will either oscillate back or be carried onward by the great stream of American life. To put it less tenderly, I think individual Jews and individual groups may still go on dreaming and suffering, but creative Judaism, which is neither religion nor nationalism, is bound to be absorbed and swallowed up in a healthy, powerful, developing civilization.

On this basis we are doomed like the ghost in Hamlet, to stalk through the world's history, a riddle to ourselves and surely a riddle to others.

We shall go on explaining this riddle. At the gate of every Jewish community, or of every community where there are Jews, there will stand a figure asking the Jew to solve the insoluble under the threat of destruction.

This uncertainty we feel in the creative effort of the Jew throughout the world. We feel that the Jew in science, for instance, owing to his peculiar position, differs somewhat from the non-Jew in science. I may illustrate in this way.

England is producing a series of scientific efforts; from time to time England produces a man who is as I may call it, scientifically, an oak, a force capable of creating a great school resting on the work and the achievements of this particular man, be it Newton or Faraday, or be it Hume. Such a tree will live and branch out scientifically, generation after generation. Only a long, unbroken tradition of intellectual effort can produce such a type.

In our scientific efforts we Jews, with some creditable and honourable exceptions, are more or less what the Germans call *bodenlos*. Our scientific effort frequently lies on the borderland between two sciences. It operates for a day and sometimes for a month or a year. It has not the character of continuity.

Our literary efforts are in many cases a replica of our economic efforts. They are the efforts of intermediaries, of people who establish themselves as clearing houses for ideas. For this reason the Jew is so prominent in the Press. He has an extraordinary flexibility. He is capable of transmitting an idea from one end of the world to the other without necessarily having an internal relationship to this idea. We cling to those intellectual pursuits which are characteristic of people who do not feel *terra firma* under their feet. That is why we are extraordinarily clever, extraordinarily quick and sometimes extraordinarily interesting, and why we frequently perform a very useful job for somebody else. That is why the Jew is often termed, by his non-Jewish friends, the salt of the earth.

The role of salt from the chemical point of view is to salt somebody's soup. Salt has still another quality. It can be taken only in a definite concentration. The moment the solution is over-saturated, down go the salt and the soup.

We are often termed a ferment. The role of a ferment is to produce a useful action in a medium which will have nothing in common with the ferment. From a biological point of view, however, there is an extremely thin line of demarcation between the ferment and the parasite. The moment the ferment increases in quantity, it ceases to be fermentative and it becomes parasitic.

This is the role which we are forced to play; this is the extraordinary, magnificently unreal programme proposed by some; to be a creative ferment and to guard against the consequences of increasing in weight or in activity so as not to become parasitic. It is a programme infinitely more difficult than building up Palestine. It is infinitely more difficult to achieve this intellectual balance, to oscillate constantly between two worlds instead of admitting simply, narrowly, *ex parte*, if you like, that if we are to live in a world different from ours, we should adapt ourselves honestly in the greatest measure possible, leaving the rest to Providence. Adaptation is one counsel, but we ought to know that it is not a counsel of perfection. We ought to know that it is a compromise; a compromise may be permitted. However, there is no use in glossing it over.

I am a chemist. I am not an authority on evolution. But I imagine that evolution means a compromise between something which is rigid and static, and something which is dynamic. It means a mutual adaptability. The dynamic gets a little more static and the static a little more dynamic, and so it gradually evolves. Evolution would therefore mean approximating to something which exists and to which it is natural to approximate.

If we leave the development of our national life to evolution, evolving towards a culture and civilization over which we have no control, to which we may contribute but which goes on with an enormous momentum, in the spectrum produced there may be left one Jewish line, but let us agree that it will be only a line. The spectrum will be non-Jewish. If our role is to supply the gamut of spectra with Jewish lines, the course suggested will suffice. But let us say so. If our role is to create a Jewish spectrum, then there must be a Jewish source of light. It becomes a question no longer of evolution but of revolution in Jewish life.

From a speech to supporters of the American Menorah Journal. *New York, February 1927.*

Achievements in Palestine

If it were possible to summarize in one sentence the position of Jewry today, I would be tempted to put it thus: the Jews of the world are penned up in their respective countries without any possibility of physical escape. Many Jews therefore seek a moral escape in non-Jewish contacts and interests, and this naturally strengthens the already powerful centrifugal forces tending towards the final break-up of Jewish life as a whole. No such calamity faces the other nations of the world, however hard their fate. Whether Russia groans under the yoke of the Tzars, or writhes under the heel of the Red Army and the Bolshevist oligarchy, the substance of the Russian people, rooted in the soil of a vast country, remains unchanged, and the people can be trusted to work out its own salvation, eventually, at whatever cost. There is always some outlook for Russia; there is none for those communities, ground between hammer and anvil, whose tradition has been utterly destroyed; who, having always had to adapt themselves to varying frameworks created by other peoples, are now powerless to manifest themselves in any life which they can call their own.

But it would be a grave misinterpretation of Jewish history for us to take account of destructive tendencies only, without having regard to the forces of resistance and defence which Jewry has always opposed to such catastrophes, even when they have threatened, as they have from time to time in the past, to overwhelm it. Even when the majority of the Jewish community seemed to be overpowered, either by physical misfortune or by moral or political forces alienating Jews from their ancient faith and traditions, there has always remained a minority which steadfastly refused to submit to the process of assimilation and dissolution. It continued, struggling heroically against heavy odds, to seek ways and means of maintaining its identity, and expressing it.

In the midst of all this there is little Palestine, which entered upon its post-war career in 1917 full of hope and confidence. Remote and unattainable, Palestine had yet been the lode-star of Jewish hopes for nearly two thousand years. In the better world that was to be created after the war, we thought we saw our most cherished dreams come true: we, the disinherited, were at long last to take our rightful place in our own land. No longer would we suffer the humiliation of seeing our best men and our highest achievements credited to our alien hosts, while every failure would unerringly be taken into account. No longer would our young men be driven as emigrants, to beg admission under a quota to some reluctant foreign land. We saw them set forth in a spirit of high endeavour, as, long ago, other men set forth from these English shores, in a little ship called the *Mayflower* – pioneers of a new nation that yet was old. For us the Balfour Declaration heralded a new era: we felt that, for the first time, the sympathies of all civilized humanity were with us. So we set to work. We hoped to build quickly, because of those to whom sheer physical room meant life. And after ten years of ardent and sustained endeavour, we find ourselves still only on the threshold of the problem, and beset by all those difficulties and disappointments which inevitably flow from the fundamental discrepancy between what it is desirable to achieve, and what it may be possible to achieve under a given set of conditions.

Yet in those ten years lying behind us we have achieved something in Palestine, something of which we have no need to be ashamed. I think we Jews have often too little idea of what it means to build up a country, a people, from the very foundations. In the *Galut*, our life has always been a superstructure, imposed upon an alien foundation; but in Palestine we have to build, in material things as in spiritual, from the ground up. And we have to learn by trial and error; there is no other way.

From a speech to Jewish Agency, British Section. London, 7 December 1931.

Slave or sovereign?

The question before us is whether man is a slave or a sovereign: is he the victim of circumstances, some of which he has been instrumental in creating; or is he – at least, can be become – the maker of his own destiny? What has the long history of the Jewish people to offer on this question?

On the surface it certainly looks as though the history of the Jewish people is a tragic illustration of man's helplessness. For what people has been so exposed to the play of external forces of the world as the Jews in these last two thousand years? If we look deeper, the lesson is quite another one.

Nations, like individuals, impress themselves upon the world in two ways: by what they *do*, and by what they *are*. The two are of course interdependent: character expresses itself in action, and action reveals character. But the ultimate influence of a nation, or an individual, is measured more by the amount of character revealed than by the stir produced in human events.

The drama of Napoleon's near conquest of Europe is superficially more impressive than the quiet moral picture of the soul of Abraham Lincoln. But Lincoln's character, working on the New World, has produced more lasting and more beneficial effects than Napoleon's achievements.

What a man *is*, means more than what a man *does*. The same is true of nations. Let us take a familiar example. Which of the two most famous western nations of antiquity, Rome and Greece, has exerted the deeper influence on western civilization? Rome *did* certain things, and Greece *was* certain things. Rome conquered the world, and administered it. Greece did little conquering, but it *was* certain things. It *was* the thinking, feeling, aesthetic spirit of the ancient world. In a certain sense – and in a certain sense only – the contradistinction between Rome and Greece also marks the difference between prophet and priest in Jewish history.

To which of these is the modern world more indebted? To the conquerors and pro-consuls of Rome, to the thinkers and scientists and poets of Greece, to the prophets of Israel or to its kings? I believe the question answers itself.

If Jewish history is studied for its specific content, what constant or *Leitmotif* do we discover? It is, I believe, the history of a people obsessed by an idea: the perfectibility of the human being. Perfectibility here, on this tiny and unhappy world of ours – not in some heaven of the future. While not denying a future existence, the Jewish philosophy concentrated itself on our particular planet. *To be* that which is right was its all-in-all.

All this did not mean that the Jewish people considered itself perfect. On the contrary, there is no people with such a literature of self-criticism as the Jews. But perfectibility, here, and now, among ourselves, has been the Jewish dream.

The persistent and obstinate monotheism of the Jews in face of all persecutions has always been an accompaniment of this belief in human perfectibility. One stern God demanding the perfection of one humanity; this is almost a summary of the Jewish credo.

Indeed, it was so summarized by Hillel, the greatest of the post-biblical sages of the pre-Christian era. Confronted by a pagan who wanted Judaism in a nutshell, as it were, Hillel replied: 'Thou shalt love thy neighbour as thyself. This is the Law; all the rest is commentary.'

Now if a man pursues an idea, he thereby asserts his freedom and his sovereignty. For if he is only the creature of external circumstance, he cannot pursue an idea; what he *is* and what he *thinks* is dictated by external circumstance. To defy external forces, to rise above circumstance, is to proclaim the sovereignty of the human spirit.

There has never been any relationship between the physical force of the Jewish people and the influence which it has exerted on the human spirit. It depended on the strength of the idea. Therefore it was, in a double sense, a proclamation of the sovereignty of man over circumstances.

Monotheism, the supreme importance of perfectibility in this sad, sub-lunar world, the refusal to be bullied by superior force, the right to persist and to suffer even as a minority, these are the leading elements in the Jewish contribution to human progress.

Not all Jews, of course, have been consistent contributors to this idea. From earliest times the lapses of Jews from the idea have been sternly pointed out and castigated by the teachers of the people. But fundamentally, the people has fulfilled this function: the assertion of the sovereignty of the human spirit over the brutality of circumstance.

There is I believe a deep connection between the character of the best

Jewish work and the Jewish spirit that I am speaking of. We can hardly conceive of a Spinoza without reference to a Jewish tradition, affecting him profoundly in spite of himself. The abstract structure of Einstein's great system presents a fascinating contrast with the brilliant empiricism and physical experiments of Rutherford. It is not too fanciful to relate Einstein to the Jewish world outlook and the Jewish search for the absolute.

The Jewish contribution to human values, wherever the Jew has been true to his character, has issued from '*being*'. Among Jews the notion of a philosopher who taught one system and lived according to another, who divorced himself from his theories, has always been unthinkable. A man was not considered a teacher merely because he was clever; if that which he said was not in keeping with the way he lived, and if the two together did not constitute an example, he could not be a teacher. If that which he *is* displeases God and man, how can that which he *says* be of any value?

The desire to seek perfection, to overcome the physical, and find harmony of being, has been the affirmative note in Jewish history. But the miracle is, that it is still there in spite of all frustration. It is still there.

Whether the affirmations of mankind will triumph over its negations, whether the creative will triumph over the destructive, one dare not, at this point in human history, prophesy too freely. But this much one can say: among those affirmations the one that issues from the long history of the Jews is of high value. As of old, the physical quantities involved are small in comparison with the vast problems of mankind; but as of old it may be that the influences so released by Jewish life may be out of all proportion to the physical quantities.

From an address to New York Herald Tribune *Forum. New York, 21 October 1947.*

Jewish contradictions
My greatest difficulty in lying here in this helpless condition is to watch and see all the mistakes that are being made in this country. You see, the Jews are a small people, a very small people, but also a great people. An ugly people, but also a beautiful people, a people that builds and destroys, people of genius, and at the same time a people of enormous stupidity. With their obstinacy they will drive through a wall, but the break in the wall always remains gaping at you. Those who strive consciously to reach the mountain top remain chained to the bottom of the hill. . . .

We Jews can do something very good, something which can be an honour to us all and to all mankind. But we mustn't spoil it. We are an

imperious people and we spoil and sometimes destroy what has taken generations to build up.
From a conversation with Meyer W. Weisgal. Rehovot, December 1951.

The Revival of Jerusalem

Weizmann paid his first visit to Jerusalem in 1907, remaining just one day. He returned in 1918 as head of the Zionist Commission while the First World War was still in progress, and with the front line only a few miles to the north. Weizmann felt oppressed by the wretched condition of the Jews in Jerusalem, who suffered both from the harsh conditions of war and the absence of communal organization. Revival of the city began early in the Mandatory period with the introduction of a secular education system, improved civic services and, above all, the establishment of the Hebrew University. The various schemes for the partition of Palestine excluded Jerusalem and its environs from either a Jewish or an Arab state. The modern city was declared the capital of the Jewish State, in defiance of the UN, in 1949, and the whole, united city was incorporated within Israel after the war of 1967.

Rome and Jerusalem
I didn't go to the Vatican, but the ancient ruins made a deep impression upon me. *Tout passe*; I [feel] no regrets about awe-inspiring Rome, powerful and beautiful. Feeble Jerusalem outlasted it. Only tourists walk about on the ruins of Rome, while on the ruins of Jerusalem new life is stirring.
From a letter to his wife. Rome, 2 April 1907.

The city captured
'You have told me of the fall of Jerusalem; it is not the "fall", it is the rise of Jerusalem. That city will now become a great centre of civilization; its future history opens up great possibilities.

'I sincerely trust that all religions which have been cradled in Jerusalem will work together in harmony. There will be difficulties about the Holy Places but these are not greater than can be overcome by the exercise of forbearance and good feeling.'
From an interview in the Daily Chronicle. *Manchester, 10 December 1917.*

'Not a Jewish city'
It is sad, very sad in Jerusalem! There are very few of us there. Neither

the heart nor the eye perceives a single Jewish institution! On the contrary, there is so much of the foreign element – strong, oppressive, threatening! The minarets and the bell-towers and the domes rising to the sky crying out that Jerusalem is not a Jewish city! There are few young Jews there, and the old ones make a dreadful impression. They are all broken-off splinters, dusty, feeble, soft, covered with age-old mould. The Jewish quarters of Jerusalem are nothing but filth and infection. The indescribable poverty, stubborn ignorance and fanaticism – the heart aches when one looks at it all! To organize Jerusalem, to bring some order into that hell – it's a job that is going to take a long time and require the strength of a giant and the patience of an angel!
From a letter to his wife. Tel Aviv–Jaffa, 18 April 1918.

Conditions in Jerusalem
The situation in Jerusalem is very sad. As you know, it has never been satisfactory, even in time of peace, and during the War it has been gradually drifting from bad to worse. The main income of the Jerusalem community, the Fund of the *Chalukah*, declined very considerably, and as no other resources were available, the pauperization of the community proceeded at a rapid pace, and one is right in saying that starvation in the most painful and literal sense of the word is rampant. The misery, dirt and squalor of the Jewish quarters is above description and it requires a gigantic effort to tackle this problem with any degree of efficiency. The various charitable institutions which have been working are at the end of their wits how to help the ever increasing needs. . . .

We are going up there tomorrow, and I hope that we shall be able to settle on some sort of plan. It is obvious that the mere distributing of alms must be stopped, and that it is necessary to offer possibilities for work. A full report on that subject will be sent to you, but I may say now that we are trying to create co-operative stores, certain workshops and also trying to remove the young children from the schools of Jerusalem, and, if possible, bring them out into the colonies. There are over 2,000 orphans in Jerusalem, many herded in orphanages, which are simply centres of disease and vermin, and the children there are in a condition which is difficult to describe.
From a letter to Louis D. Brandeis. Tel Aviv–Jaffa, 25 April 1918.

Hopes of acquiring Wailing Wall
On the Western side of the Temple site there stands what is believed to have been part of one of the original walls of the Temple. For generations and even centuries past, it has been the practice of pious

Jews to repair to this wall, especially on the eve of the Sabbath, and there to bewail the destruction of the Temple and to pray for its restoration. The Wall is in consequence known as the 'Wailing Wall'. Bound up as it is with the most sacred memories and hopes of the Jewish people, it is an object of peculiar reverence to Jews throughout the world. At present, the Wailing Wall and the neighbouring land are 'Wakf', belonging to a Moroccan corporation, and the Wall is surrounded by ill-kept, ramshackle buildings, whilst the approach to it and the space in front of it are the haunt of Arab loafers and vagrants, whose presence and conduct do not tend to the peace of mind of the Jewish devotees. The impression made on a Jew from abroad when he views the Wailing Wall is painful beyond description. The dignity and solemnity which should attach to this monument of the ancient glories of Israel are obscured by a scene which speaks only of humiliation and degradation.

The hope has long been cherished that some day the Wall and neighbouring land might pass into Jewish hands, and the site be put into a condition not unworthy of the memories and aspirations which it symbolizes. We feel that the present time, when Jewry is looking forward to a revival of its national life, would be of all times the most fitting for the carrying out of this project. We accordingly ask for permission to open investigations with a view to ascertaining how and on what terms the site can be transferred to Jewish control. If that permission is granted, we hope in due course to be able to put forward a proposal for its acquisition.

From a letter to William Ormsby-Gore. Tel Aviv–Jaffa, 1 May 1918.

The cloak of religion

I have been here in Jerusalem nearly a week trying to get some order out of this mess. There's nothing more *humiliant* than 'our' Jerusalem. Anything that could be done to desecrate and defile the sacred has been done. It is impossible to imagine so much falsehood, blasphemy, greed, so many lies, and when one realizes that Jewry is spending about four million francs a year or even more on Jerusalem, and that all this goes to maintain a system of complete moral corruption, one feels ashamed and frightened. The unenviable task of carrying on this system has fallen to our lot. We don't only receive money from Zionists. The former donors on behalf of *Chalukah* are now sending a large part of their money through us and therefore we are confronted with a difficult problem: not to accept this money at all, or if we are going to take charge of it, then to do it in our own way. Either is difficult and it is hard to escape from the dilemma. The whole system operates under the

cloak of religion. The so-called Talmud schools, *yeshivot*, devour at least £3,000 a month, which equals the budget of a good European university. Of course it's difficult to say anything before the problem has been investigated, but I have a feeling that for this money we are supporting 90 per cent parasites and perhaps 10 per cent men of talent who will, maybe, turn into something worthwhile; but to fight this system, which has developed over the centuries and become sanctified – this is what is so awful – by religious tradition, one needs tremendous strength. In any event I believe it is now our duty to begin a general revision and, taking advantage of the situation as well as of the fact that we now have power in our hands, to make the full horror of these conditions clear to the entire Jewish world by means of a scrupulous investigation. That is the main reason for my staying here.
From a letter to his wife. Jerusalem, 1 July 1918.

Symbol of a better future
We have today laid the foundation-stone of the first Hebrew University, which is to be erected on this hill overlooking the City of Jerusalem. Many of us will have had their thoughts cast back to the great historic scenes associated with Jerusalem, scenes that have become part of the heritage of mankind. It is not too fanciful to picture the souls of those who have made our history here with us today, inspiring us, urging us onward to greater and ever greater tasks. Many again will have had their attention riveted on the apparent contrast between today's ceremony and the scenes of warfare within a few miles of us. We are allowing ourselves to indulge in a mental armistice for only a brief moment, and in laying aside all thoughts of strife we try to pierce the veil of war and glance into the future. A week ago we were keeping the Fast of Ab, reminding us that the Temple had been utterly destroyed and the Jewish national political existence extinguished apparently for ever.

But throughout the long centuries, we, the stiff-necked people, have refused to acknowledge defeat, and 'Judaea Capta' is once more on the eve of triumph. Here, out of the miseries and the desolation of war, is being created the first germ of a new life. Hitherto we have been content to speak of reconstruction and restoration. We know that ravished Belgium, France devastated, Poland and Russia, must and will be restored. In this Hebrew University, however, we have gone beyond restoration and reconstruction; we are creating during the period of war something which is to serve as a symbol of a better future.

It is fitting that Great Britain, aided by her great Allies, in the midst of tribulation and sorrow, should stand sponsor to this university.

Great Britain has understood that it is just because these are times of stress, just because we tend to become lost in the events of the day, there is a need to transcend the present by this bold appeal to the world's imagination. Here what seemed but a dream a few years ago is now becoming a reality.

What is the significance of a Hebrew University – what are to be its functions, whence will it draw its students, and what language will it speak? It seems at first sight paradoxical that in a land with so sparse a population, in a land where everything still remains to be done, in a land crying out for such simplicities as ploughs, roads and harbours, we should begin by creating a centre of spiritual and intellectual development. But it is no paradox for those who know the soul of the Jew. It is true that great social and political problems still face us, and will demand their solution. We Jews know that when the mind is given fullest play, that when we have a centre for the development of Jewish consciousness, there will also come the fulfilment of our material needs. In the darkest ages of our existence we found protection and shelter within the walls of our schools and colleges, and the tormented Jew found relief and consolation in a devoted study of Jewish thought. Amidst the gloom and oppressiveness of the ghetto there stood the greatest schools of learning, where young Jews sat at the feet of our great rabbis and teachers. These schools and colleges served as reservoirs where, during the long ages of persecution, were stored an intellectual and spiritual energy which helped to maintain our national existence, and which blossomed forth for the benefit of mankind once the walls of the ghetto had fallen. The sages of Babylon and Jerusalem, Maimonides and the Gaon of Vilna, the lens-polisher of Amsterdam and Karl Marx, Heinrich Heine and Paul Ehrlich, are some of the important links in the long unbroken chain of intellectual development.

The university, as its name implies, is to teach everything the mind of man embraces. No teaching can be fruitful nowadays unless it is strengthened by a spirit of enquiry and research; and a modern university not only produces highly trained professional men, it gives unhindered and undisturbed opportunity to people with the capacity and devotion for scientific research. Our university will thus become the home of those hundreds of talented young Jews in whom the thirst for learning and critical enquiry have been ingrained by heredity throughout the ages, and who in the great multitude of cases are at present compelled to satisfy their burning need amid un-Jewish, very often unfriendly, surroundings.

A *Hebrew* University? I do not suppose that there is anyone here who can conceive of a university in Jerusalem being other than a Hebrew one. The claim that the university should be a Hebrew one rests upon the values the Jews have transmitted to the world from this land. Here, in the presence of adherents of the three great religions of the world, which amid many diversities build their faith upon the God revealed to Moses, and before this civilization founded on Jewish Law, which has paid reverence to the Hebrew prophets and has acknowledged the great mental and spiritual values of the Jewish people, the question is answered: the university is to stimulate the Jews to reach further truth. Am I too bold if today, in this place among the hills of Ephraim and Judah, I state my conviction that the seers of Israel have not utterly perished, that under the aegis of this university there will be a renaissance of the divine power of prophetic wisdom that once was ours? The university will be the focus of the rehabilitation of our Jewish consciousness, now so tenuous because it has become so world-diffused. Under the atmospheric pressure of this mound, our Jewish consciousness can become diffused without becoming feeble, our consciousness will be rekindled and our Jewish youth will be reinvigorated from Jewish sources.

Since it is to be a Hebrew University, the question hardly arises as to its language. By a strange error, people have regarded Hebrew as one of the dead languages, when in fact it never died off the lips of mankind. True, to many of us Jews it has become a second language, but for thousands of my people Hebrew is and always has been the sacred tongue, and in the streets of Tel Aviv, in the orchards of Rishon and Rehovot, on the farms of Hulda and Ben Shemen, it has already become the mother tongue. Here in Palestine, amid the Babel of languages, Hebrew stands as the one language in which every Jew can communicate with every other Jew. It is not necessary for me to dwell at this moment on the technical difficulties connected with Hebrew instruction. We are alive to them; but the experience of our Palestinian schools has already shown to us that these difficulties are surmountable. These are all points of detail which have been carefully examined and will be dealt with at the appropriate time. I have spoken of the Hebrew University where the language will be Hebrew, just as French is used at the Sorbonne, or English at Oxford. Naturally, other languages, ancient and modern, will be taught in their respective faculties; amongst these we may expect that prominent attention will be given to Arabic and other Semitic languages.

The Hebrew University, though intended primarily for Jews, will of course give an affectionate welcome to the members of every race and every creed: *My house is a house of prayer for all the nations*. Besides the usual schools and institutions which go to form a modern university, there will be some branches of science peculiarly appropriate to associate with our Hebrew University. Archaeological research, which has revealed so much of the mysterious past of Egypt and of Greece, has a harvest still to be reaped in Palestine, and our university is destined to play an important part in this field of knowledge.

The question as to the faculties with which our university may begin its career is limited to some extent by practical considerations. The beginnings of our university are not entirely lacking; we have in Jerusalem the elements of a Pasteur Institute and a Jewish Health Bureau already making valuable contributions in bacteriology and hygiene. There is the school of technology in Haifa, and the beginning of an agricultural experimental station at Athlit. It is to scientific research and its application that we can confidently look for the banishment of those twin plagues of Palestine, malaria and trachoma, and for the eradication of other indigenous diseases. It is to true scientific method that we may look for the full cultivation of this fair and fertile land, now so unproductive. Here, chemistry and bacteriology, geology and climatology will be required to join forces, so the great value of the university in the building up of our National Home is apparent. All this again reminds us of what one is likely to forget after four years of a terrible war, with its misapplication of scientific methods, that we must look to science as the healer of many wounds, and the redeemer of many evils. Side by side with scientific research the humanities will occupy a distinguished place. Ancient Jewish learning, the accumulated half-hidden treasures of our ancient philosophical, religious and juridical literature, are to be brought to light again, and freed from the dust of ages. They will be incorporated in the new life now about to develop in this country, and so our past will be linked up with the present.
Speech at the dedication of the site of the Hebrew University. Mount Scopus, 24 July 1918.

In April 1920, during the festival of Nebi Moussa, Arab demonstrations took place in Jerusalem, leading to anti-Jewish rioting with the loss of five Jewish and four Arab lives.

Electricity for Jerusalem
With reference to the £25,000 which you require for setting up an electrical installation in Jerusalem, I beg to inform you that Sir Alfred Mond and myself have undertaken to use our best endeavours to find this sum in as short a time as possible so as to enable you to begin this work with the least possible delay.
Letter to Pinhas Rutenberg. London, 28 October 1920.

Balfour inaugurates the university

The situation in Palestine was at the time somewhat tense, but the security officers assured us that apart from a fairly peaceable demonstration in the form of a strike, and the closing of a few Arab shops in Jerusalem, Haifa and Jaffa, nothing untoward was happening. Which was just as well, as our guests were beginning to arrive in considerable numbers: representatives of universities and learned societies from all over the world, not to mention a great influx of tourists. It was not easy to find rooms for all these people in Jerusalem, for hotel accommodation was still scarce, and not of the best. Still, our reception committee did its work well, and I was not aware that any complaints were made. Every resident who had an appropriate house had placed it at the committee's disposal, and one way or another we managed to see to it that our guests enjoyed reasonable comfort.

The Balfour party and the Allenbys stayed of course at Government House. Kisch, Eder and I lived through some days of rather severe tension, with the responsibility of so many distinguished people on our hands under rather difficult conditions. There was, for instance, only one road from the city to the university on Mount Scopus, and that a narrow one, with little room for cars to turn. Control of traffic was a rather alarming problem, for the number of cars travelling to and fro was a record for Jerusalem at that time. Another purely physical difficulty was the actual site chosen for the opening ceremony. There was as yet no hall which could accommodate anything approaching the number of our guests and visitors – we expected some twelve thousand to fourteen thousand people. The only place, therefore, where we could stage the ceremony was the natural amphitheatre facing a deep wadi on the north-east slope of Scopus. Round this amphitheatre we arranged tiers of seats, following the natural rock formation. Everything was rather rough and ready, but the setting had such natural beauty that no art could have improved on it.

The snag was that, to face the audience in this amphitheatre, the platform had to be on a bridge over the wadi itself. The gorge was deep, sheer and rocky; the bridge was an improvised wooden affair which inspired – in me at least – little confidence. I was told that it had been repeatedly tested, but my blood ran cold at the thought that something might give way at the crucial moment. . . . The builders, however, were convinced that the platform could safely bear two hundred or two hundred and fifty people. However, two hundred of our sturdiest young *chalutzim* volunteered to dance an energetic *hora* on the contraption. Nothing happened – except a great deal of noise – and I felt a little easier. Minute inspection of the platform failed to reveal any damage.

One final problem remained: the guarding of the tested platform during the night before the opening. Again our young *chalutzim* (members of the *Haganah* this time) came to the rescue: they established a sort of one-night camp in the wadi, and conducted frequent inspections, the last only a few minutes before the guests began to arrive.

Though accommodation might be simple, even primitive, the surroundings – the austere magnificence of the landscape which opens out before one from this part of Scopus – more than made up for it. I doubt if anyone who made the pilgrimage to Mount Scopus that day, and the arrivals began before dawn, regretted the non-existence of the Central Hall. Apart from our foreign visitors, people came from all over the country, people of every class and age and type. Only the three or four front rows of the amphitheatre were reserved; the rest were open to the public, and needless to say were thronged hours before the ceremony began. I noted with some pride the discipline and good humour shown by the crowds.

Half an hour or so before the opening time the speakers and other platform guests assembled in the Grey Hill House to don their academic robes; then they passed, a colourful little procession, through the university grove on to the platform. The party from Government House approached direct, from the opposite side. Lord Balfour's appearance set off a tremendous ovation, which was hushed into complete stillness as he took his place on the platform.

The ceremony itself is a matter of historic record, and I need not describe it here. Many of the speakers were deeply moved. One or two of them were, as was only to be expected, rather long-winded. I remember thinking at the time that Bialik (of all people!) was rather straining people's patience: he spoke in Hebrew, which to many of those present was a strange tongue. Moreover, I knew that at sunset the air would cool rapidly, and I was afraid that Lord Balfour (who was a man of seventy-seven) and some of the others might suffer, since all were bareheaded and without overcoats. However, we did finish before sundown; the crowds dispersed in orderly fashion; the guests departed to rest before the dinner party arranged for the evening; and the various committees responsible for the arrangements heaved a sigh of relief that everything had gone off without a noticeable hitch.

At dinner that evening my wife sat next to Lord Allenby. She was moved to ask him: 'Did you think my husband completely harebrained when he asked your permission for the laying of the foundation-stone in 1918?' He thought for a moment and replied: 'When I think back to that day – as I often do – I come to the conclusion that that short

ceremony inspired my army, and gave them confidence in the future.' He repeated this statement in the short speech which he made after the dinner.
From Trial and Error: *description of opening ceremony, 1 April 1925.*

A dispute in 1928 regarding Jewish arrangements for worship at the Western, or Wailing, Wall created disorders necessitating police intervention. Demonstrations by both Jews and Arabs during the succeeding months gave a political character to the dispute. On 23 August 1929 Arabs attacked the Jewish districts of Jerusalem. Violence extended to Hebron, Safed and isolated villages, so that within one week the Jewish dead numbered 133. The military and police were then able to restore order, but not before 116 Arabs had been killed. An enquiry commission was appointed under Sir Walter Shaw to investigate the disturbances, the third and most serious outbreak so far in Palestine.

Worship at Wall not the issue

The present orgy of violence is associated only casually with the worship at the Wailing Wall. That question was used by political adventurers in order to stir up fanaticism which would subserve their own interests, but it is clearly the duty of the government to see that it is disposed of without delay by a final and equitable settlement, and rendered incapable of ever in the future troubling the peace of Palestine. This should not present any serious difficulty. We have repeatedly made it clear that we fully recognize the inviolability of the Moslem Holy Places. For the religious susceptibilities of other creeds we have the same respect as we demand for our own. All we have asked is that Jews should be allowed to conduct their worship before the Wailing Wall in such manner and under such conditions as are consonant with the dignity of their religion. The Wailing Wall is the holiest of sites to Jews throughout the world. It is the last surviving fragment of their Temple, and the symbol of all they have suffered and all they have achieved in the realm of the spirit. The Mandate which gives to the government its legal authority imposes upon it a direct obligation to secure the right of the Jews – as the right of any other religious body in Palestine – to free access to their Holy Places and free exercise of worship.

In spite of all assertions to the contrary, the Moslems have no religious interest in the area before the Wall, which has been known from time immemorial as the scene of Jewish worship at that Holy Place. It is only quite recently that agitators have sought to give to it in the eyes of ignorant Moslems a fictitious religious significance by associating it with the Wailing Wall itself. This significance certain

Arab leaders are now attempting to exploit as a political weapon. The Mandatory Government can have neither the right nor the desire to lend themselves for such a purpose, and it is therefore imperative that a final settlement of this unhappy dispute be reached and proclaimed without delay.

The loss of life, the suffering and the destruction of property which have marked and accompanied the present outbreaks, appeal to the Jewish people not only for sympathy and relief, but also for statesmanship and self-sacrifice. It would be a disaster if we were to be content merely to patch up the wounds, and if our faith and our determination to build up the Jewish National Home were not increased and vitalized by this tragic experience. Out there in Palestine our brothers are bearing the brunt of the attack. They look to us to throw in ever-new reserves, to make good what has been lost, and to extend and increase what has been saved. For us the lesson of these bitter days is that we must increase the pace at which we are travelling. Time is always precious where the work in Palestine is concerned. It is now infinitely more precious than ever before. As our strength in Palestine grows, there comes a corresponding immunity from the repetition of such assaults. Two things have encouraged the Arabs: the first is the conviction that the Jewish National Home is even now only a beginning, and the second is the belief that we are still weak enough to make it possible for them to destroy us. By our own efforts we must do everything in our power to render such a state of mind impossible. We must not only make it abundantly clear that the National Home is actually in being, but, by solid, concrete achievement, by the ever-increasing acceleration of our efforts we must render ourselves too strong to invite further attacks.

From a speech at a protest rally. London, 1 September 1929.

A full-scale Arab rebellion, with a general strike, began in April 1936. Palestine remained in a condition of virtual insurrection until the Second World War. In 1937 a further investigation, by the Royal (Peel) Commission, recommended a solution based upon partition of the country into Jewish and Arab States. Jerusalem and its environs, however, would remain, together with a corridor to the sea, under British Mandate. Weizmann accepted the scheme, though with important reservations, as the only hope for peace in Palestine.

Jerusalem the spiritual force
The modern western suburbs of Jerusalem, with a Jewish population of 72,000, could be made into a Jewish enclave at one end of the British mandated territory, just as Jaffa, with its 50,000 Arab inhabitants, is

made an Arab enclave at the other. But considerations more weighty than mere numbers plead for such inclusion in the Jewish State. To the Jew, the Promised Land and Jerusalem are synonymous. It is Jerusalem that we have longed for and prayed for throughout the ages. Without it the scheme is bereft of spiritual force. These suburbs contain no Holy Places and are of no interest to any other religion. But the sentiment, which elsewhere is concentrated on Holy Places, in this case attaches to a modern town still covered by the sacred name.
From a letter to William Ormsby-Gore. London, 14 July 1937.

Appreciation for Christian support
It was a great disappointment to me that I was not able to remain in London to hear the debate in the House of Lords on Tuesday, but I have just received a copy of *Hansard*, and feel I must send you a line of most grateful thanks for your speech, and especially for your wonderful reference to Jerusalem. I feel sure that you have saved Jerusalem for us. There is really nothing I can say that can express my gratitude and that of my people for your understanding sympathy, and your powerful help. We have remembered Jerusalem for thousands of years; if and when the new Jewish Jerusalem becomes the capital of a Jewish State, we shall remember too, with blessings, the name of the man who was instrumental in saving it for us.
A letter to the Archbishop of Canterbury. Paris, 23 July 1937. (See following item for quotation.)

The UN General Assembly voted on 29 November 1947 to partition Palestine into two states, with Jerusalem and its environs as a corpus separatum *under international trusteeship. On 1 December 1947 Jerusalem came under Arab siege, broken by the Jews after five and a half months of acute hardship. It remained under threat from regular Arab forces as the State of Israel was proclaimed on 14 May 1948. The war ended with the city divided, the Old City being held by Transjordan.*

'You, the defenders'
It is with a sense of humility and sorrow that I rise to speak here among you who have suffered so much and wrought so much during this great and tragic year. Jerusalem holds a unique place in the heart of every Jew. Jerusalem is to us the quintessence of the Palestine idea. Its restoration symbolizes the redemption of Israel. Rome was to the Italians the emblem of their military conquests and political organization. Athens embodied for the Greeks the noblest their genius had wrought in art and thought. To us Jersualem has both a spiritual and a temporal significance. It is the City of God, the seat of our ancient sanctuary. But it is also the capital of David and Solomon, the City of

the Great King, the metropolis of our ancient commonwealth. To the followers of the two other great monotheistic religions, Jerusalem is a site of sacred associations and holy memories. To us it is that and more. It is the centre of our ancient national glory. It was our lodestar in all our wanderings. It embodies all that is noblest in our hopes for the future. Jerusalem is the eternal mother of the Jewish people, precious and beloved even in her desolation. When David made Jerusalem the capital of Judea, on that day there began the Jewish Commonwealth. When Titus destroyed it on the 9th of Ab, on that day there ended the Jewish Commonwealth. But even though our commonwealth was destroyed, we never gave up Jerusalem. An almost unbroken chain of Jewish settlement connects the Jerusalem of our day with the Holy City of antiquity. To countless generations of Jews in every land of their dispersion the ascent to Jerusalem was the highest that life could offer. In every generation new groups of Jews from one part or another of our far-flung Diaspora came to settle here. For over a hundred years we have formed the majority of its population. And now that, by the will of God, a Jewish Commonwealth has been re-established, is it to be conceived that Jerusalem – Jerusalem of all places – should be out of it?

Ten years ago the question first came up in connection with the Report of the Royal Commission. And in the great debate which took place on that subject in the British House of Lords the then Archbishop of Canterbury said these memorable words:

> It seems to me extremely difficult to justify fulfilling the ideals of Zionism by excluding them from any place in Zion. How is it possible for us not to sympathize in this matter with the Jews? We all remember their age-long resolve, lament and longing: 'If I forget thee, O Jerusalem, let my right hand forget its cunning.' They cannot forget Jerusalem. . . .

The Archbishop spoke the truth. We cannot forget Jersualem. And if that was true then, it is all the more true today, for in this last year we have sealed afresh our covenant with our ancient mother-city with the blood of our sons and daughters. In addition to our historical connection with Jerusalem, the unbroken chain of Jewish settlement in this city, the fact of our numerical preponderance among its inhabitants, a new link has been forged – your heroic defence of Jerusalem in this past year. It gives us the right to claim that Jerusalem is and should remain ours. Where were all those who indulged in such fine phrases about the spiritual associations of Jerusalem for the whole civilized world? Did they lift a finger to protect Jerusalem, its men and women and children, its homes and houses of prayer against the Arab shrapnel which rained death day and night on your homes for months on end? Did they make the slightest move when the Jewish quarters of the Old

City with their ancient synagogues were reduced to rubble? Did they utter one word of protest against the Jews being denied for now over a year access to the Wailing Wall, which is our holiest shrine? Do not worry, my friends. The ancient synagogues will be rebuilt, the road to the Wailing Wall will be opened. You have renewed the ancient covenant with your blood and your sacrifices. Jerusalem is ours by virtue of the blood that was shed by your sons in its defence. You suffered hunger and thirst in the broiling heat of the summer and defended Jerusalem against surrender and destruction. Not only the soldiers. You, ordinary men and women, and little children, who went about your work while the bullets flew around you, and many of you fell victims to the deadly missiles. All of you have had a share in this defence.

When I say Jerusalem is ours, I am fully conscious of the sacred associations which Jerusalem has for others than ourselves. We respect these associations. When you defended Jerusalem against havoc and destruction, you fought not only for your own people but for civilization as a whole and for all that Jerusalem means for civilization. Had it not been for your heroic defence, who knows what would have remained of its non-Jewish values! We are anxious to see these values effectively protected and we are agreeable that special arrangements be made for the Old City with its Holy Places. We would like to see this sacred zone beautified so that worshippers coming from all parts of the world to Jerusalem will derive joy and inspiration from their pilgrimage.

There would, however, appear no reason why such special arrangements for the Old City should extend also to the New City outside the Walls which has no such sacred associations. This New City has sprung up during the past hundred years essentially as a result of Jewish effort. It has become during the last thirty years the administrative and spiritual capital of the new Jewish Palestine. It houses our central national institutions, the Jewish Agency, the Jewish National Fund, the *Keren Hayesod*, the Chief Rabbinate, the Hebrew University, the Hebrew National Library, the Jewish Medical Centre and numerous learned and communal bodies. It is now also the seat of the Supreme Court. It seems utterly inconceivable that the establishment of a Jewish State in Palestine should be accompanied by the detachment from it of its spiritual centre and historical capital.

Men and women of Jerusalem, fear not for the future of your city – of our city! The words of our national hymn *Hatikvah* will yet come true:

> To be a free people in our own land –
> The Land of Zion and Jerusalem.
>
> *Speech at an official reception. Jerusalem, 1 December 1948.*

Against internationalization

Anyone familiar with international affairs knows that international regimes of this kind have invariably proved unworkable and produced nothing but insecurity, friction and economic decay. In the case of Jerusalem, a landlocked city wedged in between Israel and Transjordan, with no economic life of its own and no direct contact with the outside world, all these disastrous effects would be multiplied ten-fold.

The only significant concern which the world at large has in Jerusalem is the protection of its holy shrines and the provision of free and secure access to all who wish to visit them. In actual fact, the area containing these holy shrines represents not more than two per cent of the whole of Jerusalem, and the bulk of this sacred area is not in our possession, but in that of King Abdullah. Is it then not the height of absurdity and injustice to force an artificial and unwanted international regime upon the whole of modern Jerusalem – with its hundred thousand Jews, its Hebrew University, and all its other great Jewish institutions – merely because these holy shrines and places are situated in a small area of the city which is not in Jewish possession? We are all in favour of providing special safeguards for the protection of these holy shrines and we are willing to give adequate guarantees for their free accessibility. But we cannot agree, and we cannot be expected to agree, that our ancient Mother-city be severed from the new commonwealth of Israel. Jerusalem has been our capital since the days of David and Solomon. It was the centre of our ancient glory, as the Psalmist described it, 'beautiful in elevation, the joy of the whole earth, the city of the Great King'. Jerusalem was the tribune from which the Prophets of Israel sent forth their eternal messages to mankind: 'Out of Zion shall go forth the Law, and the Word of the Lord from Jerusalem.' When Jerusalem was destroyed, our exiled fathers by the waters of Babylon took the awesome oath: 'If I forget thee, O Jerusalem, may my right hand forget its cunning.' Throughout the long ages of our exile, Jerusalem was the lodestar of our hope. To countless generations of Jews, ascent to Jerusalem and residence within its precincts was the highest that life could offer. During eighteen centuries this attachment and aspiration formed the central theme in our life and literature. And now that our national hopes have been realized and we have again become a free nation in our ancient land, is it conceivable that Jerusalem, the home and heart of our people, be detached from the

State of Israel? It was an Archbishop of Canterbury who, a few years ago, commented on the absurdity of 'realizing Zionism without restoring Zion' to the Jewish people.

To all this has now been added the tragic experience of last year. How can any right-thinking man demand that the Jews of Jerusalem, who last year went through hunger, thirst, and deadly peril in defence of their city, should now be placed under alien rule? It was not the thirty-nine nations who recently voted to turn Jerusalem into an international regime, but the soldiers and engineers of Israel, who last year saved Jerusalem from utter destruction. No wonder that the Jews of Jerusalem are determined to remain part of Israel, as they always have been.

We are most anxious to uphold the authority of the United Nations and we shall be glad to co-operate in any solution which safeguards Christian and Moslem religious interests without depriving us of our Mother-city. Such a solution can be worked out on the common-sense principle that the Holy Places be placed under the supervision of the United Nations, while the city is governed in accordance with the wishes of the people who live in it. That was the spirit and the intent of the proposals we submitted to the General Assembly of the United Nations, by which we still stand. I hope that the United States will wield its unrivalled influence in the United Nations for helping towards such a solution.

From a letter to President Truman. Rehovot, 3 January 1950.

The Boundaries of Palestine

Palestine was generally regarded as Southern Syria and thus did not exist as an identifiable geographical entity under the Turks. With the anticipated disappearance of the Ottoman Empire in the First World War, Zionist and Arab aspirations, as well as Great Power rivalry in the region, compelled an early solution to the frontier question. Weizmann became anxious when he learned, early in 1917, of a secret Anglo-French arrangement (the Sykes-Picot Agreement) to divide the Ottoman possessions in such a way as either to give a truncated Palestine an international regime or to make it an Anglo-French condominium.

Dangers in the secret plan

The discussion turned on the question of an arrangement which is supposed to exist between Great Britain and France regarding Palestine. This arrangement had been entered into apparently almost at the beginning of the war and appears to be more or less on the following lines: That the French are to have Northern Syria down to a line drawn from Haifa to the Lake of Tiberias, the rest of Palestine south of this line down to the Egyptian frontier is to be internationalized, the Bay of Haifa with the two towns Haifa and St Jean d'Acre to be British with a British railway joining up the Bay with the Baghdad railway. Dr Weizmann submitted that this arrangement embodies all the faults of an Anglo-French and an international settlement and is moreover aggravated by the fact that Palestine is cut up into two halves and the Jewish colonizing effort which had been going on before the war for more than thirty years is annihilated.

By the separation of Galilee from Judea Palestine has been deprived of a very valuable part of the country. The Jews or the Zionists would particularly suffer because round the Lake of Tiberias the country is dotted with Jewish colonies. Although this is very grave from our point of view and we would always consider it as an unjust partition and it would certainly constitute a Jewish irredenta we would find a certain amount of compensation in the fact if at least Judea were British. For a generation or two the Jews could work under a British protection in Judea, try to develop the country as much as possible and hope for the time when some just tribunal would give them the rest of Palestine on which they have an historic claim. But if Judea instead of becoming British would be simply internationalized then this partition from a Jewish point of view is a Solomon's judgement of the worst character, the child is cut into two and both halves mutilated. But also from a general point of view it does not seem to be an admissible solution. The entry of Russian and American democracies into the war, the proclamation of anti-annexationist principles and the settlement of the map of the world on national principles on a basis of historic claims, are not in accordance with a division of Palestine which is based purely on strategic considerations.

But even from the purely strategic point of view this division does not present any advantages. The possession of the Bay of Haifa is a valuable asset from a strategic point of view as long as the hinterland is consolidated and populated by a loyal and civilized population, but if the hinterland is going to be handed over to an international regime the advanced British position will become an island and the naval base would not be able to lean on a reliable population behind it. There is

little doubt that the suggested division of Palestine would raise an outcry which will ring through from one end of the world to the other as it is contrary to all the principles which have been proclaimed by the Allies since the beginning of the war and which have lately been so strongly emphasized by America and Russia.
From a note of an interview with Lord Robert Cecil, Acting Foreign Secretary. London, 25 April 1917.

Balfour Declaration not concerned with territorial questions
No discussion about Jerusalem or any other territorial points has taken place, all the efforts both of Mr Sokolow and myself were directed towards the attaining of the declaration which as you know only lays down a principle, the actual details have never been discussed yet.
From a letter to Herbert Samuel. London, 12 December 1917.

French ambitions in Palestine
The French are making themselves as disagreeable as possible there. They pose as the conquerors of Palestine, as the Protectors of the Christians, as the modern Crusaders. Monsieur Picot, the French Political Officer whom we saw here and in Paris several times, and who professed keen sympathies towards us and the movement, is at present the soul of this French propaganda. He entered Jerusalem together with Allenby and has assumed the name of 'Haut Commissionaire de la Palestine'. Mr Picot has brought with him ready prepared French postal stamps, specially designed for the occasion, and various other little external tokens of French influence which tried to indicate the French aspirations for the future.

The British naturally resent all that but they are extremely anxious not to create more friction between them and the French than is absolutely necessary. The attitude of the French is producing another complication. The Italians have no designs on Palestine or Syria *as long as the French have none*. But they are extremely jealous of the French and they therefore immediately put up claims – quite fictitious and unreasonable – simply in order not to lag behind the French.
From a letter to Louis D. Brandeis. London, 14 January 1918.

Syrian aspirations
Count Zagheb [of the Syrian Arab Committee] volunteered certain interesting statements about the orientation of the Syrians. Firstly, there is a deadly hatred between the Moslems and the Christians; secondly, they would never forgive the English for desiring to hand over Damascus to the Hedjaz. It would constitute a terrible irredenta. Thirdly, the Count complained about lack of organization and funds

amongst the Syrians and finally, he thought that the only point of division between them and us would be the question of Galilee and the Lake of Tiberias. The Syrians are most anxious to have that. I frankly told him that this appears to me impossible, that there are very few Syrians in the district, and that with the exception of Nazareth, all this country must go to the Jews, who have developed a great colonizing activity there.
From a letter to Aaron Aaronsohn. London, 16 January 1918.

Between Rafah and Jaffa
There are great tracts of land lying between Rafah and Jaffa which are not owned by anybody in particular. According to the estimate of our friends here, only 5 per cent of these large stretches of land are cultivated and this in a sporadic manner. We have, therefore, thought it necessary to submit to the Military Authorities the proposals as outlined in the Memorandum. I realize that there is an element of risk in this affair, but should we succeed in putting under cultivation large stretches of land, even temporarily, it will give us an advantage of incalculable value. Although the whole great question of land tenure will still have to be discussed, and probably will not be discussed with any positive results until after the Peace Conference, the question of such a '*fait accompli*' would mean a great achievement.
From a letter to Nahum Sokolow. Tel Aviv–Jaffa, 8 May 1918.

Extent of Jewish Palestine
It may be that the Jews of Palestine will take part in the development of Mesopotamia and the neighbouring countries but the full economic and cultural development of Palestine can only be attained if by a Jewish Palestine is meant an integral Palestine stretching from Dan to Beersheba and from the Mediterranean to the Hedjaz railway. Unless the Jewish National Home will include the rich wheat soils of the Hauran, the wooded hills of Galilee, and the pasturage of Moab, a full and complete Jewish national life will not be possible, and it will suffer from a triple pressure from the north, the east and the south, which may eventually set up an effective barrier to a necessary and desirable Jewish expansion.
From a letter to Leopold S. Amery. London, 18 October 1918.

Proposals to Paris Peace Conference
The boundaries of Palestine shall follow the general lines set out below:
Starting on the North at a point on the Mediterranean Sea in the vicinity South of Sidon and following the watersheds of the foothills of the Lebanon as far as Jisr el Karaon, thence to El Bire, following the

dividing line between the two basins of the Wadi el Korn and the Wadi el Teim, thence in a southerly direction following the dividing line between the Eastern and Western slopes of the Hermon, to the vicinity West of Beit Jenn, then Eastward following the northern watersheds of the Nahr Mughaniye close to and West of the Hedjaz railway.

In the East a line close to and West of the Hedjaz railway terminating in the Gulf of Akaba.

In the South a frontier to be agreed upon with the Egyptian Government.

In the West the Mediterranean Sea.

The details of the delimitations, or any necessary adjustments of detail, shall be settled by a Special Commission on which there shall be Jewish representation.

From the Zionist statement to the Peace Conference, 3 February 1919, signed by Lord Rothschild, Nahum Sokolow, Chaim Weizmann and representatives of the Zionist Organization of America and the Russian Zionist Organization. It was formally submitted by the Zionist delegation appearing before the Supreme Allied Council, 27 February 1919.

Plea for a frontier on the River Litani

At the moment when, with your colleagues, you are about to engage in the final negotiations on which the fate of Palestine depends, the Zionist Organization desire to address you on a matter which causes them the deepest anxiety. It is the question of the Northern Boundary of Palestine.

The Zionist Organization have from the beginning put forth the minimum requirements essential to the realization of the Jewish National Home. It goes without saying that in no circumstances could the Sykes-Picot line be accepted by Zionists, even as a basis of negotiation. It would not only divide historic Palestine and cut off the source of the water supply of the Litani and the Jordan, but it would do far more. It would deprive the Jewish National Home of some of the most promising fields of colonization in the Jaulan [Golan] and Hauran, upon which the success of the whole project largely depends. It would take from it a number of prosperous Zionist colonies that have already been established. It would rob the assurances of the Allied and Associated Powers with respect to the Jewish National Home in Palestine of a great part of their value.

The severance of any portion of the territory in the North, which is vital to the economic life of Palestine, would give rise to a feeling of deep and lasting bitterness in the hearts of Jews, not only in Palestine but throughout the world.

While the actual boundaries of historic Palestine were subject to constant change with the varying fortunes of Israel, the natural boundaries of biblical Palestine to the North were considered to run from the desert on the East, along the slopes of the Hermon, the mountain home of the tribe of Dan, over to the Litani on the West, where the Lebanon and Anti-Lebanon first break into a series of elevated plateaux.

Today, however, the boundaries cannot be drawn exclusively on historic lines. The fact that, out of consideration for the Moslem sentiment that is attached to the Hedjaz railway, our claims to the East stop short of the historic frontier, makes it all the more necessary that there be no curtailment of our claims to the North.

Our claims to the North are imperatively demanded by the requirements of modern economic life. The whole economic future of Palestine is dependent upon its water supply for irrigation and for electric power, and the water supply must mainly be derived from the slopes of Mount Hermon, from the headwaters of the Jordan and from the Litani river.

Commissioned by the Zionist Organization, the eminent engineers, Messrs Douglas Fox and Partners, have recently sent to Palestine Sir Charles Metcalfe and Mr John [i.e. Ralph] Freeman, who have made a careful survey of its economic possibilities. The following letter gives the conclusions of their Report upon this particular matter:

'We summarize briefly below the grounds for our recommendations in respect of the Northern Frontier of Palestine.

1. Palestine is not a country of great natural wealth. It will only become prosperous and populous if the best and wisest use is made of its natural resources.
2. Palestine is seriously handicapped by being destitute of fuel. There is no coal, very little wood and only a possibility of oil.
3. The future wealth of Palestine will be derived mainly from its soil and climate, which are suitable for growing fruit and other valuable crops, but these crops require more water than is available from natural precipitation. Palestine's second handicap, therefore, is insufficiency of rainfall.
4. To compensate for these two drawbacks, nature has provided the Palestinian region with:
    (a) The waters of the Jordan for irrigation.
    (b) The falls of the Jordan for hydro-electric power.
    (c) Underground water which can be utilized to full advantage by means of (b).
    (d) The waters of the Litani for direct irrigation and/or diversion

into Jordan to supplement (a) and (b).
(e) Facilities for storage in the Valley of the Litani.
5. (a), (b) and (c) are at once required for purposes of irrigation and power.
6. While (d) and (e) are not as yet needed, their use for irrigation and power when required must be secured, if the economic future of Palestine is not to be prejudiced.
7. (c), (d) and (e) are valueless to the territory north of the proposed frontier. They can only be used beneficially in the country much further south.
8. For these reasons, we consider it essential that the Northern frontier of Palestine should include the Valley of the Litani, for a distance of about twenty-five miles above the bend, and the Western and Southern slopes of Mount Hermon, in order to ensure control of the headwaters of the Jordan, and to permit of re-afforesting this region.'

The Zionists are well acquainted with the deep interest which you, Sir, take in the present problems and the future prospects of Palestine, an interest in which your distinguished colleagues share; and they have faith that the British Government will never agree to any concession which, from the standpoint of Zionism, could only be regarded as a grave disaster. They have confidence that the British Government will never compromise the vital interests of the Jewish National Home.
A letter to David Lloyd George. London, 29 December 1919.

An Anglo-French Convention on Frontiers, signed on 23 December 1920, excluded the Litani waters from Palestine.

The question of Transjordan
May I bring to your attention a matter of vital importance to the economic future of Palestine and the upbuilding of the Jewish National Home. It is the question of the eastern and southern frontiers. The question has become especially critical in view of the agreement reached with France regarding the northern boundary which cut Palestine off from access to the Litani, deprived her of possession of the Upper Jordan and the Yarmuk and took from her the fertile plains east of the Tiberias which had heretofore been regarded as one of the most promising outlets for Jewish settlement on a large scale.

During the discussions with the French, it may be recalled, very little was said specifically about the eastern boundary south of the Hermon. It was for practical purposes assumed that so far as the territory in the east was brought within the British sphere, the needs of the Jewish National Home would be fully satisfied. Were this not the case, of course, there would have been little purpose in the struggle to secure for Palestine the right to use the Yarmuk, as the rights secured would be in large part valueless if the territory to the south also were to be taken from her jurisdiction and control. That territory must, it is clear, be settled with a fixed population, in order to give physical security and economic value to the extensive engineering works contemplated.

It must be confessed, however, that certain parts of the address delivered to the Sheikhs assembled at Es Salt last August by His Majesty's High Commissioner, which might perhaps be interpreted as suggesting the possible separation of Transjordania from Cis-Jordania, were the cause of some misgiving, but it was taken for granted that those remarks were not intended to foreshadow a fundamental change in the policy of His Majesty's Government and that they were not meant to do more than adumbrate the possible division of the country for administrative purposes into two parts – Western and Eastern Palestine. It was, nonetheless, expected that even should this eventuate, Transjordania would still fall under the general provisions of the Palestine Mandate. It is quite appreciated, however, that the administrative control of the Mandatory might assume a looser form in Transjordania than in Cis-Jordania, and that the local customs and institutions might be modified gradually as Zionist colonization proceeded. The Jewish colonists, moreover, could not expect the same security for life and property in Eastern Palestine as in Western Palestine. They could, like pioneers in all countries, be expected to defend their settlements from raids and local disturbances. The opening of Eastern Palestine to Jewish colonization would consequently, far from aggravating the military burden of the Mandatory, offer the most promising prospect of its gradual reduction and ultimate surcease, for it is only through a permanent settlement of a peaceful population upon the Transjordanian plateaux that the problem of the defence of the whole Jordan Valley can be satisfactorily solved.

Zionists have, of course, always recognized the special Moslem interests in the Hedjaz railway. It was for that reason that in our original proposals to the Peace Conference – which proposals the Emir Faisal publicly stated he considered to be moderate and proper – it was suggested that the eastern frontier be drawn close to, but west of the railway. At that time the French were not yet in Damascus, and it was thought desirable that a small corridor be provided along the railway, so as to connect the Hedjaz Kingdom with Damascus. In view of the French occupation of Damascus, His Majesty's Government may now consider that the reason for the corridor no longer exists and that it could be better for the present at least, to draw no definite eastern frontier short of the desert, but simply to provide special safeguards for the Moslem interests in the Hedjaz railway.

But if it is thought advisable to provide a corridor between Palestine and the desert, it should nonetheless be clearly recognized that the fields of Gilead, Moab and Edom, with the rivers Arnon and Jabbok, to say nothing of the Yarmuk, the use of which is guaranteed under the recently signed convention, are historically and geographically and economically linked to Palestine, and that it is upon these fields, now that the rich plains to the north have been taken from Palestine and given to France, that the success of the Jewish National Home must largely rest. Transjordania has from the earliest time been an integral and vital part of Palestine. There the tribes of Reuben, Gad and Manasseh first pitched their tents and pastured their flocks. And while Eastern Palestine may probably never have the same religious and historic significance as Western Palestine, it may bulk much larger in the economic future of the Jewish National Home. Apart from the Negev in the south, Western Palestine has no large stretches of unoccupied land where Jewish colonization can take place on a large scale. The beautiful Transjordanian plateaux, on the other hand, lie neglected and uninhabited, save for a few scattered settlements and a few roaming Bedouin tribes. The total population of the regions within the British sphere is considerably less than 200,000 and, on the average, there are fewer than eighty inhabitants per square mile. The only settled communities of any size are those about Maan, Es Salt and Kerak. Maan is not claimed for Palestine. The inhabitants of Es Salt and Kerak are chiefly Christian who desire to be linked with Palestine, rather than with the Hedjaz.

The climate of Transjordania is invigorating; the soil is rich; irrigation would be easy; and the hills are covered with forests. There Jewish settlement could proceed on a large scale without friction with the local population. The economic progress of Cis-Jordania itself is dependent upon the development of these Transjordanian plains, for they form the natural granary of all Palestine and without them Palestine can never become a self-sustaining economic unit and a real National Home. The evidence of competent and impartial authorities collected in the attached memorandum gives abundant proof of this. The linking of Transjordania with the Hedjaz Kingdom would prove disastrous to the future of Eastern Palestine as well as Western Palestine, and would in the end be of little or no value to the Hedjaz.

It is fully realized that His Majesty's Government must consider their pledges to the Arab people and the means of satisfying their legitimate aspirations. But the taking from Palestine of a few thousand square miles, scarcely inhabited and long derelict, would be scant satisfaction to Arab nationalism, while it would go far to frustrate the entire policy of His Majesty's Government regarding the Jewish National Home. Nothing need be said of the land stretching southeastwards from Maan. That, it is assumed, will be either incorporated in or allied to the Hedjaz Kingdom. But it is clear that, apart from a small corridor along the Hedjaz railway, there is no concession north of Maan, short of Damascus, to which Arab nationalism could attach any real or permanent value. The aspirations of Arab nationalism centre about Damascus and Baghdad and do not lie in Transjordania.

The southern frontier is also a matter of no little significance to the Jewish National Home. As it is vital to the economic future of Palestine that she should have an outlet to the Red Sea, the boundary should run from the vicinity of Maan southwards along the old Roman road to the Gulf of Akaba. The region in question is largely waste and is of no value to any country but Palestine. It is also of the greatest importance from the standpoint of the Jewish National Home and of general stability in the Near East that there should be some rectification of the arbitrarily drawn Turco-Egyptian frontier. In the final Egyptian settlement, the land north of El Arish, now mainly derelict but potentially rich in resources essential to Palestine's future, ought not to be allotted to Egypt, with which it is neither economically nor geographically connected and from which it is separated by a vast desert. Egyptian nationalism, it is believed, could not justly oppose a southern frontier following the Wadi El Arish, the Wadi Gerais and Wadi Hesham and terminating in the vicinity of Taba on the Gulf of Akaba.

It is confidently hoped, therefore, that there will be no thought of any further diminution of the legitimate claims of Palestine when the eastern and southern frontiers come under discussion. The unsatisfactory character of the settlement on the north makes it all the more vital that the Jewish National Home be generously dealt with on the east and south.

A letter to Winston Churchill, Colonial Secretary. London, 1 March 1921.

Transjordan was separated from Western Palestine at the Cairo Conference of March 1921. The Emir Abdulla had established himself there the previous year, and now came formally under British protection. The Churchill White Paper of June 1922 indicated that Palestine west of the Jordan alone was available for implementation of the Jewish National Home policy. The Mandate, as qualified by a British memorandum in September 1922 and approved by the League of Nations, bestowed international sanction on the separation.

'Transjordan Arabs clamour for us'

For some reason which I need not enter into, Palestine has been truncated, and a vast part has been eliminated from the scope of the Jewish clauses of the Mandate. The size of the country in which we are allowed to operate was halved overnight – indeed, was cut by more than half – and now the very same people who did that, or their supporters, turn to us and say: 'Well, you will not be able to do very much, because it is a very small country!' We have not made it small! When the project was discussed and sanctioned there was no talk of any political difference between Transjordan and Palestine. At that time, and until 1921, the Balfour Declaration applied to both countries. In fact, there are many people here who will remember the discussion of the eastern frontiers of Palestine, and we were usually told: 'You cannot discuss the eastern frontier of Palestine; there is no eastern frontier; the eastern frontier tapers down into the desert.' But suddenly a very rigid frontier was established, and a frontier which, curiously enough, is guarded one-sidedly. It is well-guarded from the west, but it is never guarded from the east. It is a door which opens only in one direction. It is open for the Arab; it is closed for the Jew. With regard, therefore, to all the arguments, which are in many cases very valid, which point to the smallness of Palestine, we admit them; the smallness of Palestine is a geographical fact, but it has a political reason for which neither the authors of the Balfour Declaration nor those who tried to help to bring about the Balfour Declaration are in any way responsible.

There is therefore a very strong moral reason for the Jews of the world to point out this fact and to say that at some date, under some conditions, Transjordan must be open to Jewish endeavour. We do not wish to carry the Balfour Declaration across the Jordan. I do not think that anybody wants to change the status of Transjordan; but to close a country which is under British Mandate to Jews is something so novel in the practice of the British Empire that we cannot understand it. It is the less understandable as the Arabs wish the Jews to come to Transjordan. There are some Arabs – in fact a great many – who do not wish the Jews to come to Western Palestine, but as far as Eastern Palestine is concerned the roles are reversed. The Palestinian Arabs do not wish the Jews to go to Transjordan, but the Transjordanian Arabs, in so far as they are vocal, are asking and clamouring for it, and they want it so much that, if the Jews do not come to Transjordan, they come to us! It may be a remote contingency, and not dependent upon us, whether Transjordan will in some circumstances, circumstances which will not affect its political status, be open to Jewish endeavour. I hope that that will happen one day; indeed, I believe it is inevitable that it will happen, and I believe and I hope that it will happen with the consent of the Arab population, which is very essential.

From a speech to a conference of the English Zionist Federation. London, 7 October 1934.

Partition the solution

It may appear to you somewhat daring if I make a tentative proposal, but my experience and my contribution to the building of Palestine embolden me to speak on the subject. There is no question about it that when Palestine was promised, when the Declaration was given, when the Mandate was written – and I should like to say that the Mandate was written not only when Mr Balfour was Foreign Secretary, it was completed in its present form under Lord Curzon, and I am quoting Lord Curzon, because Mr Balfour might be considered as biased in favour of the policy of which he is the main author, and by no stretch of the imagination could Lord Curzon be accused of any bias in that direction – at that time by 'Palestine' was understood 'Palestine and Transjordan'. Then Transjordan was cut off. As you know, the size of Transjordan is much greater than that of Palestine – more than three times. It was cut off, so to speak, at a moment's notice. And here is a sort of irony. First you amputate Palestine. You cut off a country which is three or four or five times the size of Palestine, and then you turn round on the poor Zionists and tell them, you are a small country; you cannot bring any population there; you must displace others, and we cannot allow that, and so on. I do not think it is cricket. I do not think it is fair play. Either you do not cut it off – or if you have done it, you cannot throw it in our face that we are trying to bring a population into a small country. In fact, what we have been trying to do since that time is, by ingenuity and scientific development, to increase the size of the country, and as you cannot increase it materially, or geographically, we have tried to increase it in such a way that we are trying to make two blades of grass grow where one blade grew before; in fact, to make four tomatoes grow where one was growing before, by intensifying – sometimes over-intensifying – and utilizing every little notch and every nook and cranny in Palestine, and making it produce human sustenance. That has been our business since Palestine was amputated. But it has been done, and I am not harking back to it, and I even realize that today, in order to have peace in this country, stability in the Middle East – and the Middle East is important not only for Jews and Arabs, but also for the whole of the civilized world – we have a great responsibility not to disturb the peace in this part of the world.

Knowing all that, we are – I think I am speaking the mind of a great many Jews – after a great deal of hardship, after a great deal of testing, after a great deal of evaluating the possibility of what we can do, for a form of partition which would satisfy the just demands of both the Jews and the Arabs. We realize that we cannot have the whole of Palestine. God made a promise: Palestine to the Jews. It is up to the Almighty to keep His promise in His own time. Our business is to do what we can in a very imperfect human way. I should not like to play on the sentiment of the distinguished Indian representative who sits here. I should say partition is *à la mode*. It is not only in small Palestine; it is in big India. But at least there you have something to partition. Here we have to do it with a microtome. There you can do it with a big knife.

What are the advantages of partition? It has, in my opinion, two great advantages. It is final, and it helps to dispel some of the fears of our Arab friends. I am not saying that you would easily dispel all fears. Fear is not a matter of logic. It is a matter of emotion, and emotional reaction cannot be dispelled by logical performance. But at any rate we can do all we can in order to help in future to mitigate their fear. If it is final, the Arabs will know, and the Jews will know, that they cannot encroach upon each other's domain. To us it means something else. It means equality of status with our Arab neighbours: the most important requisite for good relations between us and them. As long as they consider us inferior in political status, they will not be anxious to make peace with us. Therefore, it is a desirable solution, although it represents, as I have already pointed out, a new and great sacrifice on the part of the Jewish people. It cannot be whittled down, it cannot be bargained down, and the part of Palestine which would remain after partition must be something in which Jews could live and into which we could bring a million and a half people in a comparatively short time. It must not be a place for graves only, or graveyards, or, as you sometimes see on very full trams, 'standing-room only'.

Therefore I have a plea to make to this distinguished Committee. I respectfully pray that you will come to a decision of this kind, and above all see that this decision is carried out – and carried out quickly.

From his evidence to the UN Special Committee on Palestine. Jerusalem, 8 July 1947.

The British Connection

Help for small nations
The late Dr Herzl had great faith in English Jewry, because in England there are Judaic Jews with Gentile privileges. We have every oppor-

tunity to do work here for the Zionist movement. The English Gentiles are the best Gentiles in the world. England has helped small nations to attain their independence. It was not always done for love, but to some extent because it was profitable for England to act thus.
From a speech at a public meeting. Manchester, 26 February 1911.

Link between Britain and the Moslem world
The Eastern Question will undoubtedly be opened up; it almost is now. The latest events in Persia have drawn England into an alliance with Russia. This is not very good for us. The old paradox that the foreign policy of the Liberals is much more conservative than that of the Conservatives is being repeated. The only way for us to approach the English is to show them how vital it can be for England to have a friendly and 'strong' element in Palestine, in the Asian Near East in general, that we can be the link between England and the Moslem world. England will after all also have a lot to do with the Moslems.
From a letter to Zionist Smaller Actions Committee. Manchester, 28 December 1911.

'English Consul'
I want to go to Palestine not when I have nothing to lose here, but on the contrary after having achieved everything here. This 'everything' consists of two things: a full professorship and admission to the Royal Society. . . . I shall not conceal from you that I have yet another ambition – to become English Consul in Palestine.
From a letter to Arthur Hantke. Manchester, 25 February 1912.

Spiritual affinity
Jews all over the world trust Great Britain and look to this country as a liberator of Palestine. They know that law and order would be established there and justice would be meted out to the various races living in the country. On the other hand the Jews would not be interfered with in their colonizing activity and in their cultural development and when the Jewish population has grown strong enough it would be given by Great Britain the measure of self-government which it deserved. This wise policy of Great Britain has been sufficiently proved in all its colonies and no other nation in the world has ruled its colonies in the same manner. Under British rule great and flourishing Jewish communities have been established all over the world like the communities in Canada, South Africa and Egypt and even the American community has been established under an English-speaking race which is imbued with the same spirit of justice and fairness as the British race. The fact that England is a

biblical nation accounts for the spiritual affinity between them and the Jews.
From a note of an interview with Lord Robert Cecil, Acting Foreign Secretary. London, 25 April 1917.

Under Britain's wing
While the creation of a Jewish Commonwealth in Palestine is our final ideal – an ideal for which the whole of the Zionist Organization is working – the way to achieve it lies through a series of intermediary stages. And one of these intermediary stages, which I hope is going to come about as a result of this war, is that the fair country of Palestine will be protected by such a mighty and a just Power as Great Britain. Under the wing of this Power Jews will be able to develop, and to set up the administrative machinery which, while not interfering with the legitimate interests of the non-Jewish population, would enable us to carry out the Zionist scheme. I am entitled to state in this assembly that His Majesty's Government is ready to support our plans.
From a speech to a Zionist Conference. London, 20 May 1917.

On receiving the Balfour Declaration
We have the honour to acknowledge the receipt of the Declaration, on behalf of HM Government, in favour of the Zionist aspirations, conveyed in your letter of the 2nd inst., to Lord Rothschild 'to be brought to the knowledge of the Zionist Federation'.

The Jewish people always regarded Great Britain as a bulwark of right and justice and of the defence of the weak against the strong. They are aware of the fact that the heart of Great Britain is open to the call of distressed humanity, and that no persecution and no wrong occur, but that the sympathy of Great Britain is evoked. They remember perfectly well that the emancipation of the Jews in this country has been a shining example for other countries and that the Jewish people have never failed to find moral support from the British Government and British public opinion in the hours of their trial.

It is therefore with affectionate acknowledgement and gratitude that the Jewish people will receive the glad tidings that with regard to the real and abiding solution of the Jewish problem, and the re-establishment in Palestine of a self-governing Jewish nationality – the greatest accomplishment of emancipation in its national aspect – it is once more Great Britain that promises, at the present eventful juncture, its powerful protection to the Jewish masses who are longing for their National Home in Palestine. Indeed, no Government is more qualified and no people more called upon by its noble traditions to take the leading part in this work of civilization and national justice than are the

people and Government of Great Britain.
From a letter signed jointly with Nahum Sokolow to Arthur J. Balfour. London, 19 November 1917.

The harsh reality
I don't much like the situation I've found here. It's dangerous and difficult. The behaviour of the British towards us is shocking, and all the promises they gave us at home sound bitterly ironic here. And the worse the British treat us the greater the boldness and arrogance of the Arabs becomes; they're already raising their heads, in which the British are no doubt encouraging them. Among all the officials living here there are perhaps five–six who treat us and Zionism more or less decently; the rest are our secret or open enemies.
From a letter to his wife. Jerusalem, 29 March 1919.

What Britain can do
Those who believe, or who affect to believe, that some sort of system can be devised whereby Palestine can be 'given' to the Jewish people are talking of a Zionism which is not political but metaphysical. A country is not a thing done up in a parcel and delivered on demand. England can no more 'give' Palestine to the Jews than it can give them history or a culture. All that England can do – and is making serious efforts to do – is to create conditions whereby the Jews cannot 'take' Palestine but can grow into it again, by a natural and organic process.

England could not even give Palestine to the Jews if that country were entirely uninhabited. It could permit Jewish immigration 'as of right and not on sufferance' – which is precisely what it is doing now. The rest is in the hands of the Jewish people.
From an article in the Nation. *New York, 12 March 1924.*

The Palestine Administration
It is unfortunate that the Civil Administration in Palestine should have been, and still is, largely recruited from men who have little understanding of Zionist aims and aspirations, who come to Palestine unacquainted with and unprepared for the complex task which they have to face. I think it is to this, more than to any definite policy – let alone what is commonly known as antisemitism – that the attitude of the Palestine Administration is probably due. I have sometimes heard it said that this is merely corroborative evidence of the Machiavellian policy of His Majesty's Government, and that, while the Home Government continues to profess its adherence to the Balfour Declaration and the Mandate, it is part of its policy to select as its representatives in Palestine only such officials as can be trusted to take

no interest in, and show no sympathy for, the policy which they will have to execute. I can only say that all my experience of British Governments – and it is fairly extensive – goes to disprove any such assertion. I believe the British to be the least anti-Jewish of any people in the world; and I believe the British Government to be genuinely anxious to see the policy of the Mandate prove a success in Palestine. But we have to realize that, for the British Cabinet, Palestine is not their only concern, and that much must necessarily be left to the men on the spot – and to us. The problem of Palestine is *sui generis*, and places heavy demands on the administrators; even a British Administration meets with it for the first time.

Nevertheless, a part of any blame which may attach to the Jewish Agency for the slow progress made towards the establishment of the Jewish National Home may fairly be charged to the account of neglect, or even ill-will, on the part of some members of the Palestine Administration. Still, in remembering those who go even to the length of trying to defeat our own legitimate endeavours under the Mandate, we must not forget the debt which we owe to others – to men such as Sir Herbert Samuel, Lord Plumer, Sir Wyndham Deedes and the late Sir Gilbert Clayton.

From an address to the Seventeenth Zionist Congress. Basle, *1 July 1931*.

In the Arab rebellion
A stable, developed Jewish group here which could hold its own might prove of incalculable value to the British in a time of crisis. You may say, and perhaps rightly, 'It is not for you to tell us what our interests are', but, whether it is liked or not, I am also a member of this British Commonwealth and I did bear a certain share in time of crisis and that is my only justification for bringing up this point. I have always believed that the destinies of these two races, the small oppressed race, and the mighty, great and free race, are somehow bound up in this part of the world and, therefore, I think it is worthwhile taking a certain amount of trouble, unpleasant trouble I admit, and I would love to be able to waive it. During the last six months we felt that the only contribution we could make was to stabilize the Jewish community and make it conscious that it must not sink to the level of people who murder women and children and nurses. But is the British Empire to recede before these people? The Commission will have to judge, is this policy just, is it right; are we intruders in this country, or have we a right to be in this country? At that moment when the Commission come to the conclusion that we are intruders and have no more right to come to Palestine than we have to go to Kenya or to New York, then there

need be no more discussion.
From evidence given in camera *to the Peel Commission. Jerusalem, 23 December 1936.*

The MacDonald White Paper

A White Paper was published yesterday, and in the papers this morning, laying down the new policy which His Majesty's Government, after twenty-two years, now finds it necessary to inaugurate in Palestine. It has found it necessary to formulate and inaugurate this policy in the blackest hour of Jewish history – at a time when our enemies, cruel and relentless, seek to destroy the Jewish people body and soul, and when millions are literally living under conditions which can be called neither life nor death. At this time, at this hour, the statesmen responsible for the destinies of this country, of this great Empire, have thought it proper to initiate a new policy.

If one strips the White Paper of the mass of sophistries and verbiage which serve as a smokescreen to hide its real meaning, what it proposes to do amounts simply to this: Palestine is to become what they call a 'Palestine State' – an 'independent' Palestinian State – but this is a misnomer. If a state is to be built up of two-thirds of Arabs and one-third – and never more than one-third – of Jews, then call it what you like, but it is an Arab State. The name does not change the fundamental fact. It is no more than a poor fig-leaf to cover the nakedness of this policy. The White Paper further proceeds, in order to secure beyond a doubt the establishment of such a state, to provide that Jewish activities in Palestine have to be straitjacketed and curtailed. By order of the Mufti, supported by British statesmen, the Jewish National Home has got to be stopped and crystallized after five years; and from today – from this evening – the fundamental basis on which we are building the Jewish National Home, namely agricultural colonization, has got to be reduced to naught, or, to speak in the terms of the White Paper, has got to be left to the tender mercies of the High Commissioner of Palestine. In other words, there is to be a small delay, and then the thing is to stop; if it were dependent entirely upon the spirit and the letter of the White Paper, if the authors of the White Paper were really the masters of the destiny of Palestine, then they would have pronounced – indeed they have pronounced – the death sentence of the National Home.

From an address to a Zionist Conference. London, 18 May 1939.

The loss of the 'Struma'

This tragic event [the loss of 760 refugees in the Black Sea] is merely a link in a long chain of things which have been inflicted on us in the course of these last two or three years. And one cannot help feeling that this is a consequence of the policy which was adopted by the government shortly before the beginning of the war, the policy we have always condemned, which stands condemned morally and legally in the eyes of all well-meaning and understanding people. At the moment when the White Paper was inflicted on us in Palestine the relations between us and the Palestine Government ceased to be relations of co-operation. We are not governed in Palestine by consent any more, but by coercion. And this is one of the facts of a coercive government. But we did not ask, and have refrained from asking throughout this tragic period of war, for fundamental changes in this policy, which we condemn and with which we shall never agree. And as I said, these unfortunate 760 people could have been let into Palestine with their certificates, without in any way interfering with the White Paper. But once a government has started upon a course which is immoral and illegal, it will be forced on the downward path to commit acts for which it will be condemned in the eyes of the world. It conflicts peculiarly with all that we are saying about the great principles for which the democracies are fighting. It is a mockery and an irony to have to register facts of this kind and at the same time to read the high-sounding phrases which are being mouthed so often by the leaders of democracy.

From a speech at a protest meeting. London, 8 March 1942.

War's end brings no relief to Jews

I would like to thank you for your note of June 9th, though I confess that its contents came as a great shock to me. I had always understood from our conversations that our problem would be considered as soon as the German war was over: but your phrase 'until the victorious Allies are definitely seated at the Peace table' substitutes some indefinite date in the future. I can hardly believe this to have been your intention, because I am sure you realize what the continuance of the White Paper of 1939 is involving for the Jewish people. It bars the doors of Palestine against the surviving remnant of European Jewry, and many refugees have to wander or die, unable as they are to go to Palestine. As regards the 600,000 Jews in Palestine, the continuation of the White Paper means confinement to a territorial ghetto consisting of five per cent of the area of Western Palestine. They could hardly put up with this during the war; now it becomes unbearable. Every week in which Palestine continues to be administered under the White Paper renders the tragedy more acute. I most earnestly beg of you to bear all this in mind.

A letter to Winston Churchill. London, 15 June 1945.

Ernest Bevin's mentality

Dr Weizmann said that people who had come back from England had told him that Mr Bevin was in a terrible rage against the Jews. He was apparently suffering from a Hitler complex. He hated the Jews and wanted to down them and if he, Dr Weizmann, were to venture a prophecy, he would say that Mr Bevin would suffer Hitler's end. History had always been like that. However powerful a man might appear, in the end he came a cropper.

From a note of a discussion with Arthur Creech Jones, Colonial Secretary. New York, 18 February 1948.

Britain's guilt

When the United States attempted to secure Security Council action for stopping the Egyptian and other Arab invasions, those resolutions were defeated owing to British initiative. Great Britain is therefore responsible for allowing the Egyptian invasion to reach the point which it reached. Now that Jewish counter-measures are throwing the invaders back, Great Britain springs to the aid of the aggressor. There is also the circumstance that practically all the armaments used by Egypt in this wanton aggression were officially supplied by Great Britain in recent years. British policy has therefore been clear. Its aim has been to enable the Egyptians to advance into Palestine and to prevent them by every means from being ejected. The deep and passionate resentment at British policy which animates me today is shared unanimously by all sections of Israel's population.

From a letter to Harry S. Truman. Rehovot, 2 January 1949.

'Their historical relationship'

The association of the Jewish people with Great Britain in the establishment of the Jewish National Home has come to an end with the proclamation of the State of Israel. A new era has begun, but the record of British support for our national aspirations will for all time remain a significant chapter in the annals of the British and the Jewish peoples. As one who has been closely associated with that phase from its very inception, I heartily welcome your efforts to give new meaning and content to this historical relationship by promoting understanding, goodwill and constructive co-operation between Great Britain and the State of Israel.

From a letter to the Anglo-Israeli Association. Tel Aviv, 3 June 1952.

America and the Americans

Hope of bringing US into war against Turkey
I had several lengthy conversations with Frankfurter on the subject of America and its attitude towards our cause and he fully agreed with the necessity of the American participation in the Palestine campaign and he promised to support this view before the president. . . . I also had an opportunity of seeing Mr Lloyd George and Mr Balfour in Paris and they were in hearty agreement on the same question.
From a letter to Harry Sacher. London, 1 August 1917.

Americans barred from Zionist Commission to Palestine
I beg to submit the following extract from a telegram received from America from Justice Brandeis, President of the American Zionist Federation, regarding the participation of representatives of American Jewry in the Zionist Commission: 'New York. 27.1.18. Following from Brandeis for Weizmann. Now impossible for America to participate. Next week Felix Frankfurter will leave for London on business of War Department.'

This unwelcome change in the attitude of Americans has occurred during the last fortnight, and cannot be ascribed to any anti-Zionist influence, but to the reluctance of the State Department to agree to American Jews proceeding to Palestine, in view of the present relations between America and Turkey. As a proof of this I might add that American Jews are still giving all the financial support they can to the Commission, and letters show they are enthusiastic about the proposal. Three weeks ago they had appointed delegates of whom Felix Frankfurter was one.

You will realize that the absence of American participation would detract considerably from the value of the Commission, especially in any negotiations with the Arabs and the French, and I think every effort should be made to explain the real objects and the importance of the Commission to the American Government.
From a letter to William Ormsby-Gore. London, 30 January 1918.

Distrust of American Red Cross
It is my profound conviction that this latter group is not Red Cross at all; that is only *camouflage*. It is a political mission instigated by the same agencies that set Morgenthau in action last year. They are also half-missionaries and their staff is entirely made up of people attached to the missionary institutions in Syria. They are pro-Turk, anti-Zionist. They are financed by Schiff and Co. and other parties such as

Morgenthau, Elkus. They're trying to get their hands on all the jobs we want to do.
From a letter to his wife. Tel Aviv–Jaffa, 11 July 1918.

Washington influences

There are undoubtedly serious indications that in Washington forces are at work to frustrate and counteract Anglo-Zionist plans, and I am afraid that our own friends are not in a position to counteract this activity. This explains the refusal of President Wilson to allow the participation of American delegates on our Commission. It further explains the somewhat peculiar reticence of our American friends: I get no direct communications from them, and even the Convention did not send us a message in reply to our telegram. In fact I have heard that Pres. Wilson is at present subject to Turcophile influences. Such influences can only come from missionary quarters.
From a letter to Nahum Sokolow. Tel Aviv–Jaffa, 17 July 1918.

Displeasure with American Zionists

The leaders of American Zionism are not nationalist Jews. To them Zionism is not a movement which gives *them* a definite viewpoint of the world, which gives *them* a definite outlook on Jewish life. Zionism is to them largely a movement which tends towards the building up of a country with which they themselves have not much in common, but which they are ready to accept because it makes an appeal to the Jewish masses of which they know nothing. Uganda, Arizona, Kansas may possibly make a stronger appeal to the American leaders, but as they themselves do not intend to leave America they are of course not prepared to inflict a country on those who do desire to go and are therefore accepting Palestine. They have further not the slightest understanding for all those questions in Zionism which have contributed so much towards the real life of the movement, like the Hebrew Revival, like the desire of the Zionists to 'Judaize' the Jewish communities of the world, to wake their consciousness to fight assimilation with all its manifestations, in short for all those imponderabilia which form a national movement of which Palestine and Palestinism is merely a territorial aspect of a national-political upheaval. . . .

I need not say that the Americans very soon found themselves at variance with practically everybody, and that led to difficulties from the very outset. I was awaiting Brandeis impatiently, hoping that he will bring plans and that he will also indicate the ways and means how to carry them out. My disappointment was extremely great when I found out that they have brought nothing at all, and that apart from general, rather vague, and sometimes rather banal statements, I could not elucidate anything in the nature of a thought-out programme. In Brandeis's attitude there was a very great deal of Wilsonian generalization without the slightest desire to come down to Earth from the Sinaitic heights of generalities.

In practice their attitude amounted to that: the political role of the Zionist movement is finished; we need now new men and new methods. I agreed with Brandeis on some of these points, and have asked him to give us these men, and was ready to accept his methods, if any. He was unable to give us a single man worth having, he was unable to produce a single plan or a single new method. He remained in the position of a critic. He told us that things in Palestine were done badly, that our men there were inefficient, etc., etc. I agreed with him in the greatest part of his criticisms, but in the same time I had to insist that, apart from the criticism, we must have constructive plans, and only in carrying out these constructive plans we shall have remedied a great many of the unsatisfactory things in Palestine. Brandeis's only suggestion was to cut down everything here and in Palestine, to reduce all to a small colonizing movement, to stop many a beginning in Palestine, and then to come to the Jewish people. We contended that it would be folly now to stop our *Kvutzot*, our schools in Palestine; they all have to be improved, reorganized, but not killed. Efficiency is necessary, but it is not achieved by the simple elimination of the work. Of course there will be no mistakes if there is nothing done.

The truth as it appears now to me at least is this. The American leaders have lost their hold over their own people in America. They have preached a shallow anaemic Zionism full of sensational bluff, they spoke of Jewish states and various other 'stunts' like this. Now of course they have got no more weapons in their armoury in order to 'catch' the people. On the other hand, they have seen what European Zionism is. It is a deep national movement. They cannot follow it, and they desire to retreat. Instead of educating up their own Zionism to the height of a great movement, they attempted to cut us down so as to suit their point of view. They have failed at the conference and they will fail in their own constituency. The analogy with Wilson is almost complete. But we cannot afford a break even with these Americans, although their value at present is very small. There is no need for such a break at all, but there is a necessity to inspire the American Zionist movement with new hope and faith and to bring it down to realities.

From a letter to Herbert Samuel. London, 8–10 August 1920.

Parallels with American foreign policy

On arrival here I found a very difficult situation. Brandeis and his group (they are about fifty in all) have captured the machine of the ZO in America and have with an iron hand and, by political methods and stratagems absolutely unknown and inconceivable in Europe, kept down everything and everybody who dared to have an opinion of his own. I have never thought such a political terror possible. Anybody who expresses an opinion different from the officially recognized one is simply steamrolled out of existence and branded as a rebel, and that is the mildest term applied to an opponent. It was so amazing and overwhelming that it took me weeks to grasp it all and I was enlightened very greatly after my two visits to [Sir Auckland] Geddes, who gave me a very clear picture of American methods, politics and their state of mind. He *foretold* that I am going to have great difficulties and explained their nature. In his opinion, the attitude of B[randeis] and his colleagues to the International ZO is similar to the attitude of America to the League of Nations and to Europe. The Americans have done it all, and have won the War (have made the Zionist movement and Palestine), have done it all altruistically as they have no interest (American Jews won't go to Palestine in masses), therefore they are not anxious to take any responsibility but they would like to control it, to show us how it has to be run. Hence the insistence on controlling the American funds and their opposition to an international KH. The parallelism is very striking. *Wie es sich christelt, so jüdelt es sich!*

I cannot give you at present a full account of the negotiations which lasted about three tiresome, hellish weeks; we could not come to any agreement and I had to start the KH without the co-operation of the present 'leader' of American Zionism. But there is certainly one incontestable fact in the whole position. The masses of American Zionists and Jews have nothing in common with B. and his group, which is only a small oligarchy of men with a certain social position in this country but without influence on Jewry, with the exception of a few assimilated, non-Zionist or anti-Zionist Jews. Ninety-five per cent of American Jewry are those who understand a hundred per cent Zionism full-blooded, and are ready to follow and give money to such a Zionism and no other. I am writing this note from Boston, which is Brandeis's town, the citadel of assimilated Jewry. Last year they tried to raise here money for the Palestine Restoration Fund and exerted themselves throughout the year and have collected 28,000 dollars. At one dinner yesterday 20,000 were raised, and so it goes on in every city. We don't get big contributions, but the masses are giving in smaller sums, but in large quantities. It is a terrible exertion, but we can get from New York

alone all the money we require on one condition – that we send here a good man who will work hard and build up a Zionist Organization leaning on Jewish democracy.
From a letter to Sir Alfred Mond. Boston, 18 May 1921.

Improved atmosphere
There is no doubt in my mind that American Jews of all shades of opinion are ready to stand by us and accept willingly the programme as laid down in the Mandate. They have confidence in the British Government, and it is that which renders work here so much easier now than it was four or five years ago.
From a letter to Sir John Shuckburgh. New York, 26 December 1923.

Healthy instincts
Why do the Polish Jews keep silent and contribute nothing to the *Keren Hayesod*, expecting America to bear the brunt? Why do even the Russian Jews, many of them millionaires, sit in the hotels of Berlin, Paris and Monte Carlo, watch us drowning in our blood, and yet do nothing? They are all ready, even the Zionists among them, to criticize and backbite, grin and pick holes. Remember one thing, Dr Weltsch, I have never lost faith or watered down my Zionism but I am certainly convinced that some of the present Zionists are obsolete, incapable, and in some cases intellectually dishonest. We may succeed some day in cleaning all this up and we may not. This state of affairs explains, to me at any rate, why within the ranks of the Zionist Organization I meet with opposition of which I find none within the Jewish people at large.

I am meeting here literally thousands of people, masses of Jews with normal healthy instincts, and you will believe that I am not exaggerating when I say I have merely the physical difficulty in establishing a contact. Once the contact is established there is no difficulty in letting the current run through; and this is true for almost every class of Jew, beginning with [Louis] Marshall and finishing with an ordinary Russian Jew of East Broadway. It is a question of physical endurance; time and effort, and all the money which we need will be forthcoming. All this in spite of the fact that I am telling the people the whole truth and nothing but the truth, and laying more stress on the black side of our work than on the bright side of it. Read my speeches, ask anybody who is listening to them. I am usually reproached by the Zionists for being too pessimistic. The Jews here are willing to listen to the truth. They have confidence and they are ready to give their money and later on they will give men. They are simple and natural and therefore respond to the Zionist ideal, sometimes without knowing it. Unfortu-

nately, the Zionists in Europe are just the opposite. They are complex, intellectually perverse, sophisticated and incapable of action. They are for bitter nagging criticism, and are in the last resort shallow. They want miracles because they have no power to put their shoulders to the wheel. If the miracles are not forthcoming, they will accuse the British Government, Samuel, the Zionist leaders, everybody but themselves.
From a letter to Robert Weltsch. New York, 15 January 1924.

Social workers and 'Babbitt millionaires'
[Louis] Marshall, who is unfortunately still the pivot of the community here, has not improved with age. He is old, disgruntled, thinks it necessary to have an opinion on every subject in Jewish life – and, needless to say, the opinion is final – obstinate, although willing to do the right thing according to his lights. The controversies of last year have not improved his temper, and I am quite certain that a great many of the so-called social workers such as his son-in-law, Billikopf, and many others – a peculiar parasitical type which has grown up on the affluence of the Jewish community in this country – are influencing him against Zionism, which to them is naturally a danger. Most of the so-called social workers live on the good graces of the Babbitt millionaires who stand at the head of Jewish affairs in the various cities. The social worker is the proxy of the millionaire in all matters concerning charity, communal activities, intellectual pursuits and even religion. Within this category fall a great many rabbis.
From a letter to Berthold Feiwel and David Eder. New York, 25 November 1926.

On negotiations to neutralize Passfield White Paper
I'm conscious of the fact that a great many Zionists will refuse to accept the result of our negotiations, and – I am bold to say – almost whatever this result may be. It can never be a hundred per cent success, but it can be a basis – not a narrow one either – for further expansion in Palestine. Unfortunately mass hysteria prevails and extremism and superpatriotism *à la* Hitler and Daudet is the order of the day. Anybody who dares to preach reason and tries to face realities is howled down as a traitor. I suppose I'm the blackest of all Iscariots! This state of mind is being fostered from two centres: from Palestine by [Pinhas] Rutenberg who has gone clean off his head, and from America by the ZOA who are, perhaps, trying at present to square their accounts with me and will condemn out of hand anything which might be achieved under my guidance. I think their attitude is in great part due to this. For reasons best known to themselves they don't come here, they don't take a hand in the work, but shoot at long range.
From a letter to Felix Warburg. London, 11 December 1930.

Weizmann did not visit America between July 1933 and January 1940.

Reminiscent of German Jewry
Yesterday on the wireless I heard an announcement that Judge Samuel Rosenman, for whom I have great respect, is going to help the President with the writing of his speech. I am not afraid of antisemitism, but I thought that this announcement, coming at this time, was at least injudicious. Why am I frightened for you? Because the whole structure of American Jewry is one which is painfully reminiscent of German Jewry. I read somewhere that 70 per cent of the legal profession of New York is Jewish. The excess of white-collar workers, this close association of American Jews with desk work, is a great danger. And if I were living in America I would throw in my strength there, to remedy the situation intelligently, and by a performance which would point out to the world in an unmistakable way that Jews are creative, and that if they have not been creative, it is not their fault. And this demonstration we hope we can prove in Palestine. Forgive me for saying this, but I know your worries because they are my worries, and you should take a leaf from Palestine's book. If you could create *Chalutz* youth in America, so that instead of trying to reform everybody else American youth would reform itself, it could devote itself to converting the millions of acres of dust-bowls throughout the land – yes, the dust-bowls in Brooklyn and the Bronx. For this youth, not knowing what to do, are becoming Communists. Therefore I say: your fears should begin at home, for the creative performance in Palestine will gradually assert itself and will reflect credit on you. You have created a Frankenstein, and are ignoring the vital problems which are here.
From a discussion with American Jewish leaders. New York, 25 May 1941.

Dangers in American attitudes
I saw something of this danger in the last speech of Vice-President Wallace. Now, I am not referring to his great speech where he spoke of the people's march and the people's revolution. There was a second, shorter speech, at a church dinner. I take two parts of this speech very briefly. He traced the development of human civilization, saying there was a Hebrew civilization which was relieved by a Roman civilization, which was relieved by a British civilization, which is being relieved by an American civilization.

I am taking it very briefly, without the slightest desire to distort the statement, but I think it is substantially correct. He then went on to say that the Americans are the chosen people. He used this very expression. Now, it is not for me to criticize, but he went on to a third part. He said that we speak English but we are not British – which is quite true. But it meant more or less delimitation between America and what we usually call the Anglo-Saxon world, and he gave proof here of what he said by adding that there are 'too many Italians, too many Greeks, too many Jews, too many nations which went into the melting pot for us to be Anglo-Saxon, in spite of the fact that we speak English'.

I am not going to analyse the speech of the Vice-President, for whom I am sure everybody here has the highest possible regard. But I would like to say, for my small part, that it is not true. It is not true that in this sense the Hebrew civilization has been relieved. In other words, it means that the Hebraic civilization has been obliterated, and something else has come in its stead. Things do not happen like that in history, according to my poor lights. It is a synthesis. The bright civilization still exists. We are here to testify to that somewhat important fact. Neither has the British civilization – I am not worried about Rome, and neither am I worried about the others – disappeared. Nor can the American civilization, which is certainly beginning to take shape, go on existing without the Hebraic or the British civilization. The recognition of the organic inter-connection between these three is not sufficiently pregnant in the minds of the American statesmen. If you were to try and misinterpret – there is no limit to misinterpretation – one could say it sounded, stripped of its beautiful style, like a new brand of isolationism, on a much higher level. He added, 'the American civilization will develop according to its own laws and its own internal forces. Of course, we shall help other people.' One gets the impression, to be a little more explicit, of the utmost fear in Washington that Europe – and it is sorrowfully said – always quarrels, always gets itself into trouble. 'We'll come and clean it up, we'll give them food, we'll police Europe for a time, until these children have learned to behave.' But for the rest, no interest.

I consider this a very serious danger for us because, as I said, I believe that only by getting America to take a deep interest in the sore problems of Europe, which are also America's problems, might we possibly get on a plane of practical discussion and a practical solution of the Palestine problem.

I am throwing this idea out because I have felt it deeply all my time here. And as it was given to me to spend more time in Washington than during my usual visits, I had an opportunity of listening; and one feels this, without its being dressed up in words. Wallace perhaps did not suspect that I would read all this disparagement into his speech, but I believe it does not fall very short of the truth. And here I come to another very sensitive point. For once let us be absolutely frank and let

us say what we think without fear that it may hurt. That is not the intention. A great many Jews look upon Europe, distressed, destroyed, as something more or less beyond redemption. 'We shall have to send them wheat and bread and money and medicines, but the great community left intact is America, five million people, in a position of certain stability, freedom, power, prosperity.'
From an address to the American Zionist Emergency Committee. New York, 16 June 1942.

'I believe in the President'
America has so far shown a great deal of platonic love to us. I don't under-rate it, but it was platonic. Mostly, the Americans shrank back when it came to action. Perhaps they are busy with the war, perhaps they really don't understand as yet that the Middle East may also be an interest of theirs, but to educate the Americans to an understanding of the Zionist movement and Jewish problem even as the British understand it will still take a long time. We have to do it, for I believe in the sincerity of the President and I hope that he will have the commanding position at the Peace Table.
Ibid.

Outside the mainstream
Zionists still remain outside the mainstream of Jewish life and have not reached out beyond a narrow compass. The reason is, I think, primarily social. Zionists are recruited mainly from the lower middle class and to a smaller extent from the middle classes. The upper middle classes are still either aloof or a minority of them is hostile and ignorant. Another reason is, in my opinion, a lack of good educational literature. The Jewish press, with a few exceptions, is not on a very high level. The central organ of the Zionist movement is utterly inadequate for such times as these and for the demands which are being placed on the Zionists. It is not in consonance with the dignity and importance of an organization like the Zionist Organization of America. The labour Zionist organizations have a much better literature, but they are also even more sectarian than the general Zionists and their papers are read only by a small number. There is not a single book in America on Zionism which is up-to-date and which could be placed in the hands of intelligent Jewish or non-Jewish readers, and to which one could refer all those who wish to be better informed about the movement. The speakers again, with some very notable and distinguished exceptions, indulge most in commonplaces and sentimental phraseology and are not familiar either with the facts or with the great problems and great possibilities of Palestine and the Middle East. I believe that the sort of talks which one used to hear five or six or ten years ago do not draw any

longer, as the public is more educated and more exacting and I further believe that by giving them the true picture, even emphasizing the difficulties and dangers, one is more likely to gain their confidence and their support than by merely indulging in spread-eagle emotional outpourings which are, in my opinion, obsolete and valueless.
From a letter to Felix Frankfurter. Arrowhead Springs, California, 21 June 1941.

Britain's war in American eyes
Things are moving very rapidly here, and it is always somewhat hazardous to try and give a clear description of a dynamic state of affairs. In the three months spent in this country, one has seen great changes, both in the state of public opinion and in the actions of the administration, which is closely watching public opinion and adapts its steps to its moods. There is no slightest doubt that the President and his colleagues are determined to do all in their power in helping England to the limit of their possibility. This desire is sincere and genuine and the notion that England is the first line of defence for the United States is not merely a catch-phrase for propaganda purposes, but forms a fundamental conception determining the attitude of the government.

I doubt whether the President would like to engage American manpower into this struggle; he would naturally be happy if he could avoid it, but I am sure – and this is confirmed by some of his utterances made confidentially to his close advisers – that he sees clearly where the logic of events is driving this country, which can no longer escape the cruel necessity of taking its stand as a belligerent. The task before the President is neither easy nor simple. It is a vast and heterogeneous country. The Irish and the Germans are, in the majority, hostile to England and some of them probably friendly to the dictators. They form important groups, influential in local politics if perhaps not very powerful nationally. There are the Italians, a great many fascist in outlook, but of course there are the friendly Poles, Greeks, Czechs and Norwegians. There is also the usual group of appeasers with which we are so familiar from our own history, led primarily by [Charles] Lindbergh and [Burton K.] Wheeler, and they have gathered some momentum in these three months. They are constantly being reinforced by German propaganda and make abundant capital out of our difficulties and misfortunes. Talking to the common people – taxidrivers, or on trains or in small places – one notices that even in remote districts away from the Atlantic seaboard – there exists a remarkable unanimity amongst the small people who condemn the attitude of the minority very strongly. In the eyes of the common folk they are identified with Fascism or Nazism.

But the country is vast, and in spite of excellent communications by rail or plane, in spite of the radio, the movies and the press, it is not easy to weld and mold opinion into a harmonious whole, and this accounts for the apparent slowness with which the administration moves. It does seem slow to us, but I believe it to be very rapid, under the circumstances prevailing here. After all, there is some logic in the attitude of the non-interventionists, that the danger to America is still remote and that, given a few quiet years in which to prepare, this Colossus can ward off almost any onslaught: Why rush? etc., etc. Remembering what we ourselves preached and practised before the collapse of Czechoslovakia and even during the first year of the war, is it to be wondered that this American minority can produce a plausible argument? And I think that we should be the last to judge them severely.

There is another set of arguments which one hears from the young intelligent public – college graduates, professors and intellectuals generally. 'What kind of war is it? Is it the old imperialism under a new guise, and if we are to fight, we ought to know what is going to be the future better world. Is it really going to be a genuine democracy?' And here again these young doubters are able to point to a great many weaknesses in our structure and to portents which do not inspire them with too much confidence – like some of the vague statements uttered by our statesmen. I am not referring to Jews, about whom I shall write later, but I am speaking of the young American intellectual who is occasionally tainted with a sort of mild parlour Bolshevism but to whom democracy has a real meaning, not merely as a formal political or parliamentary way of conducting business but as a mode of life. He somehow misses it in England, which he does not know and which he judges merely by the representatives who come over here and who are not his ideal of democrats. I was anxious about this – and I don't know whether you have noticed a cablegram of mine sent some time ago to 10 Downing Street recommending that people like [Josiah] Wedgwood, Tom Williams, Ellen Wilkinson should come here, unostentatiously. They should go into the workshops, into the colleges and talk to the people and enlighten them. There are young people only too anxious to learn – they are not hardened in their opinions – but they hate being bamboozled by propaganda.

From a letter to Lord Moyne, Colonial Secretary. Arrowhead Springs, California, 21 June 1941.

Defence of Palestine
I saw Judge Rosenman at the White House on Tuesday, 4 August. . . .

Rosenman said he would like to talk to the President on the defence of Palestine, but that he is not sufficiently informed. Would we give him a short statement of what is required, and he would take the opportunity of speaking to the President. I said that a statement could be given to him, but not before the beginning of next week. I then went on to say that all the trouble for the Zionists comes from the British in Egypt and from the British Administration of Palestine, and that both these groups are naturally impressing their views on the Americans who may be there. And it is, of course, extremely difficult for the President, who has not got his own men out there, to make up his mind. And even the Americans who are in the Middle East are taking their cue from the British. To which he made the following remark: You know that I have developed in these last two years. I have come nearer to you, and if the President would permit me, I would be prepared to go out to Palestine. To which I replied, that would be a grand thing, not so much for these problems as for the whole future of Palestine. To which he replied: Of course it is very unlikely that the President would let me go, but if he does, I would like to be fully instructed and informed and put in touch with the right people; to which I naturally replied, that is the easiest thing in the world to do.

I saw Mr Morgenthau on Wednesday, 5 August in the Treasury Building, and had almost an hour with him. His secretary, Mrs Klotz, was present throughout the conversation.

Mr Morgenthau made the following communication: that soon after my visit to the President, he went to see the President himself, and devoted his conversation entirely to the question of the defence of Palestine. He did not get any satisfaction from the President – it was a most unsatisfactory visit. The President said that as long as the situation in the Middle East does not improve, he fears that any statement on his part might make the situation worse: that he has to wait until the situation improves. Then Morgenthau said, the situation has not improved. It has gone worse, because in spite of the fact that the British in the Middle East have superiority in men, in tanks and in aircraft, they somehow do not move and they do not understand modern warfare and co-operation between the three forces. They always throw in part of their tanks into the battle, become defeated and lose their equipment piece-meal. Such is the opinion of American military authorities. Take it for what it is worth. Also that Tobruk was surrendered by the South African general almost without resistance. (Dr Weizmann remarked here, parenthetically, pausing for a moment from his report on the conversation, as follows: from another source I have heard that two things happened at Tobruk: (1) the defection of

South African troops, and (2) that the Egyptians and Arabs cut the water supply off. Possibly the defection of the South African troops was a result of this.) The other difficulty in the Middle East is lack of equipment. He said there are about 60,000 Czechs and Poles who are also anxious to fight and they cannot be armed.

I then mentioned to him my conversation with Rosenman, and the remark that he would like to go to Palestine. Mr Morgenthau got up from his chair and said, 'Let me think, let me think.' After he had thought for a few minutes he said, 'It is a good thing, but he must not go alone. He must go with somebody, because on the one hand he seems to be playing with the rich German Jews, and on the other hand the American Jewish Committee is very dissatisfied that he has gone much too far with the Zionists.' Then he said, 'You know, I am a very simple and straightforward man, and this is why I am hesitant.' He said, 'I would like to go to Palestine, but only on one condition: if General Marshall would go with me.' I then asked, 'Why Marshall?' He said, 'Marshall is driven crazy by the contradictory demands which are being placed on him. There is not enough to go around, and today he is asked to send ammunition to Chile and to Brazil, tomorrow to China and after tomorrow to Russia – and the Middle East has been neglected. The Middle East is an important theatre of the war, and if Marshall would go there, there would be some definite policy.' I expressed doubts as to whether that was likely to happen, but I did say, however, that perhaps later on, when matters become a little more settled, it would be more than valuable if he would go and see Palestine with his own eyes, because at present it is not a propitious time to talk about the future, but such time may come soon; and I repeated again the arguments that the President is not informed, and that whatever information he gets is tainted with a definite bias against us.

From a note of discussion with Presidential advisers. Washington, 4 and 5 August 1942.

Washington at war

The USA was a difficult country at present. There was a great deal of disorganization, and the Opposition was at war with the President. It was a common saying that the Second Front was in Washington. There were great cleavages, and the reactionary forces were raising their heads, with the aim of destroying the New Deal. Nonetheless, he believed that if the President were to decide to stand for a fourth term, he would be adopted and would win. His impression was that the President would stand. There was an alignment of the Army, Navy and Air Force with Big Business, which had a great hold over the country. It was interesting, for instance, that in army circles they spoke of

General MacArthur as a future President. The recent racial rioting – whether the work of a Fifth Column or not – had terrified the Jews. These riots had had the well-known pattern of pogroms. Jewish life was projected against this background. It would therefore be understood that the Jews were uneasy – the more uneasy because they were leaderless. Not only the Zionists, but also the non-Zionists, had no one of outstanding rank to speak on behalf of the Jewish people. There were, of course, many excellent people – for instance there were some 6,000 Jews in the Administration, from Morgenthau down to typists, and among them were some brilliant young men. Mr [Israel] Sieff had grouped around himself a number of people in Washington who could only be compared to the small group which they had had with them in Manchester in the period between 1914 and 1916. . . .

He felt that the whole thing turned on the President and on the immediate entourage of the White House. Mr Sumner Welles had been a tremendous discovery. He had proved to be a great friend. Dr Weizmann had not experienced such friendship from a non-Jew since his discussions with Lord Balfour.

From a report to Jewish Agency headquarters. London, 5 July 1943.

Prompt recognition of Jewish State necessary

The unhappy events of the last few months will not, I hope, obscure the very great contributions that you, Mr President, have made toward a definitive and just settlement of the long and troublesome Palestine question. The leadership which the American Government took under your inspiration made possible the establishment of a Jewish State, which I am convinced will contribute markedly toward a solution of world Jewish problems, and which, I am equally convinced, is a necessary preliminary to the development of lasting peace among the peoples of the Near East.

So far as practical conditions in Palestine would permit, the Jewish people there have proceeded along the lines laid down in the United Nations Resolution of November 29, 1947. Tomorrow midnight, May 15th, the British Mandate will be terminated, the Provisional Government of the Jewish State, embodying the best endeavours of the Jewish people and arising from the Resolution of the United Nations, will assume full responsibility for preserving law and order within the boundaries of the Jewish State; for defending that area against external aggression; and for discharging the obligations of the Jewish State to the other nations of the world in accordance with international law.

Considering all the difficulties, the chances for an equitable adjustment of Arab and Jewish relationship are not unfavourable. What is required now is an end to the seeking of new solutions which invariably have retarded rather than encouraged a final settlement.

It is for these reasons that I deeply hope that the United States, which under your leadership has done so much to find a just solution, will promptly recognize the Provisional Government of the new Jewish State. The world, I think, would regard it as especially appropriate that the greatest living democracy should be the first to welcome the newest into the family of nations.
A letter to Harry S. Truman. New York, 13 May 1948.

Truman's Presidential success
Permit me to extend to you most hearty congratulations and good wishes on your re-election. We in this country have been watching the progress of the Presidential contest with bated breath, and I am sure that I am speaking the mind of the bulk of my people when I say that we feel deeply thankful that the people of the United States have given you the opportunity of shaping the policies of your country and the affairs of humanity at large during the next critical four years. We interpret their vote as an emphatic endorsement of the policy of peace, security and ordered progress in world affairs, for which you have stood since you assumed your high office, and for the continued prosecution of which men and women in every part of the globe pray with all their hearts. May you be granted health and strength to carry out your noble purpose. We have special cause to be gratified at your re-election, because we are mindful of the enlightened help which you gave to our cause in these years of our struggle. We particularly remember your unflinching advocacy of the admission of Jewish refugees to Palestine, your determined stand against the attempts to deflect you from your course, your staunch support of our admission to statehood at Lake Success, and your recognition of the fact of its establishment within an hour of our proclamation of independence.
From a letter to Harry S. Truman. Rehovot, 5 November 1948.

The Hebrew University

Although the dream of a Jewish University was born well before the creation of the Zionist Organization, it entered the stage of realization only when Weizmann, together with Berthold Feiwel and Martin Buber, made it their principal Zionist activity. They advanced a detailed case for its establishment in a pamphlet published in Berlin in

1902. The project made no headway until 1913, when Baron Edmond de Rothschild encouraged the Zionist Organization to proceed, and Weizmann was charged with direction of the campaign to found a Hebrew University.

'Third Temple'
Asher Isayevich [Ahad Ha'am] . . . considers the idea of the university dangerous in the sense that the establishment of such a centre will arouse the suspicions of states whose eyes are turned to Jerusalem. It's true that a Hebrew University and the Holy Sepulchre in one and the same place are quite incompatible, but we certainly can't give up Jerusalem. We have to take chances. To my way of thinking, this is the one slogan that can evoke a response just now – the Hebrew University. *Die Zionsuniversität auf dem Berge Zion!* The Third Temple!
From a letter to his wife. Manchester, 13 March 1913.

Dearth of intellectual leadership
About ten years ago the movement to exclude Russian-Jewish students from the universities of Central Europe began to gain ground. This situation has intensified from year to year, so that at present the Jewish student finds the gates shut almost everywhere. Hence the plight of Jewish university candidates from the East has reached a critical point. The effects upon Jews of limiting their possibilities of study, grievous though they might be today, have not yet become manifest to their full extent. The impact of this catastrophic deterioration will only become fully apparent after some years. But those who have observed recent developments must reach the conclusion that the great majority of the Jewish nation, which even today does not produce anything like an adequate intellectual force, will in the future produce such a minimum of intellectually-schooled people as to be unable to form the intelligentsia required to maintain the nation's energies. The fatal implications of such a situation to a people languishing under conditions of real deprivation and indescribable material want, often in the obscurantism of non-education, and in a state of despair, can hardly be portrayed.
From a speech at the Eleventh Zionist Congress. Vienna, 8 September 1913.

'In this our sanctuary'
The Hebrew University, while seeking to maintain the highest scientific level, must simultaneously be rendered accessible to all classes of the people. The Jewish workman and farm-labourer must be enabled to find there a possibility of continuing and completing his education in his free hours. The doors of our libraries, lecture rooms

and laboratories must be opened widely to them all, so that the university will exercise its beneficial influence on the nation as a whole. The bare nucleus of a library is already in existence here, and very valuable additions to it are at present stored in Russia and other countries. The establishment of a University Library and a University Press are contemplated soon after the war. Manifold are the preparations yet to be made. Some are already in progress. Some, like the actual building, must necessarily be postponed until the happy day of peace arrives. But from this day, the Hebrew University is a reality. Our Hebrew University, informed by Jewish learning and Jewish energy, will mould itself into an integral part of our national structure which is in process of erection. It will have a centripetal force, attracting all that is noblest in Jewry throughout the world; a unifying centre for our scattered elements. And inspiration and strength will go forth and revivify the forces latent in our distant communities. Here the wandering soul of Israel shall reach its haven; its strength no longer consumed in restless and vain wanderings, Israel shall at last remain at peace within itself and with the world. There is a Talmudic legend that tells of the Jewish soul, deprived of its body, hovering between heaven and earth. Such is our soul today; tomorrow it shall come to rest, in this our sanctuary.

From his speech at the dedication of the site of the Hebrew University. Mount Scopus, 24 July 1918.

The University began functioning on a skeleton basis in 1923, with a lecture on Relativity by Albert Einstein, who joined the Board of Governors. It was formally inaugurated by Lord Balfour in 1925 with Judah L. Magnes as Chancellor.

The Jewish approach
Naturally, I do not believe that there is a Jewish chemistry or a Jewish mathematics. It is not essential for a Jewish man of letters to write on Jewish topics. It is not necessary to drag Jewishness into everything. But there is something like a Jewish approach to problems and to the world. This Jewish approach is a possibility which can be converted into reality in the Jewish University.

We did not set out to make the Jewish University into a centre from which we can boast of Jewish achievements. We tried to create one place in the world where a normal standard could be worked out under normal conditions in an environment where we no longer have the psychic reaction of a minority. We hoped that this oscillation between Jewish life, and a constant approximation to something else, would cease; that Jewish life would become original, self-contained, approximating only to the general culture of the world. This and this alone is the value of the university.

From a speech to supporters of the American Menorah Journal. *New York, February 1927.*

Deficiencies of the University

The University at present finds itself in a very critical condition. The sources of its income are dwindling rapidly, and it is faced with the necessity of covering a Budget which, even in its severely reduced form, is still formidable in view of the prevailing financial crisis. There is therefore a danger, which in my opinion threatens the very existence of the University itself, that cuts and economies may be made in directions which are likely to cripple the scientific side of the University's work beyond all possibility of subsequent repair. It is my belief – and I say this even at the risk of being contradicted by you – that this state of affairs follows necessarily from the passive resistance which has been systematically offered throughout the years since the University's opening, to the appointment of a proper academic head of the University; and, on the other hand, from the irreparable error in policy by which the University has been committed to the setting up of a series of second-rate subjects which serve as window-dressing for the public (which is always pleased to receive a voluminous catalogue of the University's activities), but which, in substance, could be of no service to any scientific institution – even to one much more mature and more firmly established than is our poor University. A third cause of the present difficulties has been, in my view, the yielding of the authorities to the public clamour in favour of turning the University into a degree-giving institution.

May I recall to your memory – perhaps it is unnecessary – the main lines on which I tried to lay down the policy of the University in the days when I could still influence, to some extent, its progress? The policy was directed towards the slow upbuilding of an institution which should fit in harmoniously as an integral part of the general life of the country, adapting itself to the gradual growth of the National Home. I remember that I gave repeated warnings against the danger of creating a small man with a big head. This was the fundamental principle which led me, and those who co-operated with me, to open the University as a series of research institutes, and to limit those research institutes to the three fundamental subjects: mathematics, physics, and chemistry (apart, of course, from Judaica, which occupies a position *sui generis*). A University establishes its name in the world of science not by the number of students on its books, nor yet by the quantity of degrees it confers every year, but by the nature and the character and the quality of the scientific achievements which stand to the credit of its laboratories and institutions. The Hebrew University of Jerusalem would naturally be surrounded by critics; I was anxious that no one should be able to say that it was second-rate, and as the upbuilding of a first-rate University is necessarily a matter of slow growth, watched and tended with incessant care, I viewed the rapid development of various small and insignificant institutions on the Scopus with the gravest misgiving.

I think anyone conversant with academic organization would bear me out in saying that if physics, chemistry and mathematics are well taught, and solid work is done in these three subjects, then and only then has any university a sound foundation on which to erect a superstructure of other subjects. Biology, medicine, and kindred subjects are all applications of these three fundamental sciences. As we could not hope to be, in Jerusalem, with a ready-made university, *de toutes pièces*, it would have been best to be modest, and do a limited number of subjects only, but do them well, looking forward to the time when the thing would grow organically, and make headway slowly and surely through its own strength. Such a policy, of course, precludes, by its very nature, degree-giving, for which purpose you need a highly elaborate teaching-machine, and an expensive outfit.

I find, on reading the material which has come into my hands since my return from South Africa, that it seems to have been decided to create a degree in biology. Candidly, I do not know what this means. Biology is such a vast subject; I can enumerate a whole catalogue of subjects which come under that head, some knowledge of all of which would seem essential to anyone who sets out to obtain proficiency in this branch of science. But it is certainly true that the very foundation of biology, if it is to be taken seriously at all, must be mathematics, physics and chemistry. But I now see that, in view of the necessity of giving degrees in biology, and in view, on the other hand, of the financial position, it is proposed to cut out chemistry, or reduce it to a minimum. I must confess that it seems to me rather an absurd adventure to propose to confer degrees in biology on young men who, *ex hypothesi*, will be unable to obtain the necessary grounding in chemistry on which alone a serious study of biology can be founded.

There are two aspects of this matter on which I personally feel rather hurt. The first is that a final decision on this subject, with which I am known to be somewhat familiar, should have been taken without the slightest reference to me, and without any suggestion that my advice or guidance would be welcome. Apparently the biologists, among whom

Dr Kligler seems to be a moving spirit, have decided as to the wisdom of introducing this reform (if it deserves that name), and it will therefore be introduced, irrespective of whether it causes permanent harm to the University or not. I must take strong exception to the course of action adopted in this matter: it is wrong in principle; it is wrong in science; and it is certainly wrong constitutionally. I shall have something to say on this subject when the Board meets. I never thought – I say it without in any way impugning the goodwill, or the honesty or the good intentions of Dr Magnes – that Dr Magnes alone could master all the many-sided problems which must necessarily arise in a growing University, and especially in a University growing in the peculiar conditions of Palestine. It would have been, I think, in his own interests, and certainly in the interests of the institution, to enlist the help and advice of men competent in the conduct of academic affairs, and especially of men on the spot in Palestine; and to discuss and decide upon the various problems with them, as they arose.

Of course, Dr Magnes seeks advice from various friends of the University scattered over the world, and he is naturally free to choose his advisers as he pleases, but, as a matter of fact, the advice that is tendered to him comes mostly from amateurs who are not in close contact with the day-to-day requirements of the institution. I understand very well that there is at the present moment no money to pay an academic head, and I will therefore not press this point. But I cannot help saying that it would, in my opinion, be of infinitely greater value to the University to make provision for such a head in its budget than to spend the money on costly and unnecessary luxuries like degrees in biology (which I am afraid will count for very little in the scientific world), simply in order to be able to announce that the University has a certain number of 'degree-courses'. . . .

A situation now seems to have arisen in the University in which Dr Magnes finds himself unable to deal with the work, so that much of it is left to men on the spot in whose judgment it is difficult to feel the confidence that should be felt in people responsible for work of such importance. My connection with the University during the last three or four years has been purely nominal. My name figures in the Year Book as the 'President', but I neither can influence, nor have attempted to influence, the conduct of University affairs because of the resistance which has been systematically offered to any intervention, however delicate and however unselfish it may have been. I therefore find myself obliged to consider seriously the advisability of my remaining in this decorative, but rather meaningless, position. It is not my intention to do any harm to the University in its present difficult situation, but neither is it my intention to continue to cover with my name something with which I have scarcely any contact, or tacitly to acquiesce in methods of work which, in my opinion, are intolerable in an institution of the type of the Hebrew University. . . .

The second personal aspect of the matter, to which I should like to refer very briefly in this letter, is the suggestion which emanated both from you personally, and from others of my friends, and which was brought to my notice last year by Professor Einstein. You will remember, perhaps, that last year I had definitely decided to arrange, if at all possible, to work as a research chemist at the University in Jerusalem for six months in every year – i.e. for the greater part of the academic year. I had decided this without any idea of seeking any post or appointment of any kind. But if I undertook this work, it had clearly to be undertaken with a certain dignity, and I estimated that it might involve the University in an expenditure of something like £1,200 a year, which would have included laboratory expenses, salary of an assistant, and any other incidental expenses which might be required. It is true that at that time, as since, the finances of the University were precarious, and that, from the purely financial point of view, such a project may well have seemed unwelcome. On the other hand, anyone with some slight knowledge of my past might have remembered that, even in difficult times, I had often succeeded in raising very substantial sums for almost every Palestine purpose, and might not have dismissed the proposal so summarily on financial grounds alone. If at that precise moment, no money happened to be visible – and I daresay none was visible – it should have been possible, I think, to reach some sort of arrangement by which this comparatively trivial sum could have been secured; and – if I may say it without boasting – I think it might have been useful to the University in many respects if I could have made my scientific home there.

I have not, even yet, been able to get over the fact that this proposal was rather icily dismissed; to this day I have not heard a word of regret from the University authorities on the subject, though there is on record a glowingly-worded resolution, unanimously passed by the Board, to the effect that whenever the time should come when I might be able to come and work in Jerusalem, the University would extend to me a cordial welcome. If anything at the University can be said to be 'academic' it is this resolution. . . . As regards the practical side, experience has shown that my calculation of the expenses erred, if at all, on the side of generosity. I am now running a laboratory myself, here in London. It is quite a modest installation, but it answers the purpose. The total budget of this place, including the salary of my assistant and all that is necessary for somewhat advanced work, is £600 a year. I have spoken at length on this purely personal matter because I think it does go to show that there is an atmosphere prevailing at the University which is, or should be, alien to a place of learning. I shall say no more about it.

I would only like to add that I have not abandoned my intention of working in Palestine for six months of the year, and it is possible that I may be able to carry my plans into effect in the not-far-distant future. But should I succeed in this, I shall not be establishing myself within the precincts of the University of Jerusalem.
From a letter to Felix Warburg. New York, 28 June 1932.

Following protracted controversy with Magnes, in which Weizmann's displeasure at the progress of the University was shared by Einstein, Weizmann was in August 1935 appointed Dean of the Faculty of Natural Sciences.

'Nonsensical propaganda'

I would like to draw your attention to an article published in the *New Palestine* on March 27th by Dr Walter J. Fischel, 'War and Research on Mount Scopus' and the sub-title 'The Hebrew University Laboratories and Brains Trust put on Wartime Basis'. Already the sub-title is in the worst possible taste, and can do no good to the University in the eyes of men of science. But turning to the text of the article, which is written in a florid style characteristic of a high-pressure salesman, it is full of inaccuracies. For instance, on page 9, 'Remarkable discoveries have been made in extracting vitamin C from Oranges' seems ridiculous overstatement, because the preparation of vitamin C is the simplest possible thing and known for years to every chemist who has had anything to do with vitamins. Equally incorrect is the statement that the Hebrew University has found out that this vitamin neutralizes the poison produced by many disease germs. What vitamin C can do, is again very well known, and the discoveries have certainly not been made in the Hebrew University exclusively.

It goes on in the same strain, and finally winds up with the statement that vitamin C is an antidote against inorganic poisons such as phenol, which is essentially an organic substance – and really, Mr Schocken, statements like that make us look ridiculous. I could go on quoting more of the mis-statements, for instance, 'As far back as 1934 a method was worked out for obtaining sugar from peel of citrus fruits' and then it goes on explaining what the sugar is, which explanation is (a) elementary knowledge, and (b) it happens to be wrong. . . .

I would be extremely grateful to you if you would kindly indicate to

Dr Fischel that he had better restrain himself and keep, in his propaganda, to the subject about which he knows something. I am sorry to trouble you with this matter, but I am sure you would not like to see the name of the Hebrew University connected with nonsensical propaganda of this kind, which can only do harm and no good.
From a letter to S. Salman Schocken, Chairman of HU Executive Council. New York, 11 May 1942.

Doctor of Philosophy

I have been prevented till now by the pressure of affairs from conveying to you, and to your colleagues of the Hebrew University, my deep appreciation of the honour done me at the ceremony, where together with Dr Magnes I was the recipient of a degree of Doctor of Philosophy, *honoris causa*; and I am the more anxious to do so because, being at the time under great nervous and physical strain in view of the forthcoming appearance before the United Nations Commission, I was unable to address the assembly and give adequate expression to my feelings.

I need hardly tell you that my relationship to the Hebrew University makes this award my most cherished academic possession, and I am doubly appreciative for having been permitted to share in the establishment of a precedent, since this was the first occasion on which degrees *honoris causa* were conferred by the Hebrew University. Many greater names will be added to your roll of Honorary Doctors of Philosophy, but the distinction of being among the first chosen for that honour will remain. It will always symbolize for me the privilege which was mine in assisting at the humble beginnings of a great institution of learning dedicated to our people and to humanity.
A letter to Sir Leon Simon, Chairman of the HU Executive Council, who later succeeded Weizmann as Chairman of the Board of Governors. Rehovot, 10 July 1947.

The Jewish Situation between the Wars

Jews and Bolshevism

I had an interview with Sir George Clerk at the Foreign Office on the subject of the Jewish massacres which are taking place in Poland and elsewhere in Eastern Europe.

Sir George said he was aware of the facts, and that telegrams had been sent to Washington and to Paris suggesting joint action to stop these excesses. The proposal was to tell the Poles that they would jeopardize their case at the Peace Conference by ill-treating the Jews.

Sir George added that he was in favour of sending an emissary to make a thorough investigation of the facts and would do everything in his power to secure facilities for the journey of such an emissary. He quite saw that the Zionists could not remain silent on the subject, but he would prefer them to wait a little longer before starting a public agitation. And he saw a difficulty in the fact that a Zionist protest against anti-Jewish excesses may be met by the counter-charge that Jews were responsible for excesses in Russia.

I told Sir George that I fully appreciated his point of view but could not regard it as absolutely satisfactory. We were already told that Jews were responsible for Bolshevik misdoings and it did not need a protest against anti-Jewish excesses to stimulate that accusation (see *Morning Post*, etc.). The fact was that while perhaps a small faction of the Russian Jews were Bolshevists and no doubt provided the brains of Bolshevism, the overwhelming majority were anti-Bolshevist. That fact, however, was not brought to the notice of the public. The public was not told that these Bolshevik Jews massacred Jews along with others whom they chose to call Bourgeois, or that Jews had opposed the Bolsheviks, or that the people who assassinated Mirbach or tried to get rid of Trotsky were Jews. Bolshevism thrives on misery, starvation and persecution. Is it surprising that the Jews who have suffered tortures indescribable under the Tzarist regime have been driven to despair and some of them become Bolsheviks? The Jews gave more than half a million soldiers to the army of Russia, they flocked to the colours at the beginning of the war with great enthusiasm – many Jews volunteered. How did Russia treat them during the war? Russian soldiers, under the eyes of their commanders, pillaged, robbed and massacred Jewish communities. Great Jewish communities like Kovno and Vilna have been evacuated under most humiliating and trying conditions for the Jews and the Jewish population scattered through the wilds of Russia, and in many cases allowed to perish from cold and starvation. Not a single word has been uttered in the Allied Press in condemnation of the acts of Russia, then the ally of Britain and France.

From a note of a discussion with Sir George Clerk. London, 28 November 1918.

Refugees stranded

I need hardly point out to you that the effects of the new Immigration Laws in America are already being felt throughout the stricken areas in Europe. Not only do vast numbers besiege our offices, but in despair the Jews are searching for all sorts of places to make their homes. Guatemala, Mexico and Cuba are suggested, one reads of attempts to introduce Jews again in large numbers into Spain, and so on. The

conditions in Eastern and South-Eastern Europe, I mean particularly Poland, Russia and Rumania, are such that there may be trouble at any moment, and of course the Jews will be the first sufferers. Two very reliable representatives of ours have just come back from a very long tour through this particular district and the tale of woe they tell is appalling. At every port on the Black Sea, and also at many of the Channel ports here and in France, one finds hundreds and thousands of Jewish refugees stranded, debris of humanity floating about as wreckage, some of them remaining on board ships (this is happening near Greece) going from port to port in the hope of being able to land somewhere.
From a letter to Louis Marshall. London, 17 July 1924.

Crimean scheme
The Bolsheviks have with great cunning and very adroit propaganda made extensive use of the Jewish suffering for which they themselves are largely responsible, by now coming forward with an apparently generous proposal for a large settlement of Jews on the land in the Ukraine and Crimea. They have by devious ways succeeded in enlisting the support of an influential section of the Jewish community in the United States, where a fund of 15 to 25 millions of dollars is at present actually being raised for the main purpose of promoting Jewish colonization in Russia. The Crimean scheme is being heralded as a competitive and alternative project to Palestine. In a manner characteristic of American propaganda, visions are being dangled before the public which make our slow and difficult work in Palestine look insignificant as compared with the Bolshevik mirage. We have no doubt that eventually all this will result in a fiasco, but for the present it constitutes a serious embarrassment to us, divides our forces, and tends to deflect financial and moral support from Palestine.
From a letter to Sir John Shuckburgh. London, 28 May 1926.

Russian situation
For the past twenty years the position of the Jews in Russia has been growing more and more precarious. At the moment the use of the term 'community' is hardly justified, for Russian Jewry – that inexhaustible reservoir from which Jewishness once flowed in a rich stream into the communities of the West, is fast becoming de-Judaized. The economic readjustment brought about by the Bolshevist revolution in Russia, far from improving the lot of the Jews, has thrown millions of Jewish lives out of gear; for millions of Jews no place could be found in the newly created economic system of the Soviets.

I do not exaggerate when I say that the majority of Russia's three million Jewish subjects are declassed – economically, physically, and spiritually. There is no room for the trader, the middleman, the *Luftmensch*, within the framework of modern life in Russia. In the younger generation a process of adaptation is beginning: some – we are told, many – have succeeded, more or less, in adapting themselves to the new way of life, but they have done so at the cost of their Jewish traditions. Their only chance of survival has been to migrate, under one or other of the Soviet Government's schemes, from the places where they lived, and to go out as proletarian agriculturists or as organized members of the Soviet workers' army, into those vast areas of Russia where no Jewish tradition exists, or ever has existed. It is still doubtful whether any of these schemes designed to improve the conditions of Russo-Jewish life will prove successful; it is certain that, at best, they can be no more than palliatives. They leave the root of the problem still untouched.

So much for externals. Within the community itself, the Jewish religion in all its forms is rapidly disappearing. The Hebrew language is becoming an unknown, even exotic, plant; it is an offence against the state to teach it, or even to speak it, and the great centres of Jewish learning in Lithuania and White Russia have passed, or are passing, with the older generations. The breach between the old generation and the new grows wider; bonds between father and child are broken, and an abyss separates parents who think and feel in terms of ancient Jewish tradition from children who have succeeded in emancipating themselves from the pre-war period. Small wonder if, under such conditions, the number of mixed marriages among Russian Jews is rapidly increasing – perhaps 50 per cent of Russian-Jewish marriages today are outside the community. And all this is due not so much to propaganda, or to other direct action, as to sheer force of circumstances: a people scattered in small groups or isolated units among the countless millions of the Russian population has little chance of survival. Russian Jewry affords a tragic example of a Jewish community in process of dissolution; the result would seem inevitable.

From an address to the Jewish Agency, British Section. London, 7 December 1931.

About left-wing Zionism
It has been suggested to me that you regard me as belonging to the 'extreme Left'. It is about this that I should like to address you. Again, I do so not for purposes of justification – I am entitled to my views, whatever they may be, just as others are entitled to theirs. We are living in a world in which political tolerance is becoming one of the fundamentals of modern society. With the exception of one or two

despotic countries which take no part in the system of European civilization, we see Socialists, extreme or otherwise, standing at the head of great governments, playing the part of great national figures, round whom have rallied men of every shade of political opinion, and the leaders of great parties who in ordinary times stand at the opposite end of the scale. The National Government in England includes men of all parties and shades of belief, and has had the incontestable approval of the great English democracy. So that there would be no occasion for any apology on my part even if I did hold the views which appear to have been attributed to me. But in fact I do not hold such views.

The term 'extreme' is, of course, relative. One may always be 'extreme' in relation to someone else. There may be black reactionaries in Paris for whom you yourself are an 'extremist'. I have been trying to think on what this particular issue can be based, and have come to the conclusion that it can only be a result of observations, perhaps wrongly interpreted, made by members of your circle, of my activities in Palestine in the last thirteen years. Colour may have been lent to these inferences by the events of the last Congress. The last Congress was clearly divided along one definite line of cleavage: there was on the one hand a group of reactionary obscurantists – people like the pseudo-religious politicians of the *Mizrachi* – in happy combination with Jewish Fascism, as represented by the Revisionists. Their strength was further increased by a group of Americans – stupid, poisoned by personal hatreds, utterly ignorant of the problems at stake, determined only on wreaking their personal vengeance.

On the other side of the fence stood the intellectual elements, people who had carried the burden of fund-raising, political work, propaganda, during the War and after it, combined with representatives of the labour group in Palestine – those who stand in the advance trenches of the movement, and who, literally on their own shoulders, carry the weight and bear the burden of actual life in Palestine. No one who spent an hour at the Congress could fail to realize that this was the division of forces. Whatever may be one's view of the respective political opinions of the two groups, there can be no difficulty in assessing their respective contributions to the upbuilding of Palestine. On the one side you have the Ghetto politicians; on the other, the workers in Zion. As it happened, it was the second group which fought my battle, and lost it – a phenomenon not unknown elsewhere in European politics during the last four or five years. Bruening, for instance, is losing his fight against Hitler. I will not quote examples from French politics. The times are such as to encourage, in some way, the reactionary elements; I need not enter into the philosophy of it; the facts are patent.

I cannot help thinking that, in your judgment of me, you may have been influenced by events in Palestine and by some of the new slogans which reaction is bringing into the field in order to justify its existence. To give one or two illustrations: On the one side, our workmen are being accused of being grasping, domineering, of trying to obtain an undue share of the benefits which Palestine life may offer. This may or may not be true – I am not interested to constitute myself a defender of the workers – but the fact is that our workmen live modestly – more than modestly – in Palestine and whatever they have they have earned by the sweat of their brow and the labour of their hands; the work they have done has been, in the absolute sense of the word, 'theirs' – not done for them, either by Arabs or by Jews; they have led and lead clean, modest and hardworking lives, and their principal anxiety is that there should be more of them coming into Palestine month by month.

It is true that they have a powerful organization; they have shown a great deal of initiative in this direction, perfect discipline under most difficult conditions, and they have defended their specific interests forcefully and intelligently. All these things count in their favour. And I think, on the whole – there may be exceptions – that they have not subordinated the general interests of the National Movement to their own specific class interest, if such exists. They have in the past few years been the paramount constructive element in the country; they have turned wastes into gardens, and wildernesses into places of comparative safety. For that they have paid a heavy toll, often in human lives. They have made mistakes, even grave mistakes, at one time or another, but, on balance, there can be no doubt as to their great contribution to the Jewish National Home. They are admittedly viewed with suspicion in some quarters, especially by those classes who have carried into the National Home the traditions, habits and outlook of their respective ghettoes. There is also a certain animosity between them and the so-called 'old' settlers, to whom you have been a father. I should be the last to minimize the value of the pioneering spirit which in years gone by animated the 'old' colonists, and which led them to endure great hardships in the initial stages of colonizaton, while Palestine was still a backward and derelict country. But let us not forget that they had powerful and consistent support through your own well-directed munificence; they were able to pick and choose their land and their men; they were given every chance to lay the foundation for their present, and well-deserved, prosperity.

The thing which divides them fundamentally from the newer generation of pioneers is the sore and sordid question of Arab labour. You yourself have, I think, repeatedly deplored the extensive employment of Arab labour in these colonies. And it requires little imagination to see how it must appear to the young Jew who comes with high hopes to Palestine, and later suffers the hardships, perhaps, of temporary unemployment, when he sees thousands of Arabs, potential enemies, he thinks, of the settlers, working in Jewish groves and vineyards; and how his bitterness will be increased when he hears that these colonies have been built up to a great extent through the efforts of the man who occupies probably the highest position in all Jewry. A conflict which might have been amicably settled, had real endeavours been made a few years ago, has deepened and become more bitter with the passing of time, and it is this conflict, and not 'class-consciousness', which divides the two groups in Palestine. But unfortunately the cleft has been driven so deep that it cuts right through the whole life of Palestine.

This phenomenon has brought about unpleasant relations between Jew and Jew, between old and new settlers; it has created artificially two strata of society in Palestine at a time when we should have formed a compact unit, since we were surrounded by a hostile majority. I do not think one need belong to the 'extreme Left' in order to realize the value of the new generation which has come to Palestine, and to sympathize with the plight in which they find themselves. Every observer can easily see that there is a sort of bourgeoisie growing up in Palestine, which demeans itself by imitating the Western bourgeois element, without having either the traditions, or the ability, or the power, of the communities which it copies. The Jewish bourgeois in Palestine is really a man who has no money but does not care to work. And he tries to cover this fundamental vice by putting out a string of slogans as a sort of smoke-screen, which he hopes may protect him from the eyes of those who see the hollowness of his mental, moral and intellectual attitude.

From a letter to Edmond de Rothschild. London, 23 December 1931.

Threat to German Jewry

German Jews have contributed much to the economic, cultural, artistic and scientific development of their country. During the war they made (as did Jews in all countries) sacrifices at least comparable with those made by their neighbours for the lands in which they had lived, and to which they have been loyal, for generations. In Germany one would have thought the Jews had earned their right to full citizenship in the state to whose welfare they had so largely contributed.

I have spoken of the Jews, but in doing so I do not forget that they are not the only sufferers. Our sympathy must go out in equal measure to all innocent and defenceless people, be they who they may, whose liberties are – contrary, we feel sure, to the true instincts of the German nation – being endangered in Germany today.

While we, as Zionists, are naturally anxious to achieve our own national freedom, and sincerely believe in the right of every people to self-determination, we are the last to desire to meddle in the internal affairs of other nations. The German people, it goes without saying, are entirely free to regulate their own political and social life as they think fit. But as Jews we cannot remain indifferent (and it is our belief that no unbiased observer with any respect for justice and fair play can remain indifferent) when, in a great country like Germany – proud, and justly proud, of its people's high standards of culture – the economic and political existence of all Jewish citizens are alike imperilled by a policy which has inscribed antisemitism in its most primitive, one might say medieval, form as an essential part of its programme.

It is only a few days since Captain Goering, in a speech at Magdeburg, accused the Jews of organizing the 'cultural disruption of Germany'. It comes as a severe shock to civilized people, Jews or not, to find that it is possible today for a great people like the Germans to relapse into barbarism in their attitude towards a small and law-abiding minority of the citizens of their state.
From a speech at a Jewish Agency dinner. London, 2 March 1933.

'Places where they cannot live, places they cannot enter'
I should like to put briefly to you the Jewish problem as it presents itself to us today. It is a two-fold problem. It is a problem which can perhaps be expressed in one word, it is a problem of the homelessness of a people. Speaking of homelessness I should like at once to state that individual Jews, and individual groups of Jews, may have a home and sometimes a very comfortable home. Indeed, if one thinks of the small communities in the west of Europe beginning with England and continuing further down to the south, France, Switzerland, Italy, Belgium and Holland, these Jewish communities are, as compared with the existence of the Jews in Central, East and South-East Europe, in a fairly comfortable position. Then again the great Jewish community further west in America is, economically, and to a certain extent politically and morally, in a condition which allows them to work and labour without let or hindrance.

But if one draws a line and takes the Rhine as the geographical boundary almost everything to the east of the Rhine is today in a position, politically and economically, which is, if I may say so – and I am not given I think to exaggeration – something which is neither life nor death, and one may say if Europe today were in the same state as it was in 1914 before the war, with the highways and byways of Europe and the world in general open, then we should have witnessed an emigration of Jews which would probably have dwarfed the pre-war emigration, and the pre-war emigration was not small by any means. I think in 1914 there emigrated out of Russia, which then included Poland as well, something in the neighbourhood of 120,000 Jews.

They went in the majority of cases to America. They could be absorbed in a highly-developed industrial country. The emigrant found his livelihood almost immediately on arrival. This, as your Lordship and the members of the Commission are well aware, cannot happen today. The world is closed; and we have heard recently the Minister for Foreign Affairs in Poland, Colonel Beck, announcing in Geneva, and in his own country, and in England in numerous interviews which he has given, that there are a million Jews too many in Poland. This is not the place to enter into a discussion with Colonel Beck why exactly a million Jews? They are citizens of Poland; they have been connected with the fate and destinies of Poland for well nigh a thousand years. They went through all the vicissitudes through which the Polish nation went. They are out to make their contribution to Poland, good, bad or indifferent, as everybody else. Why should they be singled out as being a million too many? No doubt these elementary facts as to the state of the world today ought to be known to Colonel Beck just as they are known to every intelligent newspaper reader. What does it mean? Where can they go? Is there any place in the world which can rapidly absorb a million people, whoever they may be, Jew or non-Jew? The poor Polish peasant, perhaps ignorant and not very subtle, when he hears his own government making a pronouncement like that may possibly interpret it as meaning: here is a superfluous people standing in my way, which must be got rid of somehow.

I do not want to press the point any further. I shall not waste the time of the Commission by describing in any way what is happening in Germany. It is too well-known to need elaboration on my part. This accounts for the position of something like 3,600,000 Jews. Poland has slightly over three millions; Germany had in 1932 or 1933 something like 600,000, but that number has since diminished. If one goes further afield, and takes the Jewries of Rumania, Latvia, Lithuania, Austria, one sees practically the same picture, and it is no exaggeration on my part to say that today almost six million Jews – I am not speaking of the Jews in Persia and Morocco and such places, who are very inarticulate, one hears very little of them – in that part of the world are doomed to be pent up in places where they are not wanted, and for whom the world is divided into places where they cannot live, and places into which they

cannot enter.
From his testimony before the Royal (Peel) Commission on Palestine. Jerusalem, 25 November 1936.

'Jews don't understand'
I am distressed that the Jews don't understand the apocalyptic nature of the times. The Austrian Jews had a warning and did not take it. It always required God knows how much coaxing to get a contribution out of Louis Rothschild (I think he gave once £5,000 and all Israel was agog with it); now the Nazi thieves have stripped him bare. Our own friends in London and elsewhere will go on fiddling about in the good old way not realizing that every minute may bring about either annihilation or Redemption or both. Part of us will be destroyed and on their bones New Judea may arise! It is all terrible but it is so – I feel it even here, and can think of nothing else, but the others, even here, are much more placid when it comes to fundamentals although terribly fussy about puny matters. A new leader should arise in Israel now who should sound the call; we are already old and used up I'm afraid.
From a letter to Blanche Dugdale. Rehovot, 7 May 1938.

The Jews and the Second World War

War began with Jewish immigration to Palestine limited, under the terms of the MacDonald White Paper of May 1939, to 75,000 during the next five years. Jewish land purchase would henceforth be confined to a severely restricted area. It was intended that Palestine become an independent state within ten years, the Jews forming not more than one-third of the total population. The Jewish Agency rejected the White Paper (as did the Arabs) and Weizmann sought the waiving of its regulations so as to rescue as many Jews as possible from Nazi persecution. Simultaneously, he worked for the creation of a Jewish military formation to fight under its own flag.

'We stand by Great Britain'
In this hour of supreme crisis, the consciousness that the Jews have a contribution to make to the defence of sacred values impels me to write this letter. I wish to confirm, in the most explicit manner, the declaration which I and my colleagues have made during the last months, and especially in the last week: that the Jews 'stand by Great Britain and will fight on the side of the democracies'.

Our urgent desire is to give effect to these declarations. We wish to do so in a way entirely consonant with the general scheme of British action, and therefore would place ourselves, in matters big and small, under the co-ordinating direction of His Majesty's Government. The Jewish Agency is ready to enter into immediate arrangements for utilizing Jewish manpower, technical ability, resources, etc.

The Jewish Agency has recently had differences in the political field with the Mandatory Power. We would like these differences to give way before the greater and more pressing necessities of the time.

We ask you to accept this declaration in the spirit in which it is made.
A letter to Neville Chamberlain. London, 29 August 1939.

Enlisting Churchill's support

On the eve of my departure for America, I must write to you once more, firstly to thank you for the encouragement and help which it has been to us to know, through Brendan Bracken, that in the midst of your preoccupations, and under the severe strain of your present office, you can still maintain your interest in our cause. Secondly, I would like to leave with you my good wishes for your continued health and strength and power in the months which lie ahead. On the holder of your office lies the most continuous burden of this war. The military chiefs may have periods of respite; the man who keeps for Britain the Freedom of the Seas can never relax until victory is won.

No one can foretell with any certainty the course of the war in the near future. If it spreads to South-Eastern Europe, the Middle East can, I fear, hardly fail to become once more a major theatre of operations. If that is so, the potential value of Jewish resources in Palestine may suddenly become apparent even to those who have hitherto been raising obstacles in the way of our efforts to place them at the disposal of Britain.

But preparation takes time, as you know very well. I wished to begin it, both as regards our scientific and industrial contribution, and our military effort, as soon as I received the Prime Minister's reply to my letter sent on the outbreak of war, in which I declared our desire for a truce in the controversy over the White Paper. It has therefore been a deep disappointment to me that the Colonial Secretary seems to have set his will to prevent our offer being accepted, so far as it is in his power to do so; and by virtue of his office that power is considerable. . . .

It is quite clear to me that, in the present emergency, we cannot expect more than the maintenance of a truce as regards Palestine policy. We have been at pains to observe such a truce, but any new land legislation on the lines now under discussion, or any further tampering with immigration – which is already very difficult indeed – would seriously prejudice the future of Palestine, and make matters for the present even worse than they are. Any such steps would constitute a gross breach of the truce which we are doing our utmost to observe – a breach which could be justified, in our view, neither morally nor politically. May I here express the hope that your watchfulness will prevent any such calamity from being inflicted on us?

You have been concerned with our affairs ever since the beginning of our dealings with the British Government twenty-two years ago. You know that we have always placed our trust in your understanding of our cause and of our difficulties, and that we have always tried to show ourselves worthy of your trust.

From a letter to Winston Churchill, First Lord of the Admiralty. London, 14 December 1939.

Roosevelt's view

The appointment with President Roosevelt was arranged through Lord Lothian, who introduced Dr Weizmann and was present throughout the conversation. The talk was most friendly in character and lasted about half an hour.

The President began by saying that he had, of course, heard a good deal about Dr Weizmann, and was glad to meet him. Dr Weizmann began by dealing with his tour. He said that he had been travelling through the country and renewing old contacts, and had addressed large audiences in a number of cities. The President remarked that there were a good many Jews here who were not exactly obstructionists as far as Palestine was concerned, but who were not too friendly. Dr Weizmann said, 'Certainly that was so, but that on the whole sentiment for Palestine was very strong.' The President said, 'Yes, I agree.'

The discussion then centred on developments in Palestine. Dr Weizmann said that in the past few years they had had a shattering time there, but they had withstood the assault. The Jews had, indeed, strengthened their positions in many directions, and more than 80,000 people had come into the country in that period. He was not going to attempt to harrow the President's feelings by a description of what was happening to the Jews of Central and Eastern Europe. No doubt he knew the situation well enough, but the fact was that today Palestine and the United States were the only countries which were taking substantial numbers of immigrants. The President asked whether Dr Weizmann did not think that other countries too might absorb refugees, and referred to Colombia. Dr Weizmann said that if it were possible to settle some refugees there by all means let it be done, but none of these places could be a substitute for Palestine. He gave an example of the Argentine where, after sixty years of colonization under excellent conditions, only a very few thousand Jewish families remained on the land.

Dr Weizmann said that if one examined the situation in Europe today, eliminating those Jews who would have been swallowed up by the Russian system and disappeared, and those who would have perished – if the present rate of destruction continued – there would be two and a half millions to care for. Of these many would be aged or otherwise unsuitable for immigration. Some would find an outlet in other countries, while a certain number would in any case remain where they were. He believed that one million of the younger and more vigorous elements could over a period of years be drawn off into Palestine. This would be an immense contribution to the whole question. The problem was not really an unmanageable one if tackled with determination and with the object of aiming at a solution and not at palliatives. There were still great possibilities of development in Palestine which would enable the absorption of large numbers of immigrants. . . .

So far as the political question was concerned, the White Paper had been a nasty business, but it was not, he believed, the last word of British statesmanship, and during his tour he had tried to point out that Malcolm MacDonald was not England (Lord Lothian smiled at this). He thought that the whole issue was in the melting-pot again. The President asked: 'What about the Arabs? Can't that be settled with a little baksheesh?' Dr Weizmann said it wasn't as simple as all that. Of course they would compensate the Arabs in a reasonable way for anything they got, but there were other factors appertaining to a settlement. One result of the disturbances had been, he thought, to bring much nearer the possibility of an arrangement with their Arab neighbours; despite a campaign of violence conducted under the most favourable auspices, the latter had completely failed in their efforts to dislodge the Jews. That was a fact which was likely to have a fundamental effect on future relations with the Arabs. Already there were signs – he was not going to exaggerate them, but they were unmistakeable – that the Arabs were realizing this failure, and were casting around to see if they could not arrive at some *modus vivendi*. The

President said: 'When the war is over you will settle it. First, of course, the war must be won.'

Dr Weizmann agreed, and said that when the world again came to the conference table the Jewish question would still be staring them in the face, in all its ghastliness. He believed that the Peel Report did contain the kernel of a solution. There must be one place in the world which the Jews could call their own, and in which they should become masters of their fate. He was not going to enter into a discussion of boundaries or of the merits or demerits of partition; it could perhaps best be done within a Federal framework. At this point Lord Lothian intervened to say that he thought that was the direction in which things would move.

From a note of a discussion with Franklin D. Roosevelt. Washington, 8 February 1940.

Anthony Eden and the Jewish Army scheme

Mr Eden began by saying that he had known nothing about the negotiations which had been going on; he was surprised that they should have taken place without him. After all, he was responsible to the Cabinet for War Office affairs. He wondered whether he had been passed over, because Dr Weizmann thought him an anti-Zionist?

Dr Weizmann replied that he did not know whether Mr Eden was a Zionist or an anti-Zionist, because he had never had an opportunity of discussing anything with him. Even when Mr Eden had been in charge of the Foreign Office, when the revision of British policy in Palestine was taking shape, he had not been able to see him. Mr Eden then asked him when he had endeavoured to see him, and Dr Weizmann had given him a number of dates. He mentioned that he had seen Mr Eden's Parliamentary Private Secretary, Colonel Ponsonby, who had taken copious notes of what Dr Weizmann had said, and had even asked for a second meeting to obtain additional information. The object of taking those notes had been to arrange an appointment with Mr Eden, but such an appointment had never materialized. He had also tried to get into touch with Mr Eden through Major Cazalet.

Mr Eden apparently felt some awkwardness when these facts were brought up. Dr Weizmann had then explained fully what our request was. Mr Eden replied that it was extremely interesting, and that he should have to discuss it with the CIGS. Dr Weizmann had then told him that he had arranged to see the CIGS immediately after this talk with Mr Eden, and Mr Eden then said it might be best to bring General Dill in right away.

Before General Dill arrived, Dr Weizmann told Mr Eden that for exactly a year we had been trying to get some possibility for Jews to participate in the war. Mr Eden asked why Jews could not join the British Army. Dr Weizmann replied that British Jews were in the British Army; but he was talking about Jews from Palestine and other countries, especially America. Dr Weizmann said he had had long discussions with Lord Lloyd, who did not wish to see large numbers of Jews recruited in Palestine for fear of rousing the Arabs. He believed Lord Lloyd to be sincere in this opinion, although he did not share it himself. Mr Eden said it had been decided to form one Jewish and one Arab Battalion in Palestine. Dr Weizmann said it was grotesque that the Czechs, the Poles, the French, etc., should be allowed to fight, while the Jews were debarred from doing so because the Arabs did not want to fight for Britain.

At this stage General Dill came in, and hearing the last part of Dr Weizmann's remarks, interjected that he thought the Jews should be allowed to fight. Mr Eden said there were political reasons which had to be taken into account. Dr Weizmann said that he still remembered the time when Mr Eden had been Foreign Secretary, and knew that he must be familiar with the problems involved. The Jews could fight in Egypt and in Africa, and he proposed that a Jewish striking force should be created, which should operate on the borders of the invading countries. The Jews could perform what the Arabs had failed to do in the last war – although their activities had been much advertised. Mr Eden asked why Dr Weizmann made this statement, and Dr Weizmann suggested that Mr Eden read General Wavell's book. The Jews were eminently suitable for such work. Mr Eden said it seemed to him to be a good idea. But he did not quite understand what was meant by a 'Desert Force'. He understood the request for cadres and for recruiting in Palestine. Dr Weizmann said they must treat all the different points as part of one effort, to which Mr Eden replied that this would simplify matters.

He had, however, two objections: first, they had not a sufficient number of instructors. Dr Weizmann replied to this that he would not be surprised if the Jews were able, after a short time, to provide their own instructors if the government could give them a dozen or a dozen and a half British instructors to start with. Mr Eden said that Dr Weizmann was probably right, and General Dill nodded agreement. Mr Eden's second objection was the lack of equipment. To this Dr Weizmann replied that he had been hearing that excuse since September 1939. They would be willing to take their chance along with the other forces. Mr Eden said they could probably obtain rifles, but it would be a different matter with regard to anti-tank guns, machine guns, etc. Dr Weizmann said he was going to the USA and might be able to obtain some equipment there.

Mr Eden then asked ironically whether the Jews could not use their own arms. Dr Weizmann replied that if the British Government was hard up they might be able to do so, but of course they had no anti-tank guns.
From a report of a discussion with the Minister of War. London, 10 September 1940.

The proposal accepted
The government has at last agreed to the formation of a Jewish Army on the same basis, and I believe with the same status, as the Czech or Polish Army. Its size to begin with is to be about 10,000, assuming that 4,000 would come from Palestine and another 6,000 from the rest of the world, America in particular. This number would include the cadres which, as you know, would also come from Palestine. They are to be trained and organized *here*, and when ready would return to the Middle East. Transport does not seem to be a difficulty, as empty ships are returning from Egypt (through the Mediterranean) in considerable numbers. The PM, whom I have seen a fortnight ago, is heartily in favour of it, so are – I must add – all the other members of the Cabinet, including Beaverbrook and Halifax. With the latter I have had a long talk about the political future of Palestine on the lines of a Jewish entity within the framework of an Arab Confederation. Lord Halifax has assured me that he considers such a solution a fair one, and that Lord Lloyd's mind is moving in the same direction.
From a letter to Moshe Shertok. London, 22 September 1940.

More procrastination
I am writing to let you know that I have got no further with the War Office; they seem to think they have to wait until the [American] Presidential Elections are over. I see no reason why preliminary discussions should not take place now; it would save a great deal of time. I greatly fear that the new complications in Greece and the Balkans may make it again impossible for the War Office to find time to discuss matters with me, which means that I shall have to wait indefinitely until they make up their minds to give some thought to the details of organizing a Jewish Force. I do not wish to press them unduly; my patience is almost unlimited. But as you know, I am anxious to get to the United States as soon as possible, and they are really making me waste valuable time when I might be doing useful work over there.
From a letter to Brendan Bracken, Parliamentary Private Secretary to Churchill, now Prime Minister. London, 28 October 1940.

How Britain scorned an ally

In the war against Hitler the Jewish nation claims a place among the fighters in the forefront, and moreover, its right to fight under its own name and flag.

The Twenty-First Zionist Congress, which met at Geneva in August 1939, commissioned me to express to the British Government our desire to co-operate. I did so in a letter to Mr Chamberlain dated 29 August. I received a courteous but non-committal reply. We had to fight a political battle before Palestinian Jews were permitted to bear arms; and this battle is not over even now.

There are two aspects to the Jewish war effort: in Palestine and the Middle East, and beyond. With regard to Palestine, we have from the beginning pressed for the recruitment of the maximum number of Jews in Jewish units within the British Army, both for the defence of the country and in support of the British Forces in the Middle East. We further offered a Jewish Division to be formed in the West for service wherever required, consisting of Jewish volunteers from all free countries with a leavening of Palestinian Jews.

Mobilization of Jews in Palestine became a most vital and urgent question when, in June 1940, Italy entered the war; and still more so after the Germans reached the Eastern Mediterranean in force, in the spring of this year. The Palestinian Jews are prepared to die fighting, but not willing to let themselves be slaughtered like sheep in a shambles – co-operation is an offer, but self-defence is a claim. Certain steps for local defence have been taken by the government, and this is the most satisfactory point of my report.

I pass to the enlistment of Palestinian Jews for military service in the Middle East. At first the main thing offered by HM Government was service in two mixed 'Palestinian' units of the Pioneers, who are non-combatants. But this was not what the Jews asked for. When at last it was decided to enlist Palestinians for combat service, numerical parity between Jews and Arabs was insisted upon. And as the keenness of the Palestinian Arabs was not equal to the occasion, this rule restricted Jewish numbers to a mere fraction of what the total would otherwise have been. Since the parity rule has been relaxed new Jewish Companies have been added to The Buffs. Together with more than 1,500 in the RAF Ground Forces, and various auxiliary units, the Palestinian Jews have supplied by now some 10,000 men to the British Forces, and recruitment continues.

There is however one supremely important aspect on which, so far, we have been refused any satisfaction. Like all nations, the Jews desire to serve under their own national name and flag, doing honour to their national badge, the Shield of David, which the Nazis try to convert into a mark of shame.

But the name of 'Jew' seems to be shunned as much by those who accept our services, as it is flaunted by our enemies. The Palestinian Jews have done honourable service in France, Libya, Eritrea, Abyssinia, Greece, Crete and Syria. But have any of us been allowed the pleasure of seeing their service acknowledged? At the utmost some mention is made of 'Palestinians', so that the public does not know whether these are Jews or Arabs.

I now pass to my last chapter. Here I have nothing to record except disappointment and frustration. For a long time past there has been a pressing demand among all the free Jewries of the world for a Jewish Fighting Force in which any Jew could enlist as a Jew, for service with the British Forces, fighting under the name and flag of his race. All this time the Executive of the Jewish Agency has preserved silence. But this was not the silence of indifference or inaction.

On 1 December 1939 I made, on behalf of the Agency, an offer of a Jewish Division for service wherever required. But under the Chamberlain–MacDonald regime nothing could come of it. In the summer of 1940, under the new government, our offer was pressed once more, and in a more detailed form. In September 1940 it received the explicit approval of HM Government. Discussion of detail and preparations for carrying out the scheme followed, and reached a point at which none of us in the Agency doubted that the Jewish Fighting Force would shortly come into being. Naturally we could not join in a public agitation for something for which we held a definite promise.

Then, like a bolt from the blue, came a letter from the Colonial Secretary on 4 March, informing me that owing to lack of equipment the project must be put off for six months, but might be reconsidered again in four months. To this was added an emphatic assurance that this postponement was in no sense a reversal of the previous decision in favour of our proposal.

The original scheme was to bring the recruits for the Jewish Fighting Force to England for training, and while the framework was to be supplied by Jews seasoned in the Middle Eastern campaigns, we counted on obtaining the bulk of our recruits from across the Atlantic. Even before the postponement of 4 March the difficulties of the shipping position were apparent, and therefore the idea of training part, or the whole, of the Force in the West Indies or Canada was discussed. This necessity had become even more obvious when we raised the question once more towards the end of the six months period.

On 28 August, however, I received a further letter from Lord Moyne informing me that because of new technical difficulties the matter of the Jewish contingent would have to continue in cold storage for the present, but proposing again to consider the question in three months time. I now felt that the moment would never come when there were no technical difficulties, and I pressed for a definite decision. On 15 October I received an answer from the Colonial Secretary which in substance goes back on the promise of September 1940, and the reassurance of March 1941.

I have now given you the broad outlines of the work and the endeavours of the Jewish Agency, and the disappointments which they have suffered. We Jews are being penalized for our loyalty and devotion. There is obviously the feeling that we require no encouragement, and we are refused the rights of every nation to its name and flag. It is bitter for me to have to say this. But we do not lose hope, nor do we renounce our claim to a Jewish Fighting Force serving under its own standard. And even now I say, addressing myself especially to the Palestinian Jews: Enlist in ever-growing numbers! Work and fight, even if nameless! You are working and fighting for a great cause. And whatever others may do to us, we must not default in our duty to the common cause.

Statement to a Special Zionist Conference. London, 9 November 1941.

Jews taken for granted

On the victory of the United Nations depends the survival of the Jews nationally, and even as individuals, for in the matter of exterminating the Jews Hitler is as good as his word; and traditional ties of deep moral significance bind our people to Britain's cause. The whole-hearted support of Jewry for Great Britain has therefore always been taken for granted, and British policy in the Middle East was based by the Chamberlain Government on the principle of trying to win over the Arabs at the expense of the Jews. But the moral loss involved has not, so far, been compensated anywhere by the political gains. We shall never waver in our conviction that the White Paper is a breach of Mandate pledges in which we can never acquiesce, and which has been publicly condemned by Mr Churchill himself. But even within the framework of the implemented two parts of the White Paper of 1939, the dignity and the feelings of the Jewish people might have received consideration. Instead, these have been trampled underfoot. . . .

Palestine Jewry is asked to supply more men for the Army, and for military works and services of various kinds. This we try to do, and also to transform and develop our industries for war, and to intensify our agricultural production. For all this, labour is required; nevertheless, the immigration schedules sanctioned by the Administration have been of the most exiguous kind, and for nine months (October 1940 to July 1941) were refused altogether. This was justified on the ground that the 'circumstances of international travel' made it most difficult for prospective immigrants to reach Palestine, and that by the time they did, conditions might have changed! (See Supp. No. 2 to *Palestine Gazette* 1065, p. 1827.) The result of this neglect both of practical and humanitarian considerations is that tens of thousands of young Jews who were eager to fight and work on the British side have been left for the Nazis to kill or enslave.

From a letter to Lord Cranborne, Colonial Secretary. London, 6 March 1942.

Day of Mourning
Conference of leading Jewish organizations including American Jewish Congress, World Jewish Congress, American Jewish Committee, *Bnai Brith*, Jewish Labour Committee, *Mizrachi, Agudath Harabbonim, Agudath Israel*, Synagogue Council of America, *Poalei Zion*, have accepted and strongly support proposal [that] Wednesday December second be solemnly observed by Jews throughout the world as Day of Mourning, Fasting, prayer for Jewish victims greatest crime against humanity. Facts concerning horror directed against Jewish people unquestionably appeared [in] your local papers now have confirmation [in] Hitler's order to exterminate all Jews [in] Nazi-occupied countries by December thirty-first nineteen hundred forty-two. Almost two million already massacred. Sending you full report. In the meantime urge that you, in co-operation with all your organizations, observe December second as memorial day; [also] to secure co-operation [of] non-Jewish community and Press comments on these atrocities.

Telegram sent jointly with Stephen Wise to Va'ad Leumi. *New York, 2 December 1942.*

On a proposal by the British Government for international co-operation in solving the problem of refugees from Nazi-occupied Europe, an Anglo-American Conference took place at Bermuda in April 1943. No concrete steps ensued.

Plea to Bermuda Refugee Conference
1. In submitting this memorandum on behalf of the Jewish Agency for Palestine, we desire in the first instance to offer some observations on the scope and character of the Bermuda Conference.
2. In the light of the overwhelming tragedy which faces the more than four million Jews which, it is estimated, still survive in the Nazi-occupied countries, it was hoped that the governments of Great

Britain, the United States and the other members of the United Nations, would be ready to undertake practical steps commensurate with the vastness of the problem. Unhappily the statements of the Secretary of State for Foreign Affairs, Mr Anthony Eden, and of United States Secretary of State Mr Cordell Hull, give little support for this hope. The terms of reference for the Bermuda Conference are severely limited in scope and are intended apparently to deal only with the fringe of the problem rather than with the problem itself. While the Jewish Agency for Palestine is grateful for any measures which may be calculated to save the lives of at least some of Europe's Jews, it would be failing in its most elementary duty were it not to call attention to a situation which, overriding all ordinary political considerations, calls for a plan conceived on the broadest possible lines for the rescue of these four million Jews who are in imminent danger of physical annihilation.

3. The Jewish Agency for Palestine is deeply conscious of the fact that the sufferings occasioned by the war are part of the burden which every people must carry and that the Jews are not the only people subjected to such suffering. But it must be borne in mind that of all peoples, the Jews have been singled out for utter and complete destruction by the enemy. Should the announced policy of the enemy continue unchecked, it is not impossible that by the time the war will have been won, the largest part of the Jewish population of Europe will have been exterminated. In these circumstances it is inconceivable that the democracies, engaged as they are in a struggle for world liberation, should fail to take fullest cognizance of the plight in which the Jews in Nazi-occupied countries find themselves.

4. The Jewish Agency for Palestine is fully aware of the enormous difficulties, military and other, involved in this problem, yet it dares to hope that far-sighted statesmanship on the part of the United Nations will find a way to meet it without in any way weakening the prosecution of the war against the enemy.

5. The memorandum submitted to the Bermuda Refugee Conference by the American Joint Emergency Committee on the European situation, and by the British Joint Emergency Consultative Committee, contains a number of proposals for dealing with various aspects of the problem. In presenting this memorandum we address ourselves to the great possibilities of rescue and rehabilitation offered by Palestine. We do so in the belief that in any plans that may be adopted for coping with this situation, the contribution of Palestine can and should be a major one.

6. In the memorandum submitted by the Jewish Agency for Palestine to the Inter-Governmental Conference on Refugees called at Evian in July 1938 on the invitation of President Roosevelt, attention was drawn to the possibilities offered by Palestine for large-scale resettlement of Jewish refugees. It was pointed out that the capacity of Palestine to absorb new immigrants was not a matter of speculation but was based on the experience of several decades of colonization and the demonstrable possibilities of its rapidly developing economy. As was there emphasized too, Palestine is unique amongst the countries of possible Jewish immigration in that it is the one land to which Jews come, with international sanction, 'as of right and not on sufferance'. As the Jewish National Home it is the country above all to which Jews are entitled to claim admission.

7. In the intervening years the situation of the Jews of Europe has immeasurably deteriorated and now presents a spectacle of unbroken horror. Unhappily too, the possibilities of large-scale rescue, by emigration to and absorption in countries other than Palestine, have been shown for political and other reasons to be limited in the extreme. The statement that the world is divided into countries in which the Jews cannot live and countries which they must not enter has proven only too true. So far as Palestine is concerned, however, despite great obstacles, in spite too of the outbreak of war and the closing of the Mediterranean, there has been continued and rapid development, and a further substantial immigration has been absorbed. The Jewish population which numbered about 65,000 at the end of the last war has grown to about 550,000 today, and in the years since the rise of Hitler, Palestine has absorbed more immigrants from Germany and German-occupied Europe than any other country. It is urged that both as an *ad hoc* reception centre to which Jewish refugees may be brought and for the time being kept and maintained, and also as a place where in the long run the refugees may be absorbed into the general economy, Palestine should for the following reasons be given principal consideration:

(a) As Jews coming to the Jewish National Home they would be welcomed in every possible way by their fellow Jews there. The spirit which animates the Jewish community of Palestine in this regard was given expression in a recent manifesto in the course of which it was stated that 'the Jews of Palestine solemnly declare their willingness and readiness to extend shelter to all Jews who are leaving or who have left occupied territories, to share their bread, to open their houses and to give their garments, as everything else, to save their brothers and sisters, fathers and mothers from being led like sheep to the slaughter house'. So far as the refugees are concerned, they would feel themselves not exiles, but persons returning home. It would constitute the first step in their psychological rehabilitation.

(b) From the practical point of view, Palestine by reason of its proximity to the Balkan countries has important geographical advantages. Transportation there from South-Eastern Europe would be possible overland or by a relatively short sea-route, thus eliminating the need for large-scale shipping and greatly simplifying the transportation problem.

(c) Once in Palestine the gradual absorption and integration of these refugees into the economic life of the country could in due course be effected. It is estimated that for 50,000 there would be immediate possibilities of absorption within the framework of the present economic structure. The very great expansion of Palestine's agriculture and industry since the outbreak of the war, and the fact that 30,000 Palestine Jews are today serving in the armed forces of the United Nations, has produced an acute shortage of labour which is in no degree met by current immigration. As regards the ultimate absorption of such numbers, an aide memoire is attached marked 'A' and dated 1 February 1943 which has been previously submitted to the British Ambassador in Washington and to the United States Department of State. Very many of the refugees will, unquestionably, after all they have been through, be reluctant to return to the countries of their origin. It can hardly be intended to return them there against their will if an alternative course is open, and the great majority will almost certainly wish to remain and settle in Palestine. Thus by bringing them to Palestine in the first place, not merely is a second and wasteful transfer avoided, but the refugee is immediately placed on the road to a permanent solution of his problem.

8. We desire at this point to refer to the announcement of His Majesty's Government on 3 February 1943 of its intention to allocate 29,000 Palestine immigration certificates primarily for refugee children from the Balkan countries. The efforts of His Majesty's Government to arrange for the evacuation and transportation of these children to Palestine is warmly appreciated and it is our earnest hope that everything will be done to press forward with these arrangements with all possible speed. In this connection we would point out however the necessity for increasing the

proportion of adults, since efforts to arrange the emigration of children alone would undoubtedly encounter much greater difficulties than would that of children with parents. Moreover, the knowledge that adults are almost entirely excluded from the possibility of such evacuation plans, places them, as events have already shown even in the Balkan countries, in much greater jeopardy than might otherwise be the case. It is to be added, that in any event the immigration and maintenance of the large numbers of children contemplated, involving as it would the expenditures of great sums of money, should fall within the framework of any general scheme for financing refugee immigration which the consulting governments may be ready to undertake.

9. The major proposal set out above for a large-scale transfer of Jews to Palestine is premised of course on the abandonment of the policy adumbrated by the British Government in the White Paper of May 1939, in terms of which Jewish immigration to Palestine is limited to approximately a further 30,000 immigrants and is to cease altogether after April 1944. That policy was a part of and at one with the discarded programme of appeasement in international relations which characterized the period immediately prior to the War. The policy of the White Paper was declared by the Permanent Mandates Commission to be out of accord with the obligations accepted by Great Britain and internationally approved in the Balfour Declaration and the Mandate for Palestine. It cannot stand the test of time or of justice, and it should be abandoned forthwith.

10. In this hour of grim tragedy for the Jewish people it is our fervent prayer that the great democratic nations whose conscience has been stirred even in the midst of a terrible war by the sufferings of the Jewish people in Europe, will seek to get to the root of the problem of European Jewry as it now manifests itself. It is a problem essentially of the homelessness of a people. Twenty-five years ago, also in the midst of a war, the first great promise of redemption by giving them back a home of their own was made.

No greater contribution can be made to that problem at this time, than by doing everything possible to give practical effect to that historic promise.

Memorandum submitted to the conference. New York, 14 April 1943.

'Hitler has won'

I met General Smuts at the Hyde Park Hotel at ten o'clock this morning, and though we had not seen each other for eleven years, we met as old friends. I had, however, a considerable amount of leeway to make up in order to put before him a picture of the situation as I see it at present, and this took me about half an hour.

I described our difficulties and frustrations: the White Paper, and what it means for us, the Jewish Army, etc., and incidentally told him that because of the White Paper probably about 150,000 to 200,000 more Jews had died in torment because we could not get them out. I added that in a few months now there would be a notice over the gates of Palestine: 'No Jew need apply.' I described the gun-running trials, and told him that Englishmen and Americans were apt to return from Palestine with poisoned minds, to spread anti-Jewish, anti-Zionist, antisemitic propaganda, suggesting that the Jews were subversive, and attacking the United Nations in the midst of the war. They were trying to drive us into revolt, and at the same time they accused us of being subversive. It seemed that they were following the pattern so successfully evolved by Hitler: first defame – then you can do what you please with them.

The General listened with close attention, and at the end said that I had painted a dark picture. He thought I had changed a great deal in the years since we had met. I said it was small wonder if I had. But my attitude had taken a course precisely opposite to his own: he had started by fighting the British, and ended as one of their most important collaborators. I had devoted almost twenty-five years of my life to sincere collaboration with the British, and now everything was being done to drive me into opposition to them. I think this made an impression on him.

I said that so far as the Jews were concerned, Hitler had won the war, because he had succeeded in poisoning men's minds everywhere. He replied emphatically that Hitler was not going to win.

He asked me whether I thought the Jews still followed me? I said I believed that English, American and South African Jews still did. So far as Palestine was concerned, it was some years since I had been there, and they might regard me as coming empty-handed. But I thought they would still follow me.

From a note of a discussion with Jan C. Smuts. London, 14 October 1943.

Joel Brand, a Hungarian Zionist leader, arrived in Istanbul on 19 May 1944 with a German proposition to exchange an unspecified number of Jews, said to be about one million, in return for 10,000 trucks, food supplies and soap. Refusal would mean continuation of the Jewish extermination programme. Consultation by Britain with her allies indicated that the USA would be agreeable to such an arrangement, but Russia, fearing Anglo-American intentions, rejected it outright.

Brand was interviewed in Aleppo by Moshe Shertok (later, Sharett) who believed the offer to be authentic. But the British held Brand beyond the time-limit allowed by the Germans for the mission.

Last efforts for European Jewry

1. According to messages from the responsible Jewish group in Budapest which have reached representatives of the Jewish Agency in Istanbul, Geneva and Lisbon, 400,000 Hungarian Jews have already been deported to the death camps. The Geneva message states that most transports have gone to Birkenau in Upper Silesia, where there are four crematoriums with a capacity for gassing and burning 60,000 a day, and where, in the course of the last year, over 1,500,000 Jews from all over Europe are reported to have been killed. In and around Budapest there are still over 300,000 Jews awaiting their doom. According to the Istanbul message their deportation was to have started this week.
2. It would thus appear that the stage of temporizing, in the hope of prolonging the victims' lives, is over, and some definite steps must immediately be taken if the admittedly remote chance of saving the remnants of Hungarian Jewry is not to be missed. We realize that our proposals for action are unorthodox, and perhaps unprecedented. But we consider them warranted by the present tragedy, which is also without its parallel or precedent.
3. We have already proposed that
   (a) An intimation should be given to Germany that some appropriate body is ready to meet for discussing the rescue of Jews.
   (b) A representative of the American War Refugee Board, if necessary seconded by a British official, should be ready to meet at Istanbul a member of the Nazi group in Budapest, to explore possibilities of rescue.
   (c) Joel Brand and, if only possible, his former escort, should be allowed to return to Hungary; Brand being authorized to inform the other side of the course that will have been decided upon.
4. Since the submission of these proposals, one of our friends in Istanbul, a Palestinian, has received a message from the Jewish centre in Budapest urging him to come to Budapest for a discussion, and informing him that his safe return would be guaranteed. While fully realizing the risks involved, we would submit that he should be allowed to proceed, preferably together with Joel Brand.
5. That any Gestapo offer to release Jews must have ulterior motives – avowed or hidden – is fully appreciated. It is not, however, improbable that in the false hope of achieving those ends, they

would be prepared to let out a certain number of Jews – large or small. The whole thing may boil down to a question of money, and we believe that the ransom should be paid.

6. Apart from the question of Joel Brand's mission, we would make the following urgent suggestions:

(a) That the Allies should publish a declaration expressing their readiness to admit Jewish fugitives to all their territories, and stating that they have in this the support of neutrals (Switzerland, Sweden, Spain, and possibly Turkey), who are prepared to give temporary shelter to Jewish refugees from massacres.

(b) That the Swiss Government in particular should be asked to instruct its representatives in Hungary to inform the local authorities of such readiness, and to issue such documents to the largest possible number of people as might in the interim afford them some protection.

(c) That a stern warning to Hungarian officials, railwaymen, and the population in general, be published and broadcast, to the effect that anyone convicted of having taken part in the rounding-up, deportation and extermination of Jews will be considered to be a war criminal and treated accordingly.

(d) That Marshal Stalin be approached to issue a similar warning to Hungary on the part of the USSR.

(e) That the railway-line leading from Budapest to Birkenau, and the death camps at Birkenau and other places, should be bombed.

Aide-memoire, signed jointly with Moshe Shertok, handed to Anthony Eden, now Foreign Secretary. London, 6 July 1944.

Churchill finally acceded to Weizmann's renewed demand for a military formation on 5 August 1944, and a Jewish Brigade Group was created which saw service in the European theatre. Weizmann travelled to Palestine in November 1944, his first visit in five years.

Fragmentation in Palestine

I have seen quite a good part of the country and what I have seen produces the impression of a great advance. Just precisely at the time when a large part of the world lives under the sign of destruction, Palestine has had one of its most fruitful periods of reconstruction. It is observable everywhere: in the cities, on the farms, in the *kibbutzim*, in the *moshavim*, as well as in the old settlements.

This progress is all the more remarkable when you consider that all this has happened under the straitjacket of the White Paper. There are of course also several threatening features: (a) the high cost of living which may cause serious dislocations after the war, and (b) the political atomization of the community.

It has become almost a sport for every little group to form its own party and publish its own newspapers. Reasonable people – and there are a good many of them here – are beginning to see the absurdity of the situation and are giving serious thought to its arrest. There are, of course, many explanations for it. The concentrated intelligence and the untapped energies have not sufficient outlet, and politics serves as a convenient hand-maiden for these people. Someone remarked the other day that the 550,000 or 600,000 Jews of Palestine seem to be made up of ex-presidents and ex-secretaries of Zionist societies from all parts of the world and that on any given issue, political, economic or otherwise, each one has a view, and a very determined one at that. A newspaper editor complained to me that he receives on the average a hundred letters on any issue touched upon in his columns. That would be no tragedy (editors' waste-paper baskets are made for that), but, he added, each one of them is worth printing.

All of which leads me to one inescapable conclusion: quite apart from all the other considerations Palestine is a country which cannot live without immigration. As soon as immigration stops energies are diverted to fruitless, futile discussions and political fermentation. The people begin to stew in their own juice; they become introspective, isolated and provincial. A state of affairs not always conducive to normal, healthy development. I am convinced also that for such a healthy development the influx of young American blood is very essential. It is perhaps the central problem which will face us in the post-war period. I am saying this not only because of the ruined and devastated condition of European Jewry, but primarily because of the positive and stabilizing influence American Jewish manpower can play in the expanding economy as well as the political equilibrium of Jewish Palestine.

From a letter to Felix Frankfurter. Rehovot, 20 December 1944.

On Jewish Terrorism

By 1940, three armed Zionist organizations were identifiable in Palestine. The largest, the *Haganah*, enjoyed quasi-official recognition. It was controlled by the Jewish Agency and frequently worked with the British security forces. Of the other two, both underground groups, the

Irgun Zvai Leumi suspended activism for the duration of the war against Germany. This left the Stern Group, or *Lohamei Herut Israel*, a much smaller unit, to continue its struggle against the British undeflected. Early in 1944, when all Jewish immigration was due to cease under the terms of the MacDonald White Paper, the *Irgun* resumed operations against British installations. The Stern Group made an unsuccessful assassination attempt on the retiring High Commissioner, Sir Harold MacMichael, in August 1944.

British policy helping terrorism
The recent acts of political violence committed by certain Jewish groups in Palestine are a matter of gravest concern to the Palestine Jewish community. The overwhelming mass of our public opinion utterly condemns these outrages, and is behind the leadership in its determination to do everything in its power to stamp them out. This is our fundamental attitude, and if I now attempt an analysis of the situation, nothing I say must be taken as condoning the outrages.

If all the perpetrators could be ranked as ordinary gangsters, the matter would be much less serious, but the behaviour of some of them is self-sacrificing rather than self-seeking – they are ready to pay the supreme penalty for their acts. In the present state of tension, such proof of conviction will find its admirers, or even imitators, among the youth. Therefore, if the situation is wrongly handled, the movement may spread.

The state of mind in Palestine Jewry which makes this at all possible is a product of the unhealthy atmosphere created during the last five years by the White Paper policy, and the White Paper mentality, of the Palestine Administration. In the struggle against Hitler, and in the great tragedy of the Jews under him, the thoughts and endeavours of Palestine Jewry have centred on the saving of Jews from torture and extermination, and on the organizing of Jewish action against the enemy. In both they might have expected help from the Mandatory Power. Instead, they found British effort directed (until 1942) to hindering the escape of Jews from Nazi-occupied countries to Palestine, and (to this very day) to discouraging Jewish participation in the war. Such an attitude was bound to sour the most loyal feelings. The impression has been created that the Palestine Administration is more intent on thwarting the Jews than on fighting Hitler.

At least 3,000,000 Jews have been murdered by the Nazis; there is hardly a Jew in Palestine but had among the victims near relatives – parents, brothers, sisters, etc. – and each is bound to feel that were it not for the White Paper, and its over-implementation, his own nearest and dearest might have been saved. When millions died, a few thousand escaped, but even the thought of their rescue is marred: it is associated with the images of the *Patria* and the *Struma*, with the deportations from Athlit Camp, and exile to Mauritius. The mental torture which Palestine Jewry has suffered explains the madness of some, and the direction it takes.

This emotional background does not imply sympathy with the violent methods of the groups, which every responsible Jew, in Palestine and elsewhere, condemns. But it should be remembered in handling the situation. The Palestine authorities can arrest and shoot a hundred Jews, and after that 500, etc., but if they do so while continuing their present policy and methods in Palestine, they will implant a Sinn Fein mentality in a hundred thousand.
From a memorandum to Jan C. Smuts. London, 4 May 1944.

'Most terrible calamity'
The terrorist acts in Palestine are the most terrible calamity that could befall us; they are already doing us incalculable harm, and will do worse if they continue. I have been trying my level best, directly and indirectly, to impress upon the *Yishuv* that they have to do everything in their power to stop it.
From a letter to Abba Hillel Silver. London, 18 October 1944.

The British Minister-Resident in the Middle East, Lord Moyne, was assassinated in Cairo by Sternists on 6 November 1944. Haganah *then co-operated with the security forces in rounding up members of both underground organizations.*

After the assassination
I can hardly find words adequate to express the deep moral indignation and horror which I feel at the murder of Lord Moyne. I know that these feelings are shared by Jewry throughout the world. Whether or not the criminals prove to be Palestinian Jews, their act illumines the abyss to which terrorism leads. Political crimes of this kind are an especial abomination in that they make it possible to implicate whole communities in the guilt of a few. I can assure you that Palestine Jewry will, as its representative bodies have declared, go to the utmost limit in its power to cut out, root and branch, this evil from our midst.
A letter to Winston Churchill. London, 7 November 1944.

The new Attlee Government, which in July 1945 assumed office following victory in Europe, delayed implementation of Labour's often repeated promise to relax immigration restrictions into Palestine. As a consequence, and despite Weizmann's opposition, Haganah *joined with* Irgun *and Stern to constitute a 'Jewish*

Resistance Movement', with combined operations against the British.

Disapproval made public

I must register my complete disapproval of violence as a means of attaining our legitimate ends. We have devoted friends on both sides of the Atlantic, who firmly believe in the justice of our cause. With their support let us continue our struggle by persuasion, negotiation and constructive effort till our position as a free nation in its own country has been firmly established – till the Jewish State has become a reality.

From a statement addressed to the Jewish community of Palestine. London, 2 November 1945.

Violence escalated, with widespread Jewish operations and British countermeasures. A security swoop on 29 June 1946 resulted in the arrest of some 3,000 Jews, including several members of the Jewish Agency Executive. Weizmann was in Palestine at this time, and he sent an ultimatum to the 'Jewish Resistance Movement' to disband. This it did, though a previously agreed action, the blowing up of British HQ at the King David Hotel in Jerusalem, was undertaken on 22 July by Irgun, *with much loss of life. For a brief period Weizmann's authority was restored in the Jewish Agency, though Stern and* Irgun *were beyond its control.*

'Terror distorts Zionism'

It was the tragic destiny of our young generation to see their kinsmen brutally murdered in Europe while they stood by, helpless and impotent. They were prevented from receiving the few survivors whom Providence had spared. In their native homeland, the country of the National Home, they found themselves excluded on racial grounds from all but a small percentage of the land. A new government which had promised redress came to power in England, and mobilized its armies and fleets to hunt down the pathetic shiploads of Jewish fugitives who sought a haven where they were entitled to seek it – amongst their own people in the internationally-guaranteed National Home. The spirit which is called patriotism in other nations was deemed fanaticism in them. They saw an attempt to stunt the growth of their enterprise, to cut them off from their connections and support in the Jewish Diaspora, to hand them over to Arab rule, and condemn them to permanent minority status. As the years of war drew on, their minds were assailed by the news of unspeakable, horrible acts perpetrated upon those nearest and dearest to them. With peace came liberation – except for the Jewish people. Finally, when the immigration of 100,000 displaced Jews – urged by the Jewish Agency and repeatedly supported by the President of the United States – was made contingent on the findings of an impartial Anglo-American Committee, the positive verdict of that committee was evaded, and remains unfulfilled to this day.

It is difficult in such circumstances to retain a belief in the victory of peaceful ideals, in the supremacy of moral values. And yet I affirm, without any hesitation, that we must retain it. Zionism is a modern expression of the liberal ideal. Divorced from that ideal, it loses all purpose, all hope. When we invoke the Jewish tradition as support for our national claim, we are not free to shake off the restraints of that tradition and embark on courses which Jewish morality cannot condone. Assassination, ambush, kidnapping, the murder of innocent men, are alien to the spirit of our movement. We came to Palestine to build, not to destroy; terror distorts the essence of Zionism. It insults our history; it mocks the ideals for which a Jewish society must stand; it sullies our banner; it compromises our appeal to the world's liberal conscience. It is futile to invoke the national struggles of other nations as examples for ourselves. Not only are the circumstances different, but our purposes, too, are unique. Each people must apply its own standards to its conduct, and we are left with the task of weighing our actions in the scales of Jewish tradition. Nor must our judgment be dazzled by the glare of self-conscious heroism. Massada, for all its heroism, was a disaster in our history. It is not our purpose or our right to plunge to destruction in order to bequeath a legend of martyrdom to posterity.

Zionism was to mark the end of our glorious deaths and the beginning of a new path leading to life. Against the 'heroics' of suicidal violence I urge the courage of endurance, the heroism of superhuman restraint. I admit that it requires stronger character, more virile nerves, than are needed for acts of violence. Whether they can rise to that genuine courage, above the moral degradation of terrorism, is the challenge which history issues to our youth.

From his Presidential Statement to the Twenty-Second Zionist Congress. Basle, 9 December 1946.

Uncontrollable

I fear that terror will become the dominating feature of Jewish life, and even the Jewish Agency will be unable to control it. On the contrary, the terror may control the Jewish Agency. It is a cancer in the body politic of Palestinian Jewry. *And thou shalt burn out the evil from thy midst.* I warn you, in my twenty-eighth year of active leadership, and in the seventy-third year of my life – I can say with Dr Wise that this may possibly be the last time I shall be appealing to Congress – I warn you: check the growth of this cancer. For if not, it will devour the movement and the *Yishuv*, and will destroy all we have built up. That we must never allow to happen.

I have heard the arguments of [Moshe] Sneh. I fear them. They lead us along false paths. This is not the road. This is not the way in which Zionism came to birth.
From his reply to the debate, Twenty-Second Zionist Congress. Basle, 16 December 1946.

Weizmann failed to gain enough support at the Congress to effect his re-election as President of the Jewish Agency, which henceforth came under the joint chairmanship of David Ben-Gurion and Abba Hillel Silver.

'Dragons' teeth'
I had a talk yesterday with the two most important personages dealing with our affairs [the Colonial Secretary and the High Commissioner], and I found them both ready to use their best endeavours to bring about a satisfactory solution as early as possible. But they both came back repeatedly to the same point: no solution is possible unless and until terrorism is stopped. I realize, of course, that this constitutes a vicious circle: the announcement of a solution could stop terrorism; but you cannot announce a solution unless terrorism is stopped. It is the fate of our people always to find themselves on the horns of a dilemma. And no dilemma was ever more cruel than this one. But at all costs we have got to break through this vicious circle. . . .

I write under the strong impression left upon me by the talk I had yesterday with the two gentlemen mentioned above, and which lasted the whole evening. I used all the arguments I could muster, pressing them very hard to try and make them realize that it is unjust to visit the sins of the few upon the heads of the many. I pleaded with them with all the force at my disposal. But I greatly fear that unless terrorism is stopped, we shall find the country plunging down into absolute chaos. Those who have been preaching resistance and violence all these years, and particularly at the last Congress, little realized how dangerous was the road they were treading. They have sown dragons' teeth.
From a letter to Israel Rokach, Mayor of Tel Aviv. London, 16 January 1947.

White Paper to blame
The White Paper released certain phenomena in Jewish life which are un-Jewish, which are contrary to Jewish ethics, contrary to Jewish tradition. 'You must not kill' is something which was ingrained in us on Mount Sinai. It was inconceivable ten years ago that the Jews should break this Commandment. Unfortunately, some are breaking it today, and nobody deplores it more than most of the Jews. I hang my head in

shame when I have to speak of this fact before you, gentlemen. I hope that international action, in concert with Great Britain, will clear out this disease from our midst.
From his evidence to the UN Special Committee on Palestine. Jerusalem, 8 July 1947.

Ethics of the blood-feud
It is my conviction that the bitterness of today is a passing phase; and I am resolved – as I am sure you are too – that no word of mine, or deed, shall prolong it, and no effort of mine be spared to restore and maintain goodwill between ourselves and England. On our side – which is what concerns us – there are two things we can and must do in this direction: stop retaliation, and stop terrorism. Are our ethics to revert to the ethics of the blood-feud? What others may do is no concern of our consciences, and I would like to think that every Jew worthy of the name is resolved that by us there shall be no shedding of innocent blood.
From a speech at a fund-raising dinner. London, 20 January 1948.

Extremism born of despair
The Jews are not a people given to violence. For many centuries force has not been our weapon. Our colonization in Palestine was an outstanding achievement of non-violence. We maintained the peace even when our fields and settlements were set on fire, and peaceful men, women and children were murdered. For three long years before the Second World War we were the target of a ruthless guerilla war, which the Mandatory failed to stem. We did not retaliate. And what was the outcome? The Arab gunmen won the political battle. The British Government in the 1939 White Paper fixed a final limit to Jewish immigration, closed the bulk of Palestine to Jewish settlement and announced that within five years Palestine would be placed under Arab rule. It was then, for the first time, that the ominous saying was heard among Jews here that violence paid with the British Government. . . .

You are surprised and disgusted that we have terrorists. I can only affirm that any nation which would have to go through the cruel ordeal through which the Jews have passed under Hitler would have produced such growth as terrorism and even worse. I cannot help feeling that a good deal of the self-righteous indignation with which the British Press abounds in these days springs from an uneasy awareness – perhaps only subconscious – that the guilt rests with the accusers.
From a letter to Lady Violet Bonham-Carter. Rehovot, 13 March 1949.

Zionism and Judaism

Culture and the rabbis

Yesterday we heard here from a succession of rabbis, who claim to be the teachers of the people, that the Jewish masses are afraid of culture, they shrink away from it. From this tribune I affirm that this claim rests on self-deception. I ask these rabbinical gentlemen, with what part of the Jewish people are they in contact? Are they in touch with that part of the masses representing the future strength of this Jewish generation? Or perhaps with the part that we must no longer count on? They come together with the people only in the synagogue, but they do not go out to the popular masses. They do not see that entire masses of the people are gradually being torn away. Where were the rabbis when Jews were converting by the thousand? Why did they not come forward then as champions of Judaism? Why do they face us with mistrust when we speak of Jewish national education? Why do they seek to introduce elements into our programme that can only have a disintegrating effect? I do not acquiesce to having the word 'religious' inserted into our programme. The moment you do this you exclude a great part of the delegates from our Congress.

From a speech at the Fourth Zionist Congress. London, 16 August 1900.

Growing power of religious Zionists

If there is anything in Judaism that has become intolerable and incomprehensible to the best of Jewish youth, it is the pressure to equate its essence with the religious formalism of the Orthodox. *Mizrachi* represents the element that in the natural course of events is dying by degrees. Their fanatically religious viewpoint and way of life has no bridge leading to contemporary youth. . . .

It seems incomprehensible that you and Nordau, men who know European political movements, should treat the *Mizrachi* as the picked troops, as if they really represented a political party already half-way to maturity. Their Zionist aspiration is purely one of words. Their horizon and political perspective are so limited that they can have no understanding whatsoever of a modern approach.

Precisely because of its political immaturity, and its apparent freedom from political pretension, this group will one day use its growing power in a most unexpected and stubborn manner. It will choose a decisive moment to defy the leadership. In practice, it is already seeking to dominate our propaganda campaign, our funds, our educational activities and our voting system!

From a letter to Theodor Herzl. Geneva, 6 May 1903.

A wish for his son
It will certainly be my greatest concern to make my son a good Jew. Perhaps he will see better days, a more perfect generation of Jews. But it is not easy in this English *Galut* to give a child a true Jewish education. Everything around is so terribly un-Jewish. One will therefore have to fight the whole environment. Even the 'Jews' here are Jews only in name. But I live in the hope that my son will grow up in Palestine.
From a letter to Moses Gaster. Manchester, 11 July 1907.

Belief in fundamentals of Judaism
About the relations between the Orthodox and the Zionists. It is rather a big question, and I should like to say a few words about it, especially as I am going to Palestine, and shall have to deal very much with this question. I saw in a paper that I was credited with saying that I received a promise from the British Government not to let a single Orthodox Jew into Palestine. I would have considered it as stupidity, not as maliciously untrue, but I met a gentleman in Switzerland who represents a great non-Zionist organization. This gentleman repeated practically the same charge. He said: 'We were told that the leaders of the Zionist movement are going to put up a post near the frontier saying that no Orthodox Jew is to be allowed in.' It is almost beneath notice, but such things spread and spread, chiefly through our opponents.

It is very curious that the defence of Orthodox Jewry is taken up by those Jews who have never been near a synagogue, who have nothing to do with Judaism, who do not know a single word of Hebrew, but who have somehow put themselves up as champions of the Jews. It is also curious that there is a certain section of Orthodoxy which has an affinity for the Jew who has left Judaism altogether. It reminds me of those poor Polish Jews, and the *Poritz*. The respect they have for the *Poritz* inspires them with confidence, and they, who have never had anything to do with Jewry generally, become the champions of the Orthodox case against us. That seems to me as absurd as to see such people standing at the head of Jewish organizations or synagogues, or at the head of anything to do with the Jews. It is to me so absurd that I really cannot understand it; it is a relic of the good old times when there was no democracy.

We hear of a paper coming out edited by people who have mighty little to do with Jewish Orthodoxy, and these people will stand as the guardians of the Jewish religion. I have repeated this several times, solemnly: we who understand the value of the Jewish synagogue, the role which the synagogue is able to take in Jewish life, we shall not allow the synagogue to be transformed into a Protestant Church. We make a difference between the Jewish Orthodox and the Jewish clerical. We do not want a Jewish clerical party, but we do welcome a Jewish Orthodox party. In our schools, in our institutions, any Orthodox party which desires to unite with us for the purpose of building up Palestine will take a share according to the duties they will perform. There are no rights in the world without duties. Just as we carry a tremendous burden at present in the building up of Palestine, I hope every Orthodox and non-Orthodox Jew will bear and carry the same burden, whether the burden be financial or moral. But we cannot have people standing outside Zionism and saying: 'You build it up for us, and we shall wait until you have built it up, and then we shall come in.' They have got to do it now; it is for every Jew, whether Orthodox or non-Orthodox, to come in and build it up. I believe as much in the fundamentals of Orthodox Judaism as any of those gentlemen. We were bred in it and fought for it. If it were not for us they would have swung away from Judaism. We have saved the modern Jewish generation. We have as much merit as anybody else, and I am not going to give in to anybody else. I carry the banner of Judaism into quarters which those other people could never penetrate. Let them all come in, and if Orthodox Jewry has special requirements these will be satisfied, but they have to work hand-in-hand with us and not with our opponents and detractors.

From a speech to a Zionist Conference. London, 21 September 1919.

Partition of Palestine and Messianic hope

I now address myself to those with whom I have not always been politically at one. I speak not as a *Mizrachi*, but as a deeply religious man, although not a strict observer of the religious ritual. I make a sharp distinction between the present realities and the Messianic hope, which is part of our very selves, a hope embedded in our traditions and sanctified by the martyrdom of thousands of years, a hope which the nation cannot forget without ceasing to be a nation. A time will come when there shall be neither enemies nor frontiers, when war shall be no more, and men will be secure in the dignity of man. Then *Eretz Israel* will be ours.

I told the Commission: God has promised *Eretz Israel* to the Jews. This is our Charter. But we are men of our own time, with limited horizons, heavily laden with responsibility towards the generations to come. I told the Royal Commission that the hopes of six million Jews are centred on emigration. Then I was asked: 'But can you bring six million to Palestine?' I replied, 'No. I am acquainted with the laws of physics and chemistry, and I know the force of material factors. In our generation I divide the figure by three, and you can see in that the depth of the Jewish tragedy: two millions of youth, with their lives before them, who have lost the most elementary of rights, the right to work.'. . .

I say to my Orthodox friends: Bethink you on what ground you stand. Never in 2,000 years has the responsibility been so great as now. We have neither the wisdom, nor the strength, to bear the responsibility. But Fate has laid it upon us, and Fate does not disclose her secrets. We can only do the possible.
From a speech to the Twentieth Zionist Congress. Zurich, 4 August 1937.

Bible and Mandate
I recall Ben-Gurion at one of our meetings with the British (I think at the St James's Conference) saying that the Bible was our Mandate. It was a powerful statement and he repeated it on other occasions. However, the Bible has in the meantime ceased being our Mandate for it is not what it used to be in Judaism. We must take care, for life and death depend on the spoken word, and our casual approach to fundamental matters will not do. Perhaps I have grown old, and my simple mind, after a long time in England, has not sharpened as much as the minds of those living here. If we depend on world opinion, we cannot say on the one hand: 'The Bible is our Mandate', and on the other scorn the Bible. I am not a religious Jew from the *Mizrachi* point of view, but I am speaking of the spirit in which the *Second Aliyah* marched. They were not religious, but the digging of every well, the removal of every stone, was to them the work of the God of Israel. And so we succeeded. If we remove this spirit from the heart of the Jew I don't know what will be left.
From an address to the Zionist General Council. Jerusalem, 5 March 1945.

Theocratic state not intended
There is a small minority, amongst them some Jews, who, against the weight of evidence, refuse to recognize that the Jews are a people. They assert that the Jews are only a religious community, and argue therefore that a Jewish State would be an anomaly because it would be a 'religious' state; and because they reject the idea of a Protestant or a Catholic State, they voice their opposition to the development of a Jewish National Home into a State or Commonwealth. There never was the intention on the part of those who can speak for the Jews of Palestine and for the overwhelming majority of Jews in the diaspora that Palestine should become a 'religious' or theocratic state. We have planned our work and our institutions in Palestine on the most modern

and progressive lines. And when we speak of a Jewish State we place no stress on the religion of the individuals who will form the majority of its inhabitants, but we have in mind a secular state based on sound democratic foundations with political machinery and institutions on the pattern of those in the United States and in Western Europe.
From a letter to Harry S. Truman. New York, 12 December 1945.

'Religion shall not control the state'
Many questions will emerge in the formative stages of the State with regard to religion. There are powerful religious communities in Palestine which now, under a democratic regime, will rightly demand to assert themselves. I think it is our duty to make it clear to them from the very beginning that whereas the State will treat with the highest respect the true religious feelings of the community, it cannot put the clock back by making religion the cardinal principle in the conduct of the State. Religion should be relegated to the synagogue and the homes of those families that want it; it should occupy a special position in the schools; but it shall not control the ministries of State.

I have never feared really religious people. The genuine type has never been politically aggressive; on the contrary, he seeks no power, he is modest and retiring – and modesty was the great feature in the lives of our saintly rabbis and sages in olden times. It is the new, secularized type of rabbi, resembling somewhat a member of a clerical party in Germany, France or Belgium, who is the menace, and who will make a heavy bid for power by parading his religious convictions. It is useless to point out to such people that they transgress a fundamental principle which has been laid down by our sages: 'Thou shalt not make of the Torah a crown to glory in, or a spade to dig with.' There will be a great struggle. I foresee something which will perhaps be reminiscent of the *Kulturkampf* in Germany, but we must be firm if we are to survive; we must have a clear line of demarcation between legitimate religious aspirations and the duty of the State towards preserving such aspirations, on the one hand, and on the other hand the lust for power which is sometimes exhibited by pseudo-religious groups.
From Trial and Error.

2
Among his Contemporaries:
How Weizmann Saw Friend and Foe Within the Battleground of Zionism

Ahad Ha'am (Asher Z. Ginzberg)
His letter, my dear Dorfman, is the height of tragedy. Complete disenchantment with life, with everything. AH has left the Palestine Committee. This is enough to explain his state of mind. I am ashamed to write this, but tears came to my eyes when I was reading his words and saw how the vulgarity of contemporary Zionism and the nonentities who are in it have managed to break the spirit of such a man. AH has decided to 'retire from the world' (his own expression) and devote himself to self-analysis. He warmly sympathizes with our cause but assures us (and I fully believe him) that at present he cannot take an active part in it.
From a letter to Catherine Dorfman. Geneva, 5 July 1901.

It's very embarrassing for me to bother you again, but in view of the forthcoming improvement in my finances I hope this will be the last time. I should be very grateful if you could lend me £25.
From a letter to Ahad Ha'am. Manchester, 5 May 1912.

With Ahad Ha'am there has passed a Jewish thinker whose influence, during his generation, was probably without parallel.... He was the most honest man, intellectually, I have ever known.... Like many first-rate men he was bound to be misunderstood.... For Ahad Ha'am the *Judenstaat* was the prop to spiritual rebirth.... Ahad Ha'am saw Zionism as a problem of the renaissance.... In the days of the Balfour Declaration he was probably at his best. There the philosopher, the practical man (many forget that Ahad Ha'am was an eminently able businessman) and the sage were fused into one.... But above all I treasured his profoundly analytical mind....
From an article in New Palestine. *New York, 7 January 1927.*

Celebrated through his pen-name ('One of the People') as a Hebrew essayist, Ginzberg (1856–1927) was a Zionist theoretician who saw Palestine as the spiritual and cultural focus of the Jews rather than as a Jewish State. He left Russia for London in 1908, representing a company of tea merchants, and settled in Palestine in 1922.

Chaim Arlosoroff

You spoke in such a manner that it was much more than a speech. It was a great historic deed. And I am now happy to feel that there is someone who will at one time (I hope soon!) be able to continue the true and unsullied policy.
Note to Arlosoroff during the Seventeenth Zionist Congress. Basle, 3 July 1931.

Arlosoroff (1899–1933) was a Palestinian labour leader and Weizmann supporter. He became head of the Jewish Agency's Political Department in 1931, and was assassinated in Tel Aviv. The crime remained unsolved.

Menahem Begin

I have had an opportunity of reading an interview which the head of the *Irgun* has given to an American journalist. . . . The impression one gains in reading such an interview is that you deal with a man who is a megalomaniac suffering from a Messianic complex. Whether he is just a fanatic or a charlatan or both is difficult to say.
From a letter to Blanche Dugdale. Rehovot, 18 March 1947.

Begin (b. 1913) founded Herut *Party on establishment of Israel. Prime Minister from 1977; Nobel Prize for Peace 1978, jointly with President Anwar Sadat of Egypt.*

David Ben-Gurion

Ben-Gurion has been extremely difficult, grumbling and groaning, most secretive, always wandering off on tangents of his own – and complaining that I do not co-operate with him. As to the last, I think the reverse is true. He has been here for five months previous to my arrival, and it is extremely difficult to determine what he has been doing and what he has achieved, aside from repeating the same speech about the army which we have heard so often at various meetings in London.
From a letter to Lewis Namier. New York, 27 June 1942.

BG has stiffened on formalities and constitutional punctilios. . . . There will never be any more co-operation between us and I'm quite

certain that he is developing fascist tendencies and megalomania coupled with political hysteria.
From a letter to Berl Locker. New York, 2 August 1942.

I have no desire in this letter to expatiate at great length on the arguments and 'facts' which Mr Ben-Gurion has chosen to array against me. I am supposed to have prevented the mobilization of the *Yishuv*. I have of my own volition changed the character of our military projects. I can never say 'no' to an Englishman and therefore must never go alone to see people, must always be accompanied by a strong man who would keep watch over me. If I accept his own statement that things have gone wrong with me since the beginning of the war and that my sins and shortcomings are primarily concerned with the work for the army, which matter I handled obviously carelessly and highhandedly, the place for arguing this point out and clarifying the situation was naturally London. My activities in that respect were chiefly centred there; Ben-Gurion spent many months in London, he participated in all the meetings and shared all the disappointment with us; there were, apart from him, other people equally interested in the problem and equally keen to bring it to a successful conclusion, and if Ben-Gurion had something to criticize, and he obviously had a good deal, he should have had the courage and courtesy to bring it up then and there. He might have possibly rendered a service to the whole cause by doing it, but he has chosen to say nothing, and only when we met in New York he surprised me by remarking that he used to come to the meetings in London 'merely out of courtesy', because he attached no value to the opinions of the people there with the exception of those held by Mr Namier. 'You were simply holding court', he said, meaning to convey that I have surrounded myself with yes-men and did just as and what I liked. Even if it were true, which certainly it is not, it was his duty to raise this question in London. . . .

The idea of bringing it up in America suddenly and discussing it with people who could not possibly have known the facts except in very rough outline, after having been silent for months and months in London – this careful choosing of the ground for the delivering of a blow at a time when I was trying to grope in the maze of America-at-war, was nothing short of an attempt at political assassination, carried out deliberately, calculated coolly, and with a zeal and energy worthy of a better cause. I have watched Mr Ben-Gurion carefully during his stay here. His conduct and deportment were painfully reminiscent of the petty dictator, a type one meets with so often in public life now. They are all shaped on a definite pattern: they are humourless, thin-lipped,

morally stunted, fanatical and stubborn, apparently frustrated in some ambition, and nothing is more dangerous than a small man nursing his grievances introspectively. Mr Ben-Gurion is in a constant state of exaltation and tension, obsessed by a mission in life which is bending down his shoulders. He alone, apparently, is the self-appointed guardian of pure Zionist principles. He alone knows and represents the views of the Executive. He alone has the solution to the Zionist and Jewish problem, he alone is conscious of the tragic plight of our people. He is utterly intolerant of anybody else's views. Anybody who is unfortunate enough to question some of his statements is simply jumped upon and shouted down and he terrorizes his audience by interminable ranting speeches.
From a letter (not sent) to the Jewish Agency Executive. Ferndale, NY, 22 October 1942.

I was greatly moved by your very charming and friendly letter to me, and touched by your considerateness in taking such pains to write it by hand and in big letters. . . . I am in cordial agreement with the main lines of your policy. . . . I am happy to know that the time of your exile is at an end, and that you are now able to return to Palestine.
From a letter to Ben-Gurion. London, 6 November 1946.

I find it quite difficult to collaborate with the present Executive which . . . is less a coalition and more a Noah's Ark, with two each of all the animals – clean and unclean. . . . Unfortunately I am obliged to class David with the unclean ones as a result of the role he played.
From a letter to Marc Jarblum. London, 13 January 1947.

BG as Prime Minister and Minister of Defence has proved a great success. Whether he will be the same success in peace time I am not prepared to say; he reminds me somewhat of Winston who is good in war and less so in peace. . . . He is thoughtful, calm, resolute and a man of enormous courage.
From a letter to Sir Simon Marks. Rehovot, 24 October 1948.

Ben-Gurion (1886–1973) was a trade union organizer and labour politician. Chairman of Jewish Agency Executive 1935–48; Prime Minister and Minister of Defence 1948–53, 1955–63.

Louis D. Brandeis
He is so un-Jewish in his outlook, in his feelings, and has never attempted to realize the deep causes which have moved the Jewish masses towards Palestine. He is a colonizer purely and simply. He happens to colonize Palestine.
From a letter to Sir Herbert Samuel. London, 8 August 1920.

Brandeis tried to force his negative programme on us by all the brutal methods of which only Tammany Hall politicians are capable. On the instigation of Brandeis the Americans refused to participate in our Executive, refused to send us money.
Ibid. *Aboard SS* Celtic, *27 June 1921.*

He remains enshrined in Washington like an ikon and waits for the worshippers to come and kneel before him.
From a letter to Felix M. Warburg. London, 28 November 1931.

Justice Brandeis has often been compared with Abraham Lincoln, and indeed they had much in common besides clean-chiselled features and lofty brows. Brandeis too was a Puritan: upright, austere, of a scrupulous honesty and implacable logic. These qualities sometimes made him hard to work with; like Wilson he was apt to evolve theories based on the highest principles, from his inner consciousnes, and then expect the facts to fit in with them.
From Trial and Error.

Brandeis (1856–1941) joined the Zionist movement in 1912, and led its activities in America until 1921, when he broke with Weizmann. Justice of Supreme Court 1916–39.

Martin Buber
Martin Buber is now a professor at the Hebrew University; fifty years ago he was a young aesthete, the son of a rich father, a rather odd and exotic figure in our midst. In spite of his handsome allowance from home, he was usually in debt; for he was a connoisseur of the arts and a collector of expensive items. We were good friends, though I was rather irritated by his stilted talk, which was full of expressions and elaborate similes, without, it seemed to me, much clarity or great beauty. . . . Buber was only beginning to develop the incomparable style which, many years later, produced his remarkable translation of the Bible.
From Trial and Error.

Buber (1878–1965) was associated with Weizmann in the early Democratic Fraction. Founding editor of Berlin monthly Der Jude *1916–24; Professor of Sociology and Philosophy at Hebrew University 1938–57.*

Sir Alan Cunningham
Your Excellency's attitude in all these difficult years and continuous

goodwill and friendship to us emboldens us to send you at this historic moment our heartfelt thanks. Difficulties which arose between us and England will be forgotten, and only England's great contribution to Jewish Palestine will be remembered. We are happy that this moment coincided with your term of office.
From a telegram to Cunningham. New York, 30 November 1947.

General Cunningham (b. 1887) was the last British High Commissioner of Palestine, appointed October 1945. Formerly commanded Eighth Army in Libya.

Albert Einstein

His antagonism was to some degree directed also against me, for he complained that I had not done anything to improve what he regards as a very unsatisfactory position [the affairs of the Hebrew University].... I need not dwell on what Professor Einstein's association with our young University means for us and what it means in the eyes of the world. It was one of the happiest days of my life when I was able to secure that co-operation, and speaking for myself, there is really no length to which I would not go to bring back to our work this wonderful and lovable personality, perhaps the greatest genius the Jews have produced in recent centuries and withal so fine and noble a character.
From a letter to Felix Warburg, concerning Einstein's withdrawal from the University's Board of Governors. London, 17 January 1928.

Einstein seems to be acquiring the psychology of a prima donna who is beginning to lose her voice!
From a letter to Jacques Errera. London, 15 May 1933.

There has been a great deal of criticism of the University, chiefly on the part of Einstein. Although the form which his criticism took was perhaps not the most helpful, I can admit to you privately that in substance it was correct.
From a letter to Sarah Gertrude Millin. London, 14 January 1934.

Einstein (1879–1955) created the theory of relativity, and was awarded Nobel Prize for Physics in 1921. He delivered the first Hebrew University lecture, in 1923, and was intermittently active in its affairs.

Felix Frankfurter

You are timid because you don't feel the depth of the Jewish problem. You are not steeped in it as we are, you can go slow, you can afford to look on us as the enthusiasts, but you are 'pratical' and 'careful', you cannot afford to take any risks because you have got positions to lose –

in contradistinction to the *sans-culottes* who have nothing to lose.... That is why you are willing to reduce Zionist activities to a chartered company without profits, but will not lift it to a great movement capable of shaking the very foundations of the *Galut*, and shaking the eternal slavery to pieces.

Brandeis could have been a prophet in Israel. You have in you the making of a Lassalle. Instead, you are choosing to be only a professor in Harvard and Brandeis only a judge in the Supreme Court.
From a letter to Frankfurter. London, 27 August 1919.

Frankfurter (1882–62) was himself elected to the Supreme Court, 1939–62. Founder of New Republic, *and particularly close to President Franklin D. Roosevelt.*

Moses Gaster
Gaster behaves best of all. He is more intelligent than the others [the English Zionist leaders] and the cause above all is dear to him, and he sees all the emerging problems clearly. He sees all the difficulties, and is above petty political intrigue.
From a letter to Menahem Ussishkin. London, 17 July 1904.

I never had any doubt about your being the only man to whom I might turn in frankness and friendship. Working under your guidance these past two years, enabling me to discuss and settle so many painful problems with you, has not been in vain.... I admire the man as much as the Jew in you.
From a letter to Gaster. Manchester, 25 June 1905.

I know that Gaster is seeing ghosts, and is probably harbouring ambitious plans. The cardinal question, which I am not yet able to solve conscientiously, is: can we do without him? Is it worthwhile making the attempt to elevate him to the leadership?
From a letter to the Smaller Actions Committee. Manchester, 27 April 1913.

Haham (Chief Rabbi) of Sephardi community in Britain, Gaster (1856–1939) presided over Herzl's first public meeting in London, 1898. Well connected in political circles, he introduced Herbert Samuel and Mark Sykes, among others, to Zionism.

Lord Gort
I am even more gratified by the fine impression the new High Commissioner has made on the country. I think his warm human qualities, his tact, have already won him the respect of the Jewish

community. In the short weeks he has been here he has succeeded, I believe, in lifting somewhat the mood of the people for so many years frustrated under the sterile influence of his predecessor.
From a letter to Felix Frankfurter. Rehovot, 20 December 1944.

Field Marshal and holder of Victoria Cross, Gort (1886–1946) was High Commissioner 1944–45, retiring through ill-health. He had led British Forces in France 1939–40.

Theodor Herzl
Herzl is not a nationalist but a project conceiver. . . . He considers external conditions only, instead of the force on which we rely – the psychology of the people and the aspirations which animate it. We knew that it was impossible for us to obtain Palestine in a short time and were therefore not discouraged at the failure of this or some other attempt.
From a discussion of the East Africa project, as reported in Hatzefirah. *Basle, 29 August 1902.*

It was Herzl's enduring contribution to Zionism to have created one central parliamentary authority for Zionism.
From Trial and Error.

Author of Der Judenstaat, *publ. 1896, and founder of political Zionism, Herzl (1860–1904) was a prominent Central European journalist and playwright. He led the movement until his premature death.*

Vladimir Jabotinsky
Jabotinsky is an excellent fellow, highly intelligent, honest and very energetic, but it is a pity that the idea of a Jewish Legion has almost become his *idée fixe* and he has subordinated important Zionist interests to this idea.
From a letter to Mark Sykes. London, 15 February 1917.

The man is a public danger not only for the Zionists but for Jewry altogether.
From a letter to Leonie Landsberg. London, 30 December 1931.

He was rather ugly, immensely attractive, well-spoken, warm-hearted, generous . . . overlaid by a certain touch of the rather theatrically chivalresque, a certain queer and irrelevant knightliness.
From Trial and Error.

Jabotinsky (1880–1940), author, journalist, and founder of Jewish Legion in First World War, broke from World Zionist Organization in 1935 to establish the independent New Zionist Organization, with a maximalist programme.

T. E. Lawrence
I found in him a sympathetic understanding of Jewish aspirations in Palestine. . . . I was at once struck by the presence of this man. . . . It was therefore a great relief to me to find him not only friendly to the ideals embodied in Zionism but fully conversant with the subject. . . . Lawrence displayed great intellectual keenness and genuine interest. . . . Lawrence never regarded the policy of the Jewish National Home as in any way incompatible with assurances given to the Arabs. . . . He personally was conscious of the historic significance of the Messianic trumpet-call; it appealed to his nature.
From T. E. Lawrence by his Friends, *ed. Arnold W. Lawrence.*

'Lawrence of Arabia' (1888–1935), archaeologist and British liaison officer with Faisal, who commanded Arab revolt against Turkey (described in Seven Pillars of Wisdom*). He arranged Faisal's meetings with Weizmann.*

Sylvain Lévi
Sylvain Lévi has proved to be a wolf in sheep's clothing. He is trying to spoil everything for us, but I think it will be very hard work for him, with meagre results.
From a letter to M. Ben-Hillel Hacohen. London, 29 November 1918.

The second part of his speech [to the Council of Ten, 27 February 1919] raised three points: one, that Palestine was a small and poor land, that it already had a population of six hundred thousand Arabs, that the Jews had a higher standard of life than the Arabs and would tend to dispossess them. Two, that the Jews who would go to Palestine would be mainly Russian Jews, who were of 'explosive' tendencies. Three, that the creation of a Jewish National Home in Palestine would introduce the dangerous principle of Jewish dual rights, and this was of especial importance to France as the principal Mediterranean Power.

When M. Lévi ended his speech the rest of us felt profoundly embarrassed. . . . As we came out of the Conference precincts M. Lévi came up to me and held out his hand. Instinctively I withdrew my own and said: 'You have sought to betray us.' He got the same response from Sokolow.
From Trial and Error.

Nominee of Baron de Rothschild on the Zionist Commission of 1918, Lévi (1863–1935) was a noted Orientalist and President of Alliance Israélite Universelle *1920–35.*

Sir Harold MacMichael
I repeat what I said to you: that Sir Harold MacMichael has, in my opinion, proved himself unfit for the post he holds.
From a letter to Viscount Cranborne, Colonial Secretary. London, 6 March 1942.

The High Commissioner . . . spoke as if the Jewish problem did not exist at all – as if, as far as Palestine is concerned, it had been completely solved by the White Paper.
From a letter to Winston Churchill. New York, 2 April 1943.

MacMichael (1882–1969) was High Commissioner 1938–44. Previously Governor of Tanganyika, he later served in Malaya and Malta.

Judah L. Magnes
I would like above all to thank you for your letter. I read it at least ten times in bed – it was my favourite reading, because it breathes a freshness and zest for work that is now totally lacking in us 'old ones'. I almost feel like gushing forth in admiration for you, but shall refrain as it would be to neither of our tastes.
From a letter to Magnes. Manchester, 13 February 1906.

I have drawn his attention in very serious terms to the general indignation over his autocratic administration and constant reliance on the American money-bags, and I told him quite plainly that it would be more dignified for the University not to accept such donations rather than be perpetually dependent on the whims and threats of the donor.
From a letter to Albert Einstein. London, 9 July 1926.

That hypocrite, that Tartuffe, Magnes, lightly abandons the Balfour Declaration. He did not bleed for it, he only gained by it!
Ibid. London, 30 November 1929.

Felix [Warburg] and Magnes between them will slaughter the University if they are allowed to have their way.
From a letter to Lola Hahn-Warburg. London, 20 May 1934.

American Reform rabbi and among founders of American Jewish Committee, Magnes (1877–1948) was Chancellor of Hebrew University 1925–35, then

President. Worked for Arab–Jewish peace on basis of a bi-national or federative system for Palestine.

Louis Marshall
Although counted among the 'assimilationists', he had a very clear understanding of, and a deep sympathy for, the national endeavours of the Jewish communities in Europe who were struggling for cultural minority rights. He had learned Yiddish and followed the Yiddish Press closely, showing himself very sensitive to its criticism. Of a naturally autocratic habit of mind, firm if not obstinate on occasion, impatient of argument, he was, I felt, a man who, once convinced on the rightness of a course, would follow it unswervingly. The main difficulty in working with him lay in his tendency to procrastinate. . . . Marshall was hot-blooded, capable of generous enthusiasms as well as violent outbursts of anger.
From Trial and Error.

Marshall (1856–1929) was a leading jurist and President of American Jewish Committee from 1912. On American Jewish Delegation to Paris Peace Conference, 1919, he later led the non-Zionist negotiations for creation of the Jewish Agency in 1929, but died during its opening meeting.

Henry Morgenthau, Sr
Morgenthau is an utter ignoramus and chatterbox, who has all the manner of [David] Wolffsohn and lots of ambition.
From a letter to Ahad Ha'am. London, 7 August 1917.

German-born American philanthropist and diplomat, Morgenthau (1856–1946) was US Ambassador to Turkey 1913–16. Sent by President Wilson on mission to detach Turkey from Central Powers, 1917.

Henry Morgenthau, Jr
I do not think that England has a better friend than Secretary Morgenthau. You know how much a treasury can obstruct things, but he has done everything in order to smooth the way even at the risk of being reproached that he is doing these things as a Jew and not merely as a patriotic American. As a matter of fact he is both in a very high degree. He feels keenly that it is his duty as an American to render every possible assistance to England but he is also deeply concerned about the position of the Jews and the attitude of Great Britain towards Palestine.
From a letter to Lord Moyne, Colonial Secretary. Arrowhead Springs, California, 21 June 1941.

I have told you about my conversation with Morgenthau who wanted to bring 300,000 Jews into Palestine now, and urged me to see the President about it.... Money for such an operation could, in Morgenthau's opinion, be made available. I refused to entertain the idea, and was subjected to a good deal of criticism from him for being too timid, etc. (He used stronger language.)
From a letter to Sir Archibald Sinclair. London, 23 October 1941.

Morgenthau (1891–1967) was Secretary of Treasury 1939–45. At his prompting Roosevelt established War Refugee Board in 1944. He later led American fund-raising campaign for Israel.

Max Nordau
It is appalling that Nordau does not believe, and never did, in Herzl's work, in all his diplomacy; and that he considers himself, in the national sense, unworthy.
From a letter to Vera Khatzman. Paris, 9 July 1904.

The more I speak with Nordau, the more I am convinced of his depth and the profound tragedy he bears. Is he a major creative force at this moment, can he be relied upon in the present reckoning of forces? I doubt it. Seven years of Zionism have undermined his belief in the Jews!
From a letter to Menahem Ussishkin. London, 14 July 1904.

In our joy over the confirmation of the long, hotly-contested Palestine Mandate by the League of Nations, our thoughts go back to the days of the foundation of Zionism. In these days we have been thinking with especial reverence of you as the great champion of the Zionist idea, whose name is inseparably linked with the history of our movement.
From a letter to Nordau. London, 27 July 1922.

Writer, physician and polymath, Nordau (1849–1923) was Herzl's earliest and most celebrated follower, and among draftsmen of the Basle Programme of 1897. He refused the leadership of the movement on Herzl's death.

Baron Edmond de Rothschild
The Baron ... organized things in Palestine according to the *dernier cri*, forgetting the basic fact that in such a country one ought to begin with the modest, most necessary things and allow them to develop.
From a letter to Ahad Ha'am. Manchester, 21 May 1911.

He is a very wise old man, but a terribly *meshugener* fish. He talks enough for twenty and never lets anyone get a word in, which makes it very difficult to convince him, and one is obliged to listen to a lot of nonsense before putting a word in. All the same he's a darling, and it's a pity that he is so old.
From a letter to his wife. Paris, 1 April 1914.

The late Baron Edmond was to all intents and purposes a Zionist extremist. His one desire was to get the whole of Palestine in Jewish hands, and although he never said so publicly, he had a romantic, mystical conviction that the throne of David will be set up one day on the hills of Jerusalem. I had numerous conversations with him throughout a long period of time, stretching from the early beginning of my work during the war until practically his dying day. You can clearly understand that the last expressed wish in his will to be buried in Palestine merely emphasizes his innermost lifelong belief that he belonged here. It is probably not unknown to you that this last wish of his was one of the severest shocks he could ever have administered to the French Jewish community who looked upon Paris as their Jerusalem.
From a letter to Felix Warburg. Jerusalem, 24 January 1936.

Baron Edmond (1845–1934) began financing Jewish agricultural settlements in Palestine in 1882, proceeding to organize and control colonies directly from Paris. Major benefactor of Hebrew University. He never identified himself with Zionism, though he was made Hon. President of Jewish Agency on its formation in 1929.

James de Rothschild
It is now the dream of the Baron's life that his son James should carry on the Jewish traditions. The Baron is hoping that James will come to Palestine by way of the Jewish University.
From a letter to Yehiel Tschlenow and Shmarya Levin. Paris, 31 January 1914.

Jimmy has tried to be rather sulky and aloof and last night I had to tell him that this won't do. He has got to put his heart into the work or we shall simply leave him alone. I think it did him good.
From a letter to his wife. Aboard the Canberra with the Zionist Commission in the Mediterranean, 15 March 1918.

He's a real comedian.
Ibid. Tel Aviv, 6 April 1918.

In these stirring days my thoughts are with you and with the memory of

your late lamented father. All which you have created in Palestine in the last sixty years is the rock foundation on which we could build, and with your support and continuous interest in all branches of Palestinian activity we shall be able to face the responsibilities which have increased in proportion to our activities.
From a telegram to de Rothschild. New York, 2 December 1947.

James de Rothschild (1878–1957) served in French and British armies in First World War and was ADC to Ormsby-Gore in the Zionist Commission. Liberal MP 1929–45. He retained close interest in his family's endowments in Palestine. The Knesset building in Jerusalem was erected with funds from his estate.

Herbert Samuel

He remarked that he was not a stranger to Zionist ideas; he had been following them up a little of late years, and although he had never publicly mentioned it, he took considerable interest in the question. Since Turkey had entered into the war, he had given the problem much thought and consideration, and he thought that a realization of the Zionist dreams was possible. He believed that my demands were too modest, that big things would have to be done in Palestine; he himself would move and would expect Jewry to move immediately the military situation was cleared up. He was convinced that it would be cleared up favourably. The Jews would have to bring sacrifices and he was prepared to do so. At this point I ventured to ask in which way the plans of Mr Samuel were more ambitious than mine. Mr Samuel preferred not to enter into a discussion of his plans, as he would like to keep them 'liquid', but he suggested that the Jews would have to build railways, harbours, a university, a network of schools, etc. The university seems to make a special appeal to him. He hopes that great things may be forthcoming from a seat of learning, where the Jews can work freely on a free soil of their own. He also thinks that perhaps the Temple may be rebuilt, as a symbol of Jewish unity, of course, in a modernized form.

After listening to him, I remarked that I was pleasantly surprised to hear such words from him; that if I were a religious Jew, I should have thought the Messianic times were near; that as I came up to him I had debated in my mind whether I should speak to the Jew or the British Cabinet Minister; that I am happy to have spoken just as I did, and still happier to have heard his reply.
From a report to the Zionist Executive. London, Manchester, 7 January 1915.

Eretz Israel and Palestine are not the same thing; Samuel is High Commissioner for Palestine, and I, being your President, am the High

Commissioner for *Eretz Israel*. It is my absolute desire to work hand-in-hand with Samuel, and I think so far there is no friction between us. But there may come a time when the interests of Samuel as High Commissioner of Palestine could clash with the interest of the President of the Zionist Organization as High Commissioner for *Eretz Israel*. I imagine future development as tending towards the High Commissioner for *Eretz Israel* becoming identical with the High Commissioner for Palestine. It does not mean that I expect to get this post. Further, I state that no Zionist can hold the post of High Commissioner for Palestine. Suppose this post had been offered to me – to take a theoretical case – I should have broken faith in a fortnight. It is impossible to keep this post and be a Zionist official.

I don't for a moment question Samuel's Zionism. He is very dear to me. Because of this, and because he is an asset to us, he must be freed from these shackles, and they will have to be cut if we try to get our needs fulfilled through him.

From a speech to American Zionists. New York, 10 April 1921.

Samuel is such a coward: there he is, trembling and imploring everybody to 'make peace' with the Arabs, as if *we* were quarrelling with them!

From a letter to his wife. London, 10 August 1921.

Perhaps I am partly responsible for the Samuel chapter. In this gathering there is no one who had more to do with and was more pleased at the appointment of Sir Herbert Samuel than I. Samuel is our friend, and has worked loyally with us from the first moment. At our request, fortified by our moral support, he accepted the difficult position. We put him in that position. At this very day Samuel is decried as a Zionist leader by the Arab Delegation in a memorandum of which I have a copy. Samuel is in the unenviable position of getting kicks from both sides. Samuel has committed great mistakes, and I am ready to lay before the Political Committee my correspondence with him. You will see that we have spoken to him in words that will have more effect than this demonstration. But he is *our* Samuel; he is a product of our Judaism.

From a speech to the Twelfth Zionist Congress. Carlsbad, 5 September 1921.

Sir Herbert (later Lord) Samuel (1870–1963) held office in various governments as a leading Liberal politician 1905–32. High Commissioner for Palestine 1920–25, then active in work for Hebrew University and Jewish refugees; Order of Merit, 1958.

Moshe Shertok (later Sharett)
I was asked [by the Foreign Office] to nominate one man in Jerusalem who would centralize, sift, test, check information concerning the position in the Near East (from Egypt to Turkey inclusive) and would make suggestions. Naturally this man will be yourself.
From a letter to Shertok. London, 24 September 1939.

Shertok is able, hard-working, but utterly subservient to the views of his master – and his master may be anybody.
From a letter to C. David Ginsburg. Rehovot, 23 March 1947.

Corresponding with you is like bombarding an invisible enemy.
From a letter to Shertok. Glion, Switzerland, 9 July 1948.

Shertok (1894–1965) was head of Jewish Agency's Political Department 1933–48, then Israel's Foreign Minister until 1956. He was simultaneously Prime Minister 1954–55.

Abba Hillel Silver
Of all the personnel in American Zionism, Silver seems to be the most suitable if he could be induced to take a leading part in the general political activities of the movement.... I think Silver would be prepared to take the part assigned to him, if it can be done with dignity and without friction.
From a letter to Lewis Namier. New York, 27 June 1942.

I am sure that if anyone can inspire the movement it will be Silver.
From a letter to Numa Torczyner. London, 13 December 1943.

We have a great and important leader of American Jewry saying that it is for the *Yishuv* to decide who should struggle and where. 'We shall give moral and financial backing.' Moral, financial and political support is precious little when you send others to the barricades ... to pit themselves against British guns and tanks.
From his reply to the debate at the Twenty-Second Zionist Congress. Basle, 16 December 1946.

We are trying to form here a progressive moderate Group ... and we shall try to do the same in America – so as not to leave the filibustering Rabbi of Cleveland as the sole representative of our movement.
From a letter to Felix Frankfurter. London, 7 January 1947.

He seems to hold out hopes that America 'has come to stay' in the

Middle East, that the power of Great Britain which is 'bankrupt' is waning. He obviously wishes our poor misled *Yishuv* to believe that America is going to bring redemption. If these utterances are sincere, then they represent the worst form of wishful thinking; if they are merely propaganda, they are the worst form of demagogy.
From a letter to Eliezer Kaplan. Rehovot, 27 March 1947.

Silver (1893–1963) occupied Reform temple in Cleveland throughout his rabbinical career. President, Zionist Organization of America 1945–47; Chairman, American Section of Jewish Agency from end 1946 until 1948. He led the Zionist case before UN Political Committee in May 1947.

Nahum Sokolow

I am tormented and scourged. I have lost my centre of gravity and do not know whether to concentrate on one thing or another . . . I feel the ground underneath shaking. You are my friend, after all, so give me some advice, grant me the word of salvation – I believe in you and trust you very, very much and you will do me good.
From a letter to Sokolow. Geneva, 7 September 1903.

He took up his quarters in the Regent Palace Hotel and kept his office in his suit-case.
From Trial and Error.

Being a quasi-Jewish historian he is duly impressed by the fact that the Jews have been waiting for 2,000 years and thus he is in no hurry. Governments come and governments go but Sokolow stays on forever.
From a letter to Doris May. Merano, 20 October 1931.

In the past two years his influence has been that of an obscurantist and opportunist of the most ordinary kind. He was a dead weight! He would naturally also take part in another Executive, it makes no difference at all to him! But for the movement it does make a difference.
From a letter to Berl Locker. Zermatt, 13 August 1933.

Journalist and member of the Zionist Executive from 1911, Sokolow (1861–1936) was thus senior to Weizmann until the latter's election as President in 1920. He replaced Weizmann in that office 1931–35.

Menahem Ussishkin

Ussishkin was not so wrong when he said that in another twenty-five years it will be impossible to get Palestine unless we buy up the land now.
From a letter to Nahum Sokolow. Manchester, 19 November 1907.

I am in constant fear that Ussishkin may blurt something out and then you won't see the road for dust.
From a letter to Bella Berligne. London, 18 August 1919.

Ussishkin in USA, like a bull in a synagogue. He writes he has promises for two and a half millions and . . . is delighted. He will try hard for the Presidency on the strength of this signal 'success'. Dreamers and bluffers of the Ghetto!
From a letter to Maurice Hexter. Aboard the Ausonia *in the Mediterranean, 27 February 1931.*

Ussishkin (1863–1941), a prominent figure in Russian Zionism, headed the movement's activities in Palestine 1919–23. Subsequently he was President of Jewish National Fund, and Chairman of Zionist General Council from 1935.

Felix M. Warburg

The recent utterances of our friend Max Warburg (who for some reason best known to himself now poses as an expert on Jewish and Palestine matters), and the arrogance with which his brother [Felix] approaches any subject connected with Palestine, about which he really knows little and understands still less, are portents indicating [a] dangerous tendency. . . . The Warburgs and the Rothschilds and their methods have gone forever, and we need not attribute too much value to their names or their position or their money. . . . Let them waste their money on fantastic undertakings . . . so long as it is not Palestine.
From a letter to Simon Marks. Jerusalem, 15 December 1935.

He was a man of sterling character, charitable to a degree, a pivotal figure in the American-Jewish community, if not in very close touch with the rank and file. . . . But he was susceptible to gossip. . . . His whole upbringing militated against his taking the same view [of Palestine] as we did. . . . Warburg was one of their most valuable assets in communal work, and they greatly feared to lose him under the impact of a new idea.
From Trial and Error.

Warburg (1871–1937), German-American banker and philanthropist, was the leading American non-Zionist in the Jewish Agency, making substantial contributions towards development of the Hebrew University and economic projects in Palestine. His brother and business partner Max (1867–1946) had a distinguished career in German public service, remaining during the Nazi era to direct Jewish welfare activities.

Sir Arthur Wauchope
He is obviously the best High Commissioner we have had since 1920, and he is a man who is clearly unlikely to be bamboozled, or to allow his mind to be poisoned, by petty official intrigue.
From a letter to Chaim Arlosoroff. London, 28 June 1932.

Your acceptance of a further term of office in this country fulfils in the happiest way my own hope for a brighter opening of the New Year, and I would like to offer you my warm personal congratulations – all the warmer because I hope and believe that you will yourself find almost as much satisfaction in continuing to live and work for Palestine as we in Palestine shall feel in having you at the helm.
From a letter to Wauchope. Rehovot, 1 January 1935.

The HC is very disturbed about the international situation, and he feels he must take some precautionary measure so as not to flood the country with too many immigrants on one side, and to keep the Arabs sweet on the other. Possibly he is rather worried about our negative attitude on the question of the Legislative Council.
From a letter to Israel M. Sieff. Rehovot, 22 January 1936.

The HC has got cold feet, and when a man is frightened he is neither logical nor just.
From a letter to Lewis Namier. Rehovot, 5 February 1936.

General Wauchope (1874–1947) was High Commissioner November 1931–March 1938.

Orde Wingate
Orde Wingate has gone to Egypt as a staff officer to Wavell. So far I have not succeeded in retaining him definitely as an organizer of the Jewish Army.... A great deal will depend upon his relations with Wavell. I have impressed that upon Orde repeatedly; he must try and work with W., just as Lawrence did with Allenby. You must go to Egypt and see to that.
From a letter to Moshe Shertok. London, 22 September 1940.

He and I often found ourselves taking different views on matters of tactics. He was young; he was impatient.... We had a good many frank and heated arguments. Sometimes I would feel I had to try to

make him see that many of his own difficulties, like ours, were due to lack of restraint, and at working at too high a tension. But I doubt if I succeeded in convincing him. For he was consumed with a sacred fire, which illumined his whole life and being. His contacts with the young Jewish settlers ... were intimate and cordial ... he became for them not only a leader, but something of a national hero; legends grew up around him. ... When he came back after the Abyssinian campaign, I found him, in spite of his brilliant achievements, very depressed in mind – in some ways, indeed, a sick man. ... He never lost sight of his one great hope: that some day he would be called to command a Jewish Force in Palestine. ... When such men die, their going leaves a sense of loneliness which nothing can dispel.
From an article in New Judaea. *London, April 1944.*

Wingate (1903–44) was a professional soldier who led British regulars and Haganah *members in action against Arab terrorists during 1938–39. He died, holding rank of major-general, in a plane accident in Burma while commanding 'Chindits'.*

Stephen S. Wise
In his usual way he thundered forth a long speech, full of banalities, which was much more appropriate for a mass meeting than for a small gathering consisting of about fifty people without a gallery. Dr Wise, however, carried his gallery with him.
From a letter to Felix Warburg. London, 28 December 1928.

I am reluctantly compelled ... to register my protest against the speech of Dr Wise on Friday, July 3rd. His speech contained statements and allusions which, in my considered opinion, are neither justified nor legally or morally admissible in an assembly such as the Congress. He overstepped the bounds of parliamentary freedom of speech. ... All that was left to me to do at the time was to leave the hall.
From a letter to Leo Motzkin, chairman at the Seventeenth Zionist Congress. Basle, 5 July 1931.

We look to the Zionists in the USA under your brilliant leadership for guidance, help and support – moral, political and material – and I know that you will stand by us – as you always did – in this hour of our history.
From a letter to Wise. Paris, 27 January 1937.

Wise (1874–1949) was America's leading Reform rabbi, a pioneer of Zionism in the USA and influential in Democratic politics during the Wilson and Roosevelt administrations. Long an opponent of Weizmann, he drew close to the leader from 1935, to become his devotee.

David Wolffsohn
Wolffsohn travels round the world, abusing everything and everybody, and this is called Zionism.
From a letter to Menahem Ussishkin. Manchester, 22 May 1910.

I also heard a piece of news that Wolffsohn has syphilis and I made a joke about it of which I hope you'll approve. '*Wolffsohn ist sehr Ehrlich.*' It's all around Berlin already and will, I hope, reach Wolffsohn.
From a letter to his wife. Berlin, 5 April 1911.

Wolffsohn (1855–1914) was a close friend of Herzl, succeeding him as leader 1905–11. A timber-merchant and banker in Cologne, he was dislodged by Weizmann and other Russian Zionists. Ehrlich ('honourable') puns with Paul Ehrlich, discoverer of the syphilis cure salvarsan.

Israel Zangwill
Mr Zangwill is the real ideologist of East Africa. He goes much further than the leaders would wish. In a certain sense he is even opposed to Palestine, on the grounds that it would require the re-establishment of the ancient Jewish form of worship with all its rites, such as sacrifices, etc.; we could not, therefore, lead a modern life there. He is not acquainted with the evolution of Judaism as a whole; Zionism, according to him, depends on accidents. He does not know the people he believes he is serving. But after a discussion lasting some hours, he took it in silence when I told him: 'You may well be the photographer of the Ghetto, but you are not its psychologist.' I hope that he can henceforth be discounted as a politician and as a fighter for Africa, for, being a man of intellect, he is beginning to feel the inner contradictions and will think twice before taking another step. Like Nordau, he is completely hypnotized by Herzl.
From a letter to Moses Gaster. Geneva, 24 October 1903.

It is so English-American: the speeches of Mr Zangwill; kettledrums and trumpets and tinsel for a crowd listening with bated breath to the announcement of a new kind of shoe polish.
Ibid. Manchester, 15 January 1907.

Author of the internationally acclaimed Children of the Ghetto, *Zangwill (1864–1926) was Herzl's earliest British champion. On the East Africa issue he broke with the Zionist Organization and formed the Jewish Territorial Organization, to seek a homeland for the Jews elsewhere than in Palestine.*

3
The Leader Observed

A Portrait in Composite

Sir Norman Angell
I recall vividly a remark made by a well-known French writer after hearing an address by Weizmann and the discussion which followed, at Chatham House, the headquarters of the Royal Institute of International Affairs. Walking home afterwards, the Frenchman said to me, 'How does it happen that a Russian Jew, born in conditions and environment so remote from those of England, should be as British as all that?'

I asked him just what he meant, and he went on to elaborate: 'Here was a man presenting a cause which we know means a great deal more to him than any matter of life or death, and presenting it to a gathering of the British ruling orders – to Cabinet ministers, ex-Cabinet ministers, members of Parliament, notables of the bar and the press. And never once did he raise his voice or become declamatory or violent. Nor was he ingratiating. He did not beg, he did not threaten. His voice was neither smile nor frown. Such passion as you glimpsed at times was a cold and restrained passion. A Frenchman would have pounded the table and thundered and gesticulated and called upon high heaven to witness the infamy of the policies of which those present had been guilty; and called down vengeance on their heads. But Weizmann was the Englishman – and the English aristocrat at that: cold, restrained, impersonal.'

This quality in Weizmann would perhaps be more noticeable to a Frenchman than to an Englishman. In so far as the picture just drawn is a true one, I believe it to be fortunate for the cause of Zionism.
From a contribution to Chaim Weizmann, Statesman and Scientist, *ed. Meyer W. Weisgal.*

David Ben-Gurion
It is my view that while Dr Weizmann can render invaluable services in concerted action, he can do incalculable harm when he acts alone. He

does not always grasp realities when he is confronted with a new situation, and may give an unexpected answer without realizing what it means. He wants to seem reasonable always and not only to be reasonable to an Englishman. He is as much a political Zionist as anybody else, but he cannot free himself entirely from the Ahad Ha'amist school to which he belonged for a long time. When he hears conversations he hears more what he would like to hear than what he does hear. On many occasions his reports are unduly optimistic. He identifies personal position and personal courtesies with political courtesies.
From the Minutes of a private meeting. New York, 27 June 1942.

Weizmann's moderation was evident only when he spoke to us, to his brethren, to the Zionists, to our Congresses – for he thought he knew our limitations. But when he spoke to the non-Jewish world, he was neither moderate nor humble – in the less nice sense of that word. I never failed to be astonished, when I was with him at meetings with Cabinet Ministers, by his inner forcefulness, by his determined manner. He could be angry with these men of power – and he had occasion to be only too often – but his anger emerged with such natural dignity that it was always deeply moving. Here was no fawning suppliant. Here was a proud representative of a historic people demanding the righting of age-long wrongs.
From a discussion with Moshe Pearlman in Ben-Gurion Looks Back.

Sir Isaiah Berlin
He believed in a kind of unswerving, energetic, passionate gradualism. He was wholly dominated by his wish to build a modern state for his people and grew to be the most representative Jew of his time, inasmuch as he possessed that most important qualification for leadership, that is, of being recognized by all Jews, whether they approved of his ideas or not, as being wholly and indubitably one of themselves. His sympathies were wide enough to do justice to all types of Jews – Western bankers, Russian intellectuals, American businessmen, professors, rabbis, barons, artists, above all the masses in the Pale and in the ghettoes of London and New York, and in this respect he differed from such Zionists as Herzl and Brandeis, Jabotinsky and Einstein, Baron Edmond de Rothschild and his equally distinguished and fascinating son, James.

Assimilationists and anti-Zionists, religious zealots and cynical or embarrassed cosmopolitans, opposed or ignored him, but did not doubt his sincerity or devotion. His appearance, his gait, his manner-

isms, his clothes, his voice, his accent, his turns of speech were recognized as their own by the masses, and despite his mordant and, indeed, savage wit, his sometimes ruthless cutting of Gordian knots, his ill-concealed impatience – despite all these, his natural dignity and pride, and, towards the end, the immense prestige of his position, endeared him to the people. No one denied this representative quality, something that he possessed in common with other men who stood close to the centre of national feeling, such as Garibaldi, Masaryk, Venizelos. He was on good terms with reality, and his love of familiarity with the people was untouched by self-consciousness, still less by self-hatred.
From a lecture at the Hebrew University. Jerusalem, 1970.

Philip Marshall Brown
Like Disraeli, he occasionally reveals the temperament and the characteristics of an Oriental.
Quoted in The Realities of American–Palestine Relations, *by Frank Manuel.*

Martin Buber
At that time, forty-three years ago, in the 'heroic' period of Zionism, when you, friend of my youth, and I jointly fought against Theodor Herzl, the man we yet recognized and revered as our leader, and against the bulk of the movement, what was our impulse then? Was it not our inability to put up any longer with those fascinating slogans, since Reality had revealed itself to us – the hard reality of the hour, with its task both difficult and unpretentious? And, later on, what was it raised you, Chaim Weizmann, to the position of leader but this sense of, and will to, Reality, originally common only to us, to our small group, resulting in the decisive demand not to create 'conditions' first and then 'things' – as Herzl had intended – but things first and then the appropriate conditions – always things first and then conditions?
From a contribution to Chaim Weizmann, A Tribute on his Seventieth Birthday, *ed. Paul Goodman.*

Lord Robert Cecil (Viscount Cecil of Chelwood)
It is impossible to reproduce in writing the subdued enthusiasm with which Dr Weizmann spoke or the extraordinary impressiveness of his attitude, which made one forget his rather repellent and even sordid exterior.
From a note in Foreign Office files. London, 18 August 1915.

Winston Churchill
There is the figure of Dr Weizmann, that dynamic Jew whom I have

known so long, the ablest and wisest leader of the cause of Zionism, his whole life devoted to the cause, his son killed in the battle for our common freedom. I ardently hope his authority will be respected by Zionists in this dark hour, and that the government will keep in touch with him, and make everyone of his compatriots feel how much he is respected here. It is perfectly clear that in that case we shall have the best opportunity of carrying the matter forward.
From a speech in the House of Commons. London, 1 August 1946. Hansard, *Fifth Series, vol. 426, col. 1254.*

Those of us who have been Zionists since the days before the Balfour Declaration know what a heavy loss Israel has sustained in the death of Dr Chaim Weizmann, who was famed and respected throughout the free world, and whose son was killed fighting for us. Weizmann led his people back to the Promised Land where we have seen them invincibly installed in a sovereign state.
From his speech at the Lord Mayor's Banquet. London, 10 November 1952.

Richard H. S. Crossman
Today we had Weizmann, who looks like a weary and more humane version of Lenin, very tired, very ill, too old and too pro-British to control his extremists. He spoke for two hours with a magnificent mixture of passion and scientific detachment. Here is a Jew who frankly admits that every Jew carries the virus of antisemitism with him and founds his case for a Jewish commonwealth on that fact. He is the first witness who has frankly and openly admitted that the issue is not between right and wrong but between the greater and the lesser injustice.
From an account of evidence submitted to the Anglo-American Committee of Enquiry, in Palestine Mission.

Mrs Edgar (Blanche) Dugdale
Found Chaim very depressed. Antisemitism growing in Paris. All the world disturbed and Jews the scapegoats everywhere. 'I felt' he said (when alone with me) 'as if an iron band were round my throat.' All the tragedy of Jewry is in Chaim's eyes at such moments.
From her diary entry for 13 July 1936, in Baffy, *ed. N. A. Rose.*

What a curious genius his is – rising to greatest heights then by some foolish, unpremeditated act undoing his own work and making one wonder whether it is instinct – or intellect – which is uppermost with him. I have seen it again and again!
Ibid., *entry for 31 August 1936.*

Abba Eban

He was never a pacifist. He was concerned not with what violence would do to its victims, but with what it might do to its practitioners. During his final years he saw Israel's youth forced to seek its glories in the 'traditional' fields of national struggle. The virtues of peace and learning, stubborn toil and progressive advance towards excellence, were necessarily superseded in the national priorities by more urgent concerns. At the same time a Canaanite heresy arose. In some quarters the Jewish diaspora was despised.

He feared lest Israelis might seek to live within the limits of their geography rather than in the enlarging perspectives of their far flung history. Zionism, which for him had meant a large vision – the renewal of Jewish creativity within the family of nations – became a slogan of derision. Mass immigration demanded a quantitative rather than a qualitative approach to the solution of social problems.

It is idle to deny that under these stresses there has been an objective estrangement between Weizmann's ideals and Israel's young reality. But there is ample evidence that it is a temporary estrangement. Thomas Jefferson, to whom Weizmann corresponds in our national history, made magnanimous provision for his own eclipse. 'No generation has the right to commit another to its own conceptions of political virtue or human destiny.' But there comes a time when the tangent is corrected and the old deep fountains are revisited with a sense of new discovery.

In Israeli youth today there is a search for deeper satisfaction and more mature fulfilments than are to be found in a military camaraderie or siege, however rich in its implications of honour, responsibility and sacrifice. The generation calls for a message compounded of creative humanism and scientific truth. In his unique synthesis of these visions Weizmann, ten years after death, emerges as the most modern figure in the Zionist Pantheon. The hour of his maximal influence may be still to come.

From a speech at a public meeting. London, 8 November 1962.

Daily Express

Zaharoff and Venizelos have gone, and their secret influence has been cut out of our government. But a more powerful foreigner remains. . . . The last of the foreigners surpasses them both in his genius for exerting a hidden mastery over the minds of our simple British politicians. His name has never been whispered in the ears of the electors. They are hardly aware of his existence. Yet he has entangled the British taxpayer in a net which can only be cut by resolute and ruthless popular action.

Who is this man of mystery? His name is Dr Chaim Weizmann. He is the President of the Zionist Organization. His genius it was that lured us step by step into the morass of Palestine. His genius it is that keeps us there, and will keep us there until we sink up to the neck in irretrievable disaster. The Great Chaim is one of those master-minds who dominate the destinies of nations.
From a front-page article. London, 28 October 1922.

Felix Frankfurter
Weizmann the scientist has outstripped the imagination of Kipling the poet. For Weizmann, rooted as he is in Eastern religion and Western scientific culture, proves that not only may East and West meet; they may become fused in a single person. And Dr Weizmann would be the first to insist that there is nothing unique about such fusion.
From his foreword to Chaim Weizmann, Statesman and Scientist, *ed. Meyer Weisgal.*

Nahum Goldmann
Pragmatic as he was in the concrete day-to-day work of resettling Palestine, in politics he was an artist, fascinating Jews and gentiles alike by his charm and sparkling intelligence. He could characterize a man – and dispose of him – in a single word. Like all great artists, he was extremely subjective, not to say egocentric. Without realizing it, he constructed a world of his own and placed himself at its centre. When he took action he was not an intellectual making a firm distinction between subject and object, but an artist identifying himself with his medium. Zionism was an expression of Weizmann's personality. The famous sentence '*l'état c'est moi*' was applicable to him as to few other men. His own destiny and that of the movement were to him one and the same. When he had to resign from leadership of the movement in 1931, he was not so much angry as completely surprised. Ten minutes before the vote of censure he would not have thought it possible that a majority of the Zionist Congress could demand his resignation. To him it was as if, by doing so, the movement had dissolved itself.
From his autobiography.

Theodor Herzl
I regard you, Dr Weizmann, as a person who has been temporarily misled, but nevertheless a useful force who will once more find his way back and proceed along the right road together with all of us. But I am becoming ever more strongly convinced that not all the gentlemen in your group are in this category, and I am ready for the time when,

sooner or later, they will be lost to our movement.
From a letter to Weizmann. Vienna, 14 May 1903.

Vladimir Jabotinsky
Weizmann has never understood the political position in the country, never realized the significance of previous events as precedent for the future; during those two years of continuous pogrom he had stifled the outbursts of protest until the impudence of our enemies grew and ripened and took deep roots, and we became *hefker* [ownerless property] in their eyes. During last Passover he saw for himself the results of his tactics – but even after the slaughter he did neither learn nor forget. And now he is continuing his blind policy that is bound to bring us ever greater damage.
In an 'Open Letter' sent May 1920 from his Acre imprisonment, reproduced in The Jabotinsky Story, *vol. I, by Joseph Schechtman.*

Harold Laski
He has faults, he has committed blunders, he has sometimes failed through trusting too much, as he has sometimes failed through trusting too little. He has not always evaded those special sins to which a political leader is liable; he has sometimes, I think, like most statesmen, heard a little too easily in the echo of his own speech the voice of history. But, when all this is taken into account, the Palestine of today is the outcome of his devotion, as the Palestine of tomorrow will be the outcome of his faith. He has given to the Jewish people in a tragic half-century that kind of last full measure of unremitting service that Lenin gave to the new Russia, that Keir Hardie gave to Socialism in Britain, that Jaurès gave to Socialism in France.
From a contribution to Chaim Weizmann, A Tribute on his Seventieth Birthday, *ed. Paul Goodman.*

T. E. Lawrence
You wish me to deny statements which a third person declares I made to Dr Weizmann. I will do nothing of the sort. . . . Especially as I suspect you want my denials only to assure yourself and triumph over Dr Weizmann, a great man whose boots neither you nor I, my dear Bishop, are fit to black.
From a draft letter [? June 1922] to the Anglican Bishop of Jerusalem, reproduced in The Letters of T. E. Lawrence, *ed. David Garnett.*

Louis Lipsky
American oratory has its own standards. Foreigners do not appreciate it. It stems from the rough and ready West. Its dependence upon sound

suggests the open spaces. Dr Weizmann did not qualify as an American orator. His voice was not resonant. He had few gestures. He used no groping introductions or exalted perorations. He hated the impersonation of emotion. He had no ear for the rhythmic phrase. He acquired the English gift for understatement. He did not propagandize himself as a person. He was not made for stage effects.

In spite of these limitations, no Jewish speaker ever made the same deep and lasting impression – even in the United States. Dr Weizmann spoke as if his words were the issue of suffering. He made the impression of a murky flame that had to be fanned to give heat. Shmarya Levin had burning passion; Sokolow was a master of brilliant narrative and analysis and of sly humour; Ussishkin took his audience by storm with sledge-hammer blows; Bialik spun exciting ideas and fascinated his listeners with figures of speech that did not require form to make them live. Dr Weizmann had none of these qualities. He established an identification of himself with what his words were trying to convey. He seemed to be able to capture the wisdom of Jewish life. He drew his thoughts out of an invisible responsibility. There was prophetic significance in his phrases – a mystery striving to explain itself. There was a stateliness in his speech which was unique. He seemed to speak ex-cathedra for the silent Jewish people.

From A Gallery of Zionist Profiles.

David Lloyd George
As Chairman of the Munitions of War Committee I took this matter greatly to heart. While I was casting about for some solution of the [shortage of acetone] difficulty, I ran against the late C. P. Scott, Editor of the *Manchester Guardian*. He was a friend in whose wisdom I had implicit faith. I told him of my problem and that I was on the look-out for a resourceful chemist who would help me to solve it. He said: 'There is a very remarkable professor of chemistry in the University of Manchester willing to place his services at the disposal of the State. I must tell you, however, that he was born somewhere near the Vistula, and I am not sure on which side. His name is Weizmann.' Scott could guarantee that whatever the country of origin, Weizmann was thoroughly devoted to the cause of the Allies, that the one thing he really cared about was Zionism, and that he was convinced that in the victory of the Allies alone was there any hope for his people. I knew Mr Scott to be one of the shrewdest judges of men I had ever met. The world renown of his great paper had been built up on the soundness of his judgment – of men as well as of affairs. But I also trusted his patriotism implicitly. Pacifist as he was he believed in the essential

justice of our intervention in this War. I took his word about Professor Weizmann and invited him to London to see me. I took to him at once. He is now a man of international fame. He was then quite unknown to the general public, but as soon as I met him I realized that he was a very remarkable personality. His brow gave assurance of a fine intellect and his open countenance gave confidence in his complete sincerity. I told him that we were in a chemical dilemma and asked him to assist us. I explained the shortage in wood alcohol and what it meant in munitionment. Could he help? Dr Weizmann said he did not know, but he would try. He could produce acetone by a fermentation process on a laboratory scale, but it would require some time before he could guarantee successful production on a manufacturing scale.

'How long can you give me?' he asked. I said: 'I cannot give you very long. It is pressing.' Weizmann replied: 'I will go at it night and day.'

In a few weeks' time he came to me and said: 'The problem is solved.' After a prolonged study of the micro-flora existing on maize and other cereals, also of those occurring in the soil, he had succeeded in isolating an organism capable of transforming the starch of cereals, particularly that of maize, into a mixture of acetone butyl alcohol. The generations of these organisms die very quickly, and in quite a short time, working night and day as he had promised, he had secured a culture which would enable us to get our acetone from maize. . . .

When our difficulties were solved through Dr Weizmann's genius, I said to him: 'You have rendered great service to the State, and I should like to ask the Prime Minister to recommend you to His Majesty for some honour.' He said: 'There is nothing I want for myself.' 'But is there nothing we can do as a recognition of your valuable assistance to the country?' I asked. He replied: 'Yes, I would like you to do something for my people.' He then explained his aspirations as to the repatriation of the Jews to the sacred land they had made famous. That was the fount and origin of the famous declaration about the National Home for Jews in Palestine.
From War Memoirs.

Malcolm MacDonald
In spite of the bitter hostility which Chaim Weizmann felt towards part of my policy regarding Palestine in the pre-War years, and his consequent strong dislike of me following our earlier period of warm friendship, my deep affection as well as high admiration for him never changed; and it remains ardent today.
From a letter to Barnet Litvinoff. Sevenoaks, Kent, 3 July 1976.

Richard Meinertzhagen
The visit of Dr Weizmann had a marked effect, not only on his own people but on the Arab inhabitants of Palestine. He was able to co-ordinate Zionist effort, and moderate the extremist and too-progressive elements. He got into personal contact with many of the Arab notables in Palestine and did a great deal to dispel the many illusory ideas on Zionism which have been saturating Palestine from foreign and badly-informed sources. He established a cordial relationship with the Palestine Administration.
In a report to Earl Curzon. Cairo, 13 January 1920. From Documents on British Foreign Policy, *First Series, vol. IV.*

Max Nordau
The Greater Actions Committee has taken it upon itself to represent the Congress, to have power to speak in the name of the Jewish people and thus to confirm the mandates of Weizmann and Sokolow and pursue a policy toward concessions to England. It's a degraded farce. . . . Any half-way independent utterance is received with jeers and neighs by the sycophants or by the roars of mere fools. But what do you expect? The mediocre Jew is no different than the mediocre non-Jew.
From a letter to his wife, 16 February 1920, published in Max Nordau, *by Anna and Maxa Nordau.*

Arthur Ruppin
Weizmann has twice invited his closer friends, myself included, for discussions. He is depressed and considers the moral and aesthetic level in Palestine to be low. . . . Weizmann told us that he was ready to be nominated as a candidate for the presidency of the Zionist Organization at the next Congress. The Labour supporters are pleased with this. I am also in favour of Weizmann. I am only sorry to see how many weaknesses this great man has.
Diary note, 18 January 1935, in Memoirs, Diaries, Letters, *ed. Alex Bein.*

Harry Sacher
He was never happy as a colleague. He disliked seeking counsel, and he had no gift for reporting. He preferred to make decisions for himself, and he was impatient of criticism. These characteristics were to cause him much embarrassment later, when he was the official head of the Zionist Organization, associated with elected colleagues, and faced with a representative Congress. But in those war years he was spared these unwelcome restrictions, and he was justified by success. Sokolow was the roving ambassador, Weizmann the statesman. His faith was

justified and his leadership crowned when on November 2, 1917, the Balfour Declaration was announced to the world. It was a miracle of statesmanship, and seldom has anything of the like been achieved.
From Zionist Portraits and Other Essays.

Israel M. Sieff
He seemed always to be possessed of what may be called a 'divine discontent'. It dominated him. He was restless, probing, attempting, experimenting, pushing forward. He was both a man of ideas and a man of action. He was continually self-questioning and self-criticizing. He was controlled by a spirit which, at one and the same time, drove and informed him. Yet, whilst he was analytical and questioning, he never lost his positive and constructive approach.
From an article in Jerusalem Post, *2 November 1954.*

Abba Hillel Silver
Though a leader of a movement of national rebirth and resurgence, he has consistently resisted that vehement flood of romanticism which has swept away so many of the noble ideals of mankind. He has proclaimed no provocative political ethnology, no conceited race mythology, no *Kultur* principle like that which has been the undoing of Germany.
From a contribution to Chaim Weizmann, Statesman and Scientist, *ed. Meyer Weisgal.*

Jan C. Smuts
He is the greatest Jewish leader since Moses.
Quoted by Sarah Gertrude Millin in a letter to Weizmann. Johannesburg, 16 September 1935.

Vice-President Henry A. Wallace
My mind runs to a name familiar to you all – Chaim Weizmann, who came over to this country because he saw us on the point of making some very serious mistakes with regard to our rubber programme and because he felt that oil could not do it by itself. And so he brought in alcohol to do the job . . . he came to me at that time and I made connections for him. I know that he made it possible for us to avoid a very serious mistake in terms of the war effort.
From a radio broadcast. Washington, 10 March 1944.

Sir Arthur Wauchope
Dr Weizmann spoke very seriously without pause and for the main part of forty minutes calmly and impressively. . . .
   Dr Weizmann then spoke of his supreme contempt for all the Arab

leaders, and their complete lack of patriotism as shown by the bitterness of inter-party conflict, and their readiness to accept Jewish money.

I did not say so, but, as a matter of fact, no city suffers from so many parties and from greater party bitterness than Tel Aviv. I am always told that Arabs accept Jewish gold, and I have no doubt some do, but it is a curious fact that the present Arab leaders are all poor men.
From a report to the Colonial Secretary. Jerusalem, 6 May 1936.

Sir Charles Webster
No one will dispute that Dr Weizmann was the main creator of the National Home and without the National Home there could have been no State of Israel today. But even now I doubt whether this part of his great achievements has ever received in contemporary history all the recognition that it deserves. It was in my opinion the greatest act of diplomatic statesmanship of the First World War. That period produced several great leaders of small nationalities who obtained much for their peoples when the world was transformed by the conflict between the great powers. But none of them, in my view, not even the two most renowned amongst them, Masaryk and Venizelos, can compare in stature with Dr Weizmann.
From a lecture. Rehovot, 27 November 1955.

Meyer W. Weisgal
A curious thing happened. The opposition which for weeks and months has been assiduously preparing for its day of triumph was not jubilant over its victory. It was, instead, depressed. Even the bitterest foe felt intuitively a sense of remorse. But what the opposition did not realize was that this attempt at political assassination would become the symbol of Weizmann's apotheosis. For the movement there was only confusion, uncertainty, and a general questioning: 'What will Weizmann do now? Will he return to the Congress? Will he sulk in his tent?'

The closing session was convened. Weizmann was no longer on the rostrum – that three-tiered, improvised platform, dominated in the background by a huge likeness of Herzl which gave the Zionist Congress the dignity and solemnity of a great national assembly. Weizmann in his familiar posture, his left hand over his brow, staring seemingly into emptiness, was missing. A strange, almost guilty feeling pervaded the Congress hall. The delegates' seats were sparsely occupied. The left wing of the Congress hall was entirely empty. The presiding officer rapped the gavel and asked the ushers to gather in the delegates from the lobbies and from their various caucuses. Gradually the seats began to fill up. But the left wing was still largely empty. Suddenly two ushers opened a side door and the figure of Weizmann, tall, stately, his expression grave, emerged, followed by a hundred or more delegates of the Labour Zionist wing. Slowly, and in measured step, as was his wont, he walked at the head of this group to the section reserved for the Labour delegation. The atmosphere became electric. An ovation began, spreading in waves from the galleries to the hall, and thence to the platform. The whole Congress was engulfed in it. Weizmann remained seated. The applause gathered volume and continued till he was compelled to rise from his seat. It was the signal for a renewed acclamation. The delegates wept and in effusive continental fashion embraced and kissed each other. At that Congress, in the moment of his defeat, Weizmann was anointed the leader of his people.

From his report on Weizmann's defeat at the 1931 Zionist Congress, reproduced in . . . So Far.

Sumner Welles
I have found Dr Weizmann the most constructive of all the Jewish leaders with regard to the Palestine question. He believes, as I think you do, that the solution of this problem should, if possible, be found by agreement between the Jews and Arabs.

From a letter to Roosevelt. Washington, 19 May 1943.

Robert Weltsch
Weizmann became irritated when other men, among them those whom he for one reason or another regarded as his antagonists, expressed views that were in fact similar to his own, but that he himself could not easily put forth because he saw also the other side of the matter, which the others ignored. He also thoroughly disliked the puritan type of American Jew, which was humourless and moralizing and often seemed self-righteous. So he was alienated from two men with whom he had many views in common but with whom he was unable to co-operate: Louis Brandeis and Judah Magnes. They were in some way representative of the two main objectives of Zionism: Brandeis in the quest for new men outside the Zionist Organization and for an economic programme, Magnes in the field of Arab policy. Much of the period 1919–29 was embittered by Weizmann's resentment against these men.

From his contribution to Chaim Weizmann, A Biography by Several Hands, *ed. Meyer W. Weisgal and Joel Carmichael.*

Stephen S. Wise
I could not believe that what happened could conceivably come to pass; that England and America would jointly be rebuked and rebutted by Congress and that Dr Weizmann, our foremost statesman, and wisest leader – though without the support of Press agents – would be dropped as pilot when most needed. The voting meant little or nothing. The barest majority, whipped together by electioneering devices worthy of an American political convention at its worst, voted to make it impossible for Dr Weizmann to go to the London Conference and, therefore, to retain the leadership. Many who voted 'no' would have preferred to vote in the affirmative if caucus bondage had not intervened to rob them of their freedom.

From a statement on Weizmann's dismissal by the 1946 Zionist Congress, quoted by Evening Standard. *London, 5 January 1947.*

4
Steps to the Balfour Declaration

At the outbreak of war on 4 August 1914, Weizmann's status in Zionism was the insignificant one of member of the Greater Actions Committee, a large grouping formed from delegates of all countries represented in the World Zionist Organization. He was also a Vice-President of the English Zionist Federation (EZF), a body reduced by internal divisions and personality conflicts to virtual non-existence. The Zionist Executive, also known as the Smaller (or Inner) Actions Committee, was located in Berlin. The largest Zionist constituencies were Russia, enemy of Germany, and the neutral United States.

1914
18 October
In a letter to Shmarya Levin, a member of the Zionist Executive then stationed in New York and an Austrian subject, Weizmann condemns a move by the Berlin headquarters to establish a bureau in neutral Copenhagen. This would enable Berlin to retain contact with Zionist bodies throughout the world, but in Weizmann's view it would give their movement a German coloration. He states that a 'Prussian' victory would be fatal to all Jewish hopes.
19 October
He proposes to Israel Zangwill, an opponent of the Zionist Organization, joint action in preparing the Jews to voice their demands for justice in anticipation of an eventual peace conference. He expresses his conviction that Britain will be victorious and Palestine will come within her influence. The celebrated author is unimpressed. He questions Weizmann's credentials in speaking for the Zionists and declines to act as suggested.
11 November
With Turkey's entry into the war on 29 October, and Prime Minister Herbert Asquith's declaration that this signalled the end of the Turkish

Empire, he contends in a letter to prominent Zionists in America (one of whom, Isaac Straus, has recently arrived from Berlin as an agent of the Central Powers) that the Jews should openly lodge their claim to Palestine. American Zionist policy, however, reflects America's neutrality in the war. It is against any action that might help hated Russia, affront Turkey and prejudice the situation of the Jewish community in Palestine. The Americans wish to bring the headquarters of the movement to New York for the duration, and to this end have constituted themselves a Provisional Executive Committee for General Zionist Affairs (PEC) under the chairmanship of Louis D. Brandeis.

12 November

Weizmann tells C. P. Scott, editor of the *Manchester Guardian*, that Palestine as a British dependency in the hands of the Jews could become an 'Asiatic Belgium'. Scott, a Liberal opposed to the further expansion of British imperialism, is unconvinced, but he offers to put Weizmann in touch with his friend Lloyd George, who is Chancellor of the Exchequer.

17 November

A. J. Balfour, former Conservative Prime Minister now in opposition, informs Professor Samuel Alexander of Manchester University that he has the 'liveliest and most pleasant recollections' of Weizmann, and would be glad to hear of his proposals.

25 November

Weizmann acquaints James de Rothschild, son of Baron Edmond, with his ideas for Palestine. James advises against enlisting the help of American Jews who, he says, are regarded in Britain as pro-German.

10 December

At Lloyd George's behest Weizmann meets with Herbert Samuel, President of the Local Government Board and the first professing Jew in the British Cabinet (Disraeli having been baptized). Samuel reveals that he has already put it to the Foreign Secretary (Sir Edward Grey) and Lloyd George that a Jewish State might be established in Palestine, through Britain's good offices. Weizmann is amazed that a so-called 'assimilated' Jew should have ideas similar to his own, and discovers that Samuel's tutor in these matters has been Moses Gaster, head of Britain's Sephardi community.

12 December

Balfour tells Weizmann that a Jewish State 'is not a dream, it is a great cause and I understand it'. Weizmann has hitherto kept only a small group of personal friends (Harry Sacher, Simon Marks, Israel Sieff, all centred in Manchester, and Leon Simon and Ahad Ha'am) informed of his moves. He now includes Gaster, though not the EZF's chairman Joseph Cowen. But two members of the Zionist Executive, Nahum Sokolow and Yehiel Tschlenow, both Russian citizens, are due in London.

22 December
He enlists Dorothy de Rothschild, twenty-year-old wife of James (then on military service in France) to sound out the British Rothschilds and their influential connections as to their readiness to help. She propagates his cause in political circles.

28 December
Weizmann visits Baron Edmond in Paris and finds him positive and sympathetic, though concerned lest public discussion rouse the fears of Catholic opinion in France.

1915

7 January
Weizmann gives Sokolow and Tschlenow, now in London, a report of his activities to date, barely hinting at a possible Zionist alliance with Britain but emphasizing difficulties in forging a united front with the non-Zionist leaders of Anglo-Jewry.

15 January
Together with Samuel, he discusses his plans with Lloyd George.

25 January
Samuel sends the Prime Minister a memorandum advocating the annexation of Palestine and restoration of the Jews there. Asquith is dismissive, but Lloyd George approves. Grey is dubious about British control, because of French susceptibilities.

While in Paris for a meeting with Baron Edmond Weizmann discusses his plan with the British Ambassador, Sir Francis Bertie, who makes a diary note of Weizmann's 'absurd scheme'.

29 January
Weizmann rebukes Judah Magnes, of the New York PEC, for ascribing the difficulties Palestine's Jews are experiencing with the Turks to his activities in England. He states that such ideas as he is pursuing have been ventilated in the British Press since Turkey joined the Central Powers.

Late January
Weizmann learns that Levin has been publicly criticizing him in America for his activities.

4 February
Gaster complains to Weizmann that he is not being kept informed, and he reproves the latter for accepting re-election as Vice-President of

EZF, a body with which Gaster has a long-standing feud.

9 February
Weizmann's scientific experiments in fermentation are inspected in Manchester by a representative of the Nobel Explosives Company, who sends a favourable report to the Admiralty.

14 February
Fearing that Liberal opinion could prevent Britain's espousal of a Jewish Palestine under this country's protection, Weizmann argues with Scott that such an arrangement would meet with no opposition from Russia. France, he says, has no justification for claiming Palestine but should be satisfied with Syria, including the Beyrout area. He warns Scott against the hazards of an international regime for Palestine. This begins a long process of persuasion of sceptical British figures, including Balfour.

19 February
Dardanelles campaign initiated. The operation is joined on 26 April by a Palestinian transport unit, the Zion Mule Corps, mobilized in Alexandria by Joseph Trumpeldor from among Jews of Russian citizenship. Meanwhile Brandeis, in the interests of the Jews still residing in Palestine, sends a message to the Porte via Henry Morgenthau, US Ambassador, pledging the Zionists' 'unqualified loyalty' to Turkey.

March
Samuel circulates a revised proposal to the Cabinet. This, much modified from the original concept of a Jewish State, advocates a British protectorate with carefully regulated immigration leading eventually to a 'measure of Jewish self-government'. Asquith remains unconvinced, noting that its only other partisan is Lloyd George 'who does not care a damn for the Jews but thinks it an outrage to let the Holy Places pass into the possession or under the protectorate of "agnostic, atheistic France" '.

18 March
Weizmann again presses the logic of a British protectorate on Scott, stressing that with greater British influence in the whole of Arabia from Egypt to the Persian Gulf the Jews would prove, as he later told Scott in a letter, 'the best possible agent'. Weizmann is now disregarding the Copenhagen Bureau of the Zionist Organization and the American PEC as well as the Berlin Executive, ostensibly on the grounds that the presence in England of Sokolow and Tschlenow made London the centre of the movement. The two Executive members are spending much time in fruitless negotiation with non-Zionist Anglo-Jewish leaders for a united Jewish front. He also advises them against taking

up an invitation to proceed to America. He has begun working with the Admiralty on large-scale trials of his acetone process.
16 May
Tschlenow leaves for Copenhagen but Weizmann refuses his invitation to join him there. Sokolow remains in London.
25 May
Asquith forms Coalition Government in which Samuel loses his Cabinet rank. Balfour enters Cabinet and assumes Admiralty portfolio in succession to Winston Churchill, who has resigned over the Dardanelles débâcle. Lloyd George becomes Minister of Munitions.
Early June
On Scott's recommendation Lloyd George discusses Britain's explosives shortage with Weizmann.
Late June
Vladimir Jabotinsky is in London pressing his plan for a Jewish Legion, which he has been canvassing without success among the French in Paris. Called to Copenhagen by Tschlenow, he refuses a demand that he drop his Legion scheme.
Mid-July
Weizmann takes up residence in London to work with the Admiralty and Ministry of Munitions.
18 August
He convinces Lord Robert Cecil, Under-Secretary of State for Foreign Affairs, of the importance to England of the fulfilment of Zionist hopes. Sacher leaves London to rejoin the *Manchester Guardian*; he is simultaneously editing a book, for which Weizmann undertakes to find the finance, that will explain Zionism to the British. With a grant from Baron Edmond it is published in 1916 as *Zionism and the Jewish Future*.

1916
23 January
Together with Cowen, Weizmann forms a Zionist consultative committee in London. Although Sokolow and Gaster are among its members, it appears to have had little to do except give an appearance of Zionist harmony in discussions still proceeding with other Anglo-Jewish bodies. It is also delegated to prepare a platform of Zionist aims. The committee dissolved itself in January 1917, the gulf separating Zionists and non-Zionists as wide as ever.
March
The Zion Mule Corps is disbanded. About 120 members come to Britain with Trumpeldor to enrol in the British Army. This gives added force to Jabotinsky's agitation for a Jewish Legion. He has the support

of Weizmann almost alone among the leaders of British Zionism, who fear the project as possibly compromising their citizenship. In New York the *Maccabean*, the official Zionist organ, describes Jabotinsky as 'guilty of an absurdity as well as of a disloyal act'. The British military are themselves distrustful of 'foreign legions', and headway is slow.

March–June
Weizmann is fully engaged with chemical work, bringing him into easier contact with Lloyd George and Whitehall officials. Scott is helping him to lodge a financial claim with the government for his contribution to the war effort. There is a lull in the campaign for a British protectorate over Palestine, in part due to ill-feeling against immigrant Jews of Russian citizenship who are exempt from Britain's conscription law but are reluctant to volunteer for army service. This is particularly embarrassing for Samuel, now back in the Cabinet as Home Secretary, and he appeals to Weizmann and others for help in persuading Jews of Russian nationality to enlist, lest they be deported. Jabotinsky contends that a Legion would entice them to serve.

6 December
Lloyd George becomes Prime Minister, with Balfour as Foreign Secretary. Samuel, loyal to Asquith, declines to continue in the government.

End December
Weizmann's closest supporters, mainly the Manchester group, form the British Palestine Committee and initiate a publication *Palestine*, edited by Sacher. Its proclaimed policy is 'to reset the ancient glories of the Jewish nation in the freedom of a new British dominion in Palestine'.

1917

21 January
Jabotinsky and Trumpeldor send a formal petition to Lloyd George to create a Jewish Legion. This contains a reference to Weizmann as approving the project. Jabotinsky himself enlists the following day, joining the Zion Mule Corps veterans. Trumpeldor decides to return to Russia and enlist there.

28 January
Weizmann, through the good offices of James Malcolm, an Armenian nationalist working in London for his people's liberation, meets Sir Mark Sykes of the Cabinet Secretariat. An expert in Middle East affairs, Sykes had in 1916 negotiated a secret agreement with François Georges-Picot for a division of the Turkish Empire that would give Britain and France outright ownership of some areas and spheres of

interest in the rest. A truncated Palestine is to be either an Anglo-French condominium or to be given an international regime comprising England, France, Russia and perhaps Italy. Previously, in October 1915, Britain had made a commitment to the Shereef of Mecca to recognize his rule in Arabia in return for an Arab revolt against their Turkish overlord. This, the McMahon pledge, left a coastal area, including Palestine, likewise in an ambiguous situation. Sykes intimates to Weizmann that there is a commitment to the French, and while sympathetic to Zionist propaganda, he pleads for circumspection.

4 February
By agreement with Cowen, Weizmann expresses readiness to assume the Presidency of the EZF, provided he can have his own people (mainly the Manchester group plus Leon Simon) on its Council. He thus achieves a recognizable status at last to strengthen his hand.

7 February
Sykes meets leading Zionists, together with Samuel, Lord Rothschild and James de Rothschild, at Gaster's home. They ask for an exclusively British protectorate over Palestine, and are dismayed to learn that the country's destiny has to some extent already been settled with the French. Sykes suggests a mission to Paris, to convince the French of a Jewish Palestine but playing down the question of suzerainty. Sokolow assumes the errand. Weizmann informs Jabotinsky accordingly, intimating his hope also of an eventual Jewish Legion.

13 February
The first issue of *Palestine* appears advocating a Jewish entity with preferred frontiers that include Damascus and continue southwards well to the east of the Hedjaz railway. Sykes and Weizmann are incensed, as this will heighten French suspicions of a British conspiracy with Zionism.

20 March
The Russian Revolution (of Lvov and Kerensky) encourages Weizmann to believe he can now persuade the Zionists in that country to speak freely of a British protectorate and, he tells Scott, 'the Zionist Organization there will become a very great power'. It will also help the mood in America, he says. He therefore wants to have his discussions with government figures placed on a formal basis. He wishes also to accompany Sykes out East so that he might enter into negotiations with leading Arabs in Palestine as the country is conquered.

22 March
In a discussion with Weizmann, Balfour foresees problems with France and Italy. Failing agreement, Balfour hopes for an Anglo-American

protectorate. Weizmann opposes this too, and is informed that Lloyd George too wants exclusive British control.

26 March
He emphasizes to Sykes, at the request of Jabotinsky, that the Zion Mule Corps veterans be sent after training to the Egyptian Expeditionary Force, and not to the Western Front as contemplated.

27 March
First British attack on Gaza. Lloyd George confirms his ambition for a British Palestine to Weizmann. Most British newspapers publish articles in support of this plan.

2 April
America declares war on Germany as an 'Associate' of the Allies, though not against Turkey.

3 April
Together with Scott, Weizmann breakfasts with Lloyd George. The Prime Minister emphasizes his opposition to a French stake in Palestine. He too wants Jewish volunteers to be sent to the Egyptian Front.

4 April
Sokolow reports from Paris that the French are determined to have all Palestine.

8 April
Weizmann begins pleading with Brandeis to reinforce his efforts with expressions of support, both personal from Brandeis himself and official from the US Government, for a Jewish Palestine under British aegis. But these are not forthcoming.

16 April
Scott informs Weizmann of the details of the Sykes-Picot Agreement and advises him not to travel East without authoritative notification of the government's intentions regarding Palestine.

27 April
As with Brandeis, Weizmann presses Tschlenow to speak out in the desired vein in Russia. But he is troubled by Sokolow's reports from Paris, which have suddenly assumed a more optimistic form and refer to 'satisfactory negotiations'. Sokolow has been sending similar messages to Brandeis and Tschlenow, and Weizmann suspects that Sokolow may have been trapped into acceptance of French, or at least Anglo-French, suzerainty of Palestine. This contradicts his own line of an exclusively British connection, and he wires Sokolow to return to London forthwith. The latter, now in Rome, replies that his discussions have omitted questions of future suzerainty, and he points to his audience with the Pope as assurance that the Vatican will offer no

insurmountable opposition to their plans.

4 May
Weizmann receives a report from a Zionist representative in Zurich concerning Vatican efforts, in association with Catholics from Germany, Austria and Italy, to exclude Britain from Palestine and secure the country's internationalization under Papal protection. He informs Sir Ronald Graham of the Foreign Office accordingly.

7, 10 May
Balfour is in Washington, and has two discussions with Brandeis. The latter's note of the meetings states that Balfour admired and had affection for Weizmann and would do all he could to advance the Zionist cause, and that Balfour hoped for Anglo-American suzerainty but feared Franco-Italian objections. (Brandeis, having discussed Zionism with President Wilson on 6 May, also recorded that Wilson was sympathetic to its aims and would make a public statement 'at the proper time'. No such statement was in fact made before the Balfour Declaration, nor did Brandeis make one on his own behalf.)

20 May
Weizmann convenes Extraordinary Zionist Conference in London to make a public statement that it is premature to have a Jewish State in Palestine, but they hope that as a result of the war Britain will become the protector of Palestine; the Zionist scheme will be implemented without impairing the legitimate interests of the non-Jewish population.

24 May
Alarmed by Weizmann's progress in governmental circles, Britain's foremost anti-Zionist spokesmen in Jewish ranks, David L. Alexander of the Board of Deputies and Claude C. Montefiore of the Anglo-Jewish Association, publish a letter in *The Times* repudiating Zionism and any proposal to give Jewish settlers in Palestine special rights.

28 May
Weizmann, Lord Rothschild and Chief Rabbi J. H. Hertz reply in *The Times* with their own letters. In the ensuing furore Alexander and Montefiore concede defeat, the former by resigning the Presidency of the Board of Deputies. The Conjoint Foreign Committee, through which they have been fighting the Zionists, is dissolved.

29 May
As EZF President, Weizmann requests the Director of Military Intelligence to exempt his closest colleagues (Marks, Sieff, Sacher, Simon, Albert M. Hyamson and Samuel Landman) from military service, 'six men without whose assistance the cause of the Zionist movement in this country could not be carried on'. The exemptions are granted.

June
Despite sustained representation to Tschlenow, Weizmann fails to secure from the All-Russian Zionist Conference in Petrograd an endorsement of his plan for a British protectorate of Palestine. In fact Tschlenow is by no means convinced the war will end in British victory, and in his speech guards against any reference to Turkey's possible loss of Palestine.

19 June
Weizmann and Lord Rothschild impress upon Balfour that a British declaration of support for Zionism is now opportune. Graham has already advised the War Cabinet of the importance of a pro-Zionist declaration, particularly in Russia. Balfour asks Weizmann to submit a draft, which must not identify a possible Suzerain Power.

Weizmann is by now apprised that Henry Morgenthau, accompanied by two Zionists (Felix Frankfurter and Eliahu Lewin-Epstein) is proceeding to Europe with a plan to detach Turkey from the Central Powers; Turkey, by making a separate peace, would retain her possessions. The mission is disguised as an investigation into the welfare needs of Palestine's Jews. Weizmann is officially delegated by the British Government to join the mission and scotch the plan.

29 June
Weizmann travels to Gibraltar where the Morgenthau mission is abandoned, both through his representations and because Morgenthau himself has second thoughts on its feasibility.

17 July
Edwin Montagu, Herbert Samuel's fiercely anti-Zionist cousin, joins the Cabinet as Secretary of State for India.

18 July
In Weizmann's absence abroad, a formula, devised by Sokolow and others, is submitted by Lord Rothschild to Balfour for a British announcement accepting the principle that Palestine 'be reconstituted as the national home of the Jewish people'.

28 July
Following agreement with Russia to repatriate Russian citizens who refuse to enlist in England, the War Office announces the formation of a Jewish Regiment.

29 July
Returning home via Paris, Weizmann meets Lloyd George and Balfour there, and hints at the possibility of an American declaration of war upon Turkey and despatch of a force containing a large Jewish contingent to reinforce the Palestine campaign.

Late July
Weizmann and Sokolow form another Political Committee of prominent Zionists in London. They emphasize that it would have advisory functions only, without access to confidential information given to the two principals.

1 August
Weizmann indicates in a letter to Ahad Ha'am that Frankfurter will discuss American participation in the Palestine theatre with Wilson, and that Lloyd George and Balfour are agreeable to Weizmann himself visiting the US to expedite the scheme. He says: 'The Arabs are now giving [the British] a lot of help. This does us no good and we must help them too.'

17 August
He angrily resigns from the EZF and Political Committee in protest at their objections to the formation of the Jewish Legion, but is prevailed upon to stay. In the light of Jewish objections, Legion volunteers are integrated anonymously in the Royal Fusiliers.

September
The situation in Russia suggests the possibility of a separate peace, and prompts Scott to warn Weizmann that this would make it inopportune to press the Palestine question. Weizmann contends that a declaration now will help Britain both in Russia and America.

3 September
Draft of declaration, with alternative government versions, before War Cabinet. Lloyd George and Balfour are absent, and Montagu fights against it. It is resolved to contact President Wilson for his reaction.

12 September
Weizmann wires the text of the draft announcement to Brandeis, asking for his intercession with Wilson. But Wilson's reply, heavily non-committal, has already been received by the Cabinet.

16 September
Weizmann attacks Montagu, 'a great Hindu nationalist', in letters to Philip Kerr, personal aide to Lloyd George, and on 3 October to Balfour.

28 September
With Scott's help, Weizmann has a brief meeting with Lloyd George, in consequence of which the latter again places the Palestine question on the Cabinet agenda.

4 October
Further discussion in the War Cabinet, with Montagu re-stating his opposition. It is decided to send a further revised draft to Wilson, and circulate it also among Zionist and non-Zionist Jewish personalities in England.

9 October
Weizmann sends the new draft to Brandeis, to Israel Rosov (the leading Russian Zionist in Petrograd in the absence of Tschlenow) and to Baron Edmond de Rothschild, calling for 'enthusiastic endorsement' to prevent further delay. Rosov and Baron Edmond reply approvingly; Brandeis replies that Wilson's approval has been given, but not for publication.

23 October
To rebut a last-minute opposition campaign, Weizmann furnishes Graham with a copious list of Jewish organizations, at home and abroad, which have passed resolutions in support of Palestine as a National Home under British protection.

31 October
War Cabinet authorizes Balfour to issue a declaration of support for Zionist aspirations. Montagu sends a protest from India.

2 November
The Balfour Declaration delivered to Lord Rothschild.

5
As Chronicler of his Age

Childhood in the Pale of Settlement
Motol was situated in one of the darkest and most forlorn corners of the Pale of Settlement, that prison house created by Czarist Russia for the largest part of its Jewish population. Throughout the centuries alternations of bitter oppression and comparative freedom – how comparative a free people would hardly understand – had deepened the consciousness of exile in these scattered communities, which were held together by a common destiny and common dreams. Motol was typical Pale, typical countryside. Here, in this half-town, half-village, I lived from the time of my birth, in 1874, till the age of eleven; and here I wove my first pictures of the Jewish and gentile worlds.

The life of the Jewish child in a Russian town of those times has been described over and over again in Jewish literature, and is not unfamiliar to the general reader. Like all Jewish boys I went to *cheder*, beginning at the age of four. Like nearly all *cheders*, mine was a squalid, one-room school, which also constituted the sole quarters of the teacher's family. If my *cheder* differed from others, it was perhaps in the possession of a family goat which took shelter with us in cold weather. And if my first *Rebbi*, or teacher, differed from others, it was in the degree of his pedagogic incompetence. If our schoolroom was usually hung with lines of washing, if the teacher's numerous children rolled about on the floor, if the din was deafening and incessant, that was nothing out of the ordinary. Nor was it anything out of the ordinary that neither the tumult nor the overcrowding affected our peace of mind or our powers of concentration.

In the spring and autumn, when the *cheder* was a tiny island set in a sea of mud, and in the winter, when it was almost blotted out by snow, I had to be carried there by a servant, or by my older brother. Once there, I stayed immured within its walls, along with the other children, from early morning till evening. We took lunch with us and consumed it in a short pause in the proceedings, often with the books still opened in front of us. On dark winter afternoons our studies could only be pursued by artificial light, and as candles were something of a luxury, and oil lamps practically unobtainable, each pupil was in turn assessed a pound of candles as a contribution to the education of the younger generation.

In the course of my *cheder* years I had several teachers, and by the time I was eleven, or even before, considerable demands were made on my intellectual powers. I was expected to understand – I never did, properly – the intricacies of the Law as laid down in the Babylonian Talmud and as expounded and knocked into me by a *Rebbi* who was both ferocious and exacting, and certainly far from lucid in his expositions. He was always at a loss to understand why things needed to be explained at all; he felt that every Jewish boy should be able to pick up such things, which were as easy as they were sacred, by natural instinct, or at least just by glancing down the pages. I did not share his view, but was too badly terrorized to join issue with him as to his methods – if, indeed, I was at all aware of their inadequacy.

I did not relish the Talmudic teaching, but I adored that of the Prophets, for which I attended another *cheder*. There the teacher was humane and kindly, with a real enthusiasm for his subject. This enthusiasm he managed to communicate to his pupils, though here, too, school and surroundings were of the most depressing character. It is to this teacher, who became a lifelong friend of mine, that I am primarily indebted for my knowledge of the Hebrew Bible, and for my early and lasting devotion to Hebrew literature.
From Trial and Error.

How Herzl became a true Zionist
Herzl became a Palestine Zionist the moment the Kishinev delegates said 'No' at the Uganda Congress. The vote was by name. My late father voted 'Yes'. I voted after him with 'No'. Then the names of the two delegates from Kishinev were called and both said: 'Lo' ('No'). Poor Herzl grew pale, and then he became a true Zionist. He understood the depth of the tragedy and the depth of the idea, and then he resolved upon beginning practical work in the country, even if slowly, even if only symbolically, with a few hundred pounds. I can remember Herzl saying after the vote: 'I do not understand; the rope is round their neck, and still they say "No".' Yes, the rope was (and still is) round our necks, and yet we said 'No'. For we knew very well: that same British Government would make us another offer – and they, in fact, have made that offer. Another reminiscence: A week after the vote I travelled to London fourth class (because there was no fifth). I went to Downing Street (I was living in Whitechapel) and I saw there the

Director of the Department for the African Colonies, Percy by name. In my broken French, I tried to find out his opinion about the Uganda plan. This Englishman, of one of the noblest families in the country, and a religious Christian, said: 'If I were a Jew, I would not give one sou nor one man for this cause. For you cannot exchange Palestine for some other country.'
From a speech at Czernowitz. 12 December 1927.

Impressions of Edwardian London
I arrived today in this monstrous London, and have hardly managed to do a thing. I find it very difficult to find my way and have not settled down yet. The hotels here charge exorbitant prices . . . I have been rushing about madly, and there is slush here, foul weather, fog, din and uproar, and a language which is not exactly comprehensible to me. . . . I am now in Whitechapel. Lord, what horror! Stench, foul smells, emaciated Jewish faces. A mixture of a London avenue and Jewish poverty in the suburbs of Vilna.
From a letter to his fiancée. London, 8 October 1903.

Darling, I have never in my life felt so well as here. It is not without reason that I was striving to get here. This is the hub of the world and, really, you sense the breathing of a giant, the city of cities.
From a letter to his fiancée. 12 October 1903.

Poverty and fear in the ghetto
Everything here is so dull that one impatiently awaits news from those places where the sun always shines. . . . Every time I walk through the town I return home with a broken heart. There is not a single animated face, not a single smile; all around there are only dead shadows. I wonder what keeps people alive! You see a small shop with three roubles worth of merchandise, and a whole family has to live on the profits of such a 'business'. Moreover, they have to live in fear of their lives and to experience all the horrors of Easter and similar festivals. . . . Things are in a fine state when one has to be glad that a week has passed tranquilly, without any Jewish blood being shed. You can well imagine the psychology of people living permanently in such nervous tension. . . . One is compelled to marvel at the great moral force that lives in the hungry Jew. In such conditions others would have turned into beasts long ago!
From a letter to his fiancée. Pinsk, 14 April 1904.

May Day in Manchester
This day is merely a children's holiday, a festival of horses and

donkeys. No mention of a workers' holiday. Not even the Social-Democratic organizations observe May 1st, and the factories keep working. On the other hand, they deck out all the horses. All the children (about 200,000) assemble in a huge square and are offered treats and entertainments by the city. They go from house to house, dancing and playing, receiving sweets and money. Then there is a donkey show, and the best (!) donkey (four-legged) receives a prize and marches in solemn procession through the city. That's all! England is an exception in everything. Besides, these are very ancient customs, dating back to time immemorial.
From a letter to his fiancée. Manchester, 5 May 1906.

The decline of British power
English society as such lacks the intellectual vigour one finds in Germany or France. The English Labour movement, with 1½ million adherents, has not produced even one Jaurès or Bebel. The country is governed by an oligarchy of the ancient hereditary nobility, and everything is made to fit the system. The main centres of education in England, Oxford and Cambridge, with their unrivalled resources and institutions, also incorporate countless relics from the Scholastic epoch. People like us, and myself particularly, find all this very difficult to accept.
From a letter to his fiancée. Manchester, 8 September 1905.

The problem as expounded in the document [on Britain's imperial role] is chiefly concerned with the organization of the dominions and leaves the nucleus of forty-seven million British taxpayers alone; it creates so to say a 'periphery' and assumes the presence of a strong centripetal force which will hold together the complex organism. Doubtless there is such a force – language, culture, origin, ties with the mother country, which are not easily broken up. But in the same time, as a perfectly detached observer I cannot help thinking that there are centrifugal forces making for a detachment of the dominions from the centre and unless they are strongly counteracted an artificial organization would not counterpoise such forces. The mother country is not in all matters the leading element and allows America, Germany, to gain the hegemony for certain things. England is the '*Kulturträger*' in its own colonies only to a certain degree, American and Germanic influences penetrate there slowly but the process is a steady one and on the increase.

I am not an admirer of the German cultural ideals, but I admire the organization and efficiency of Germany and I am firmly convinced that unless a complete reorganization of the forty-seven million British taxpayers takes place Germany may beat us afterwards even if this war is won completely by the Allies. Every day the Germans gain two hours over the British, because their working day is longer; every week he gains a day, because he has no week-end; he is keen, enterprising and despite of the military organization is full of initiative. He loves work for the sake of work; he is an enthusiast of work and this virtue penetrates right through all the strata of the nation. It is deplorable that this wonderful motor is using itself up now for destructive purposes. I admit that the warlike tendencies have to be destroyed, but the virtues of Germany will remain, blossom out again and if the military caste is destroyed a new and great Germany will arise, which may conquer the world without firing a shot. One cannot protect England against the spiritual invasion with dreadnoughts, submarines or destroyers, even with an army and a munitions department with a dozen of Lloyd Georges at its head.

England has the best human material in the world. I am teaching at a British University and have an opportunity of closely observing the younger generation. I lived for many years in Germany, Russia, Switzerland, know France and I am able to make comparisons. The English material is head and shoulder above the Continental, but to put it brutally is going to waste in many respects. The system of education has to be recast, beginning with the elementary school and finishing with Oxford and Cambridge, beginning with the workshop and finishing with the high office of the Premier. The love to work has to be implanted and England has to realize that it must not be satisfied with occupying a 2nd class seat and thinking that it is a first.

I am not criticizing. I love and admire and believe in England too much to be a critic, but it grieves me to see many things, which make for the disadvantage of England. This 'muddling through' which is almost glorified as a national virtue cannot last for ever. In the present war this 'system' costs England many thousands of lives and the savings of two centuries.

From a letter to Alfred Zimmern. Manchester, 4 July 1915.

Jews in Turkish Palestine
I returned this morning from a tour of the Jewish colonies in Judea (Petach-Tikvah, Rishon-le-Zion, Rehovot). I very much regret not having gone to the colonies directly instead of spending 1½ days in Jaffa, where people concern themselves only with squabbles, gossip and homemade politics, and know only one thing: tearing everything apart. In the colonies one feels altogether different. It's worth a lifetime to

glimpse the work of Jewish hands, to see how, after twenty years of toil, former sand and swamps support flourishing orchards, to see Jewish farmers. I understood many things much better, more clearly; the potentiality of Palestine is immense. It is difficult to describe it, Verusenka; I must tell you all about it in the minutest detail, and transmit to you at least a little of the sunshine of Palestine. It is impossible not to feel well in a colony. My general conclusion is briefly the following: if everything progresses so slowly, with such difficulties, the fault lies not with the *soil of Palestine*, nor even with the political conditions in the country (indisputably difficult), but rather with *ourselves – and only ourselves*. If our Jewish capitalists, say even only the Zionist capitalists, were to invest their capital in Palestine, if only in part, there is no doubt that the lifeline of Palestine – all the coastal strip – would be in Jewish hands within twenty-five years. No force in the world would then be able to destroy what was built.

I am not shutting my eyes to the tremendous difficulties, the obstacles, the hard life, but my conviction is strong and unwavering. Let the Jews want it, and everything will be ours!
From a letter to his wife. Jaffa, 14 September 1907.

Jewish anti-Zionists
They have a perfect right to hold anti-national opinions, but the objectionable feature in their policy is, and it is this which fills me with great anxiety, that whereas they themselves won't do anything to further the Zionist or even the Palestinian cause, they will try their utmost to hamper us in our work when the decisive moment comes. Of course, their opposition is illogical; if people say that they are not nationalist Jews, they have no right to prevent other people from acting as nationalist Jews, especially as they are a small minority, I would say a plutocratic oligarchy, living in the West, detached from the masses in the East, from the sorrows and joys of these masses, from their aspirations and ideals. These Western organizations have built up a series of institutions and formulae, which they call 'Judaism', which is free of any real Jewish contents. The Synagogue in the West, which is practically the only powerful symbol of Judaism, is nothing but a copy of the Church, and it is the aspiration and ambition of the heads of the synagogues in most cases to make it as near to the Church as possible. The communities here have done nothing to stop the slow but sure process of disintegration, which is going on and finds itself expressed in baptism, mixed marriages, etc. They have done nothing to foster and develop Jewish learning, Jewish literature, Jewish knowledge, and in this way the Anglo-French communities have fallen far behind even the

German assimilant communities. Whereas you can point in Germany to a magnificent series of great Jewish names, who have excelled and are excelling in Jewish learning, you cannot find many either here or in France, especially in this country. The process of dissolution is only rendered less visible through the constant influx of people from the East.
From a letter to Moses Gaster. Manchester, 6 March 1915.

Meeting with Faisal
I made the acquaintance of Faisal, son of the King of the Hedjaz. He is the first real Arab nationalist I have met. He is a leader! He's quite intelligent and a very honest man, handsome as a picture! He is not interested in Palestine, but on the other hand he wants Damascus and the whole of northern Syria. He talked with great animosity against the French, who want to get their hands on Syria. He expects a great deal from collaboration with the Jews! He is contemptuous of the Palestinian Arabs whom he doesn't even regard as Arabs!

The country I passed through, where the Anglo-Arab army is now operating –'the south-eastern part of Transjordan – is a vast plain with plenty of water and absolutely nothing else: not a house or a hut or a tree. One sees only nomadic Bedouin. But the soil is very fertile and this vast stretch of land could become a granary for a great number of people. The climate there is wonderful, it's more than 2,000 metres above sea level. I went almost as far as the Turkish lines near Ma'an, I was in an Arab camp and watched the army's movements through field-glasses. The day I arrived a German plane flew over the Arab lines, threw out a white flag and landed, and a Turk brought a letter to the Shereef from Djemal Pasha. In the letter the Turks offered the Shereef heaps of gold.

The trip was extremely interesting, even though the voyage along the Red Sea, which lasted about five days there and back, was pretty tiring. Sometimes a wind would blow for hours from the glowing mountains of the Sinai Peninsula and you'd feel as if you were actually standing near a red-hot oven. I saw Sinai from a distance. It is a magnificent, menacing, bare rock. I saw it at sunset, and it was literally fiery red, sombre and imposing. I don't know, but it may be that feelings connected with all these places are so sacred and profound that everything seems more grandiose than it really is. And so in the evening after a heavy day, I sometimes walk alone on the beach near Jaffa and the sea. The evenings here are marvellous, even after a hot day. Absolute calm reigns. The wonderful Palestinian sky, the beautiful sea, the great silence – then indeed one seems to hear the voices of the dead

rising from the tomb, the voices of our prophets, sages and judges foretelling the future.
From a letter to his wife. Tel Aviv–Jaffa, 17 June 1918.

Recruiting staff for Zionist service
An Arab will take an administrative job at a very low salary. A Jew always comes to me with a long list of requests before he will do the Jewish people and myself a favour and accept any position below that of a general.
From a letter to Ahad Ha'am. Tel Aviv–Jaffa, 3 August 1918.

Boarding a transatlantic liner in the twenties
How fortunate that you did not accompany me on the launch on Saturday, and wisely returned to Exeter, where I hope you stayed safely. When we went to the harbour at 7.30 p.m., I was told that the launch would only be leaving at 10 p.m., because the boat was late. I returned to the hotel, had a light dinner, and tried to telephone Exeter, hoping to speak to you, but unfortunately it turned out that the telephone at Exeter was out of order, and I had to forgo that pleasure. I was feeling so extremely sad that I would have given a great deal to have heard your voices. At 10 we left, and would you believe it: the launch sailed out into the open sea, but still no ship! We tossed about in that small vessel for 1½ hours, and it became very cold and choppy. Finally, around midnight, the ship arrived, and the launch began manoeuvring towards the large boat. By this time the wind had become much stronger, most of the passengers were sick, and the small craft was rocking heavily. The French crew of the *Paris* gave our launch some senseless orders. At long last the English captain of our launch lost patience and demanded that the captain of the *Paris* come out and see for himself that one could not risk embarking the passengers, as it was quite impossible to lower the gangway. After a lengthy exchange of insults, very typical of the *entente cordiale*, the captain of the *Paris* put in an appearance and declared that it was very easy to fix a ladder, and that should the English refuse to do this he would leave the passengers to their fate and sail off. The poor passengers were by then so exhausted and frozen, so sick, that they would gladly have returned to Plymouth – I among them. At that moment our small craft struck the *Paris* with such violence that even the Frenchman saw reason and decided to take his large ship into port. So we returned to port, where the *Paris* joined us, and the passengers were embarked in five minutes. But by the time the whole business was over it was 3 a.m. On board the *Paris* we were given some hot coffee, and then I went immediately to bed, feeling very

angry, exhausted, frozen, and extremely sick.
From a letter to his family. SS Paris, *1 March 1923.*

How the Zionist Executive worked
I am all alone here. Halpern is down with influenza in Berlin and Feiwel is ill here. Both are in bed. There's a rumour that Sokolow is here, but nobody has seen him. If I want to take a decision, I stand in front of a mirror and hold a conference with my reflection, and that is how the 'organization' is run.
From a letter to Leonie and Alfred Landsberg. London, 2 November 1925.

The British administrator in Palestine
Directly we have trouble with the Arabs, the arbiter has got to be the British Government. I state this on the basis of very painful experience. We could get along with the British alone or the Arabs alone, but never with the British plus the Arabs. Not because they do not like us. We are a difficult people, the Arabs are easy. The British know how to handle them, they have a recipe with which they have built up their empire. We give the British trouble. We present innumerable problems. We make the administrator think. And when you make a man think every hour of the day he hates you for it. In Palestine, under the Samuel Administration, I had an excellent case to prove the point. The immigration officer, a splendid man, a *Goy*, a friend of mine doing his level best to further immigration, came to me and said: 'I have room for 400–600 Jews who should replace Egyptian labourers.' It was an excellent opportunity, but they would have had to work on *Shabbas*. So I had to argue with him about our Sabbath rules. He could not understand it. It was troublesome; he was disappointed. He meant to bring in 600 Jews; either they would have had to starve or the *Shabbas* would have had to go by the board. It is a typical case.
From a statement to American Zionists. New York, 10 April 1921.

This attempt to degrade the promise of a National Home for the Jewish people to minority status in an Arab Palestine is mainly due to the peculiar relationship between the British and the Arabs on the one side, and the British and the Jews on the other. The British in Palestine have never clearly explained to the Arab population the real meaning and implications of the Balfour Declaration; at best they have been rather apologetic about the policy they were appointed to carry out; at worst, some of them have been openly hostile to it. Among British administrators and politicians in the Near and Middle East, there is a school of thought which is all too ready to ascribe every difficulty encountered by

British policy in Egypt, India, or elsewhere, to the Jewish National Home in Palestine. The Arabs have been quick to seize on this evidence of weakness, and, with the help of the Axis Powers, have succeeded in whipping up an agitation which at times has assumed threatening dimensions. The Arabs had to be pacified at any price, and the Jews had to foot the bill. To the Palestinian administrator the Arab presents no problems; he is a 'native', and the methods which have proved their efficacy in various backward British dependencies can be applied to him with their usual success. The Jew does not fall into the same category. He has come to Palestine to construct there a modern civilization, and has brought with him a number of new, complex, and baffling problems. He is 'difficult', critical, always anxious to be trying something new, and he does not fit into the time-honoured framework of administrative routine which has proved serviceable in Nigeria or Iraq.

From an article in Foreign Affairs. *New York, January 1942.*

'Mein Kampf' and the English reader

I personally have not the slightest apprehension as to the effect of Hitler's book on English readers if they are presented with it in its entirety. I have subjected myself to the painful task of reading it from cover to cover, and I can only say that in the whole of my reading I have never encountered a literary production so abominable. I have not the slightest doubt as to what the average Englishman who reads the book, as it stands, will think of those comi-manic perorations, those crude commonplaces, those pseudo-scientific biological and historical generalizations, just as I have little doubt about the verdict of any average neurologist on the mentality of their author.

It is all the more distressing to find that by the method of careful selection employed, a number of fairly plausible passages have been arranged to give the impression to the English reader of *The Times* – who will not touch the book – that Hitler is perhaps rather a radical, but on the whole by no means unreasonable political thinker and agitator. I find it very painful to say so, but I am sure that anyone who reads the leading article in last Monday's *Times* can hardly help feeling that some such impression has already been made on at least one, and certainly most competent, reader of these extracts. The air of plausibility with which Hitler's allegations against the Jews are invested in the leading article's summary, the suggestion inevitably conveyed by it that Hitler's barbarism is something in the nature of a healthy reaction against a sordid and unmanly sexualism, attributed largely to the Jews (a suggestion reinforced to the minds of English readers by references to pacifist writings in this country) – all these must lead the reader of *The Times*, who from the daily reports of your Berlin Correspondent, and from all your previous editorial utterances, has been led to form a very definite picture of Hitlerism, to revise his conception, and see the Nazi creed in a much more favourable light. . . .

I should like to add one word about Hitler's reference to England. I know perfectly well that it is very easy to select from the book a string of quotations showing the author as a friend of the British Empire, and as an opponent of German overseas development. But I challenge any reader of the book to quote a single instance from any part of it which shows him to have any genuine appreciation of the real character of British democracy and the British Empire, or any real goodwill towards them. His estimates of the British Empire and of British policy are the well-known German commonplaces; Britain playing off one European power against another, maintaining the balance of power, designing policies of encirclement. He needs the support of Great Britain for an alliance against France, and for the establishment of a German Colonial Empire in Eastern Europe. Hence, he cynically urges that every concession should be made to conciliate British diplomacy in other spheres. The true character of British policy is as much a closed book to him as is the true meaning of the British democratic system, which he loses no opportunity of deriding. The conception of an Empire based on freedom and yet governed by order defies his intellectual and moral capacities.

From a letter to Geoffrey Dawson, editor of The Times. *London, 27 July 1933.*

Arranging a Zionist Actions Committee meeting

It was quite unnecessary to disturb my afternoon slumber by the telephone – which always gives me a jar – and to suggest beginning of Sept. in Palestine which BG ought to know by now is an impossible date for me. If 25 Aug. in Zurich is not suitable – and I would be happy if this were the case – let us have the AC in Palestine about a week or so before the Commission begins its work there. You know that I take a benevolent but very detached interest in the AC. . . . In reality I know what will happen. As soon as I have made my statement they will get a fit, the flood gates of eloquence will open, I shall be barged into; they will argue with me thinking I'm the Mandatory Power. In due course I shall be called a traitor. Being already hardened and immunized against such an appellation we shall part company on most affectionate but nevertheless decisive terms, each one of us trying for a better 'ole.

I don't see why we could not do it by correspondence. I'm prepared to write to the AC and be called names in absentia, which may be more convenient to both sides. They can be more outspoken and I need not listen to it.

In future – I mean in Carlsbad – I intend to go to a nursing home where telephones are non extant. What I thought of you when you woke me up this afternoon would make a sailor blush. I strongly urge you to take a holiday very soon for the good of yourself and everybody else.

From a letter to Arthur Lourie. Paris, 28 July 1936.

The desertion of the Jewish intelligentsia

I felt it would be a great accession of moral strength and a valuable source of technical knowledge if we could offer to the Hebrew University, or to the Sieff Institute, Albert Einstein the physicist, James Franck of Göttingen, the mathematician Hermann Weyl, the physicist Placzek, the chemist Wiegener, to mention but a few names. But somehow I failed to convince them. Some of them found homes in England, at Oxford, Cambridge, Manchester, Birmingham; others, as we have seen, in America. That was comprehensible; but there were other places chosen in preference to Palestine which were utterly beyond me.

Zurich was the centre which dealt with academic refugees, and thither I went to consult the members of the Swiss committee. There I learned early one morning that James Franck was in the city, a refugee – and that he and his wife were breakfasting with my friend, Professor Richard Baer, the physicist. Without waiting for an invitation I barged in on them and found the two gentlemen and Mrs Franck immersed in a discussion about the merits of going to – Turkey! Whether Franck was considering the idea for himself, or whether he was recommending it to others, I couldn't make out, but at that moment I entirely lost my good manners. I could not contain myself, and exclaimed: 'I can understand it if you want to go to Oxford, Cambridge, New York or Chicago. But if you go to Turkey you will find the scientific conditions there much worse than in Palestine – you might as well accept our invitation to go to Palestine.' Franck objected that there was no security of tenure in Palestine, to which I promptly replied that tenure in Palestine would be more secure than in most other countries – not excluding the Western ones. 'It is true,' I said, 'our university has not got government support, but if men like you came out, a great physics institute would be built round you, and after a certain time you would not lack for anything.'

It was interesting to watch Mrs Franck during this conversation. She was a Swedish Jewess, very blonde, and obviously very proud of her

'Nordic' descent. She thought that I was trying to reduce her husband to a condition too awful for words. She kept looking daggers at me, and I had to give up the consultation. I felt then as I had felt in the early days of Zionism. Just as the rich Jews never came to us until we were a 'practical' proposition, so these intellectually rich Jews thought that Palestine would be detrimental to their careers. True, the German catastrophe had greatly altered the situation, and Palestine was absorbing more refugees than all other countries combined; yet the inertia, the weight of prejudice, was such that many of them preferred Turkey to the Hebrew University in Palestine.
From Trial and Error.

It was my hope that now, of all times, the great Jewish intellectuals would rally round the Palestine effort. They would have a great contribution to make just now, and the unhappy people is entitled to look to its great and gifted sons for vigorous support; but – and I must be forgiven this comparison – just as those in possession of earthly goods have come to us either not at all or in small numbers, so those intellectually blessed are slow in coming. In the war the best went into the battlefield; never before has such a war of annihilation been forecast for a people as it has been for us – and yet not all have come!

I hope you will not hold these candid words against me! I wish you good health and hope that you will soon come to us, if only for a long visit.

Toscanini was here; he came despite his great age and regardless of all obstacles; he brought us comfort. I believe one is justified in applying to him the words of Anatole France: *Pour un moment il était la conscience humaine.*
From a letter to Albert Einstein. Rehovot, 28 April 1938.

The Hollywood phenomenon
Two great organs shape public opinion, like the moving picture industry and the broadcasting systems, and both are controlled by Jews. As for the first, this control is in hands, into which one would not like to entrust such a delicate and important mechanism, which could accomplish a great deal in the direction of a proper education of the American people. It is not surprising that well-educated Americans, free from prejudice, resent bitterly such a phenomenon like Hollywood, of which I caught a glimpse during my tour. I am certain that the others would on a whole produce an equally unpleasant Hollywood, but they are the majority – are always right; and we, the minority, are always wrong.
From a letter to Felix Frankfurter. Arrowhead Springs, California, 21 June 1941.

Echoes of gunfire

The last sentence of my remarks was punctuated by the noise of gunfire. It is the second time in my life that this has happened. In July 1918 it was my great privilege to lay the foundation stone of the Hebrew University on Mount Scopus, and every sentence of my short speech was punctuated by guns which were easily to be heard on the mountains – though they were five or six miles away. These guns led to an overwhelming victory, and I hope the guns we have heard today are the precursors of the victory to come.

Concluding an address to the Board of Deputies of British Jews. London, 18 June 1944.

6
Advocate of his People

Before the creation of the State of Israel in 1948 the Zionist movement was severely handicapped by its lack of diplomatic status. Its representatives did not enjoy the courtesies of automatic access to national leaders, and it frequently had to resort to intermediaries to plead its cause. Weizmann, however, developed close relationships with many world statesmen. He could thus lay his case directly before many of the most powerful men of his time (though Churchill refused to help him secure an interview with Stalin early in 1945) and the movement reflected in their eyes the character and personality of its advocate. Weizmann's effectiveness in this regard was the basis of his strength in the Jewish world. It also bred resentment among Jews who denied the validity of Zionism or who subscribed to the cause but opposed his policies and style of leadership.

The statesmen named below featured prominently in Weizmann's activities to secure international endorsement for the Jews' return to Palestine.

Arthur James Balfour
Weizmann's introduction to Balfour was effected by Charles Dreyfus, who was leader both of the Jewish community and the Conservative Party in Manchester when the young chemist arrived there in 1904. The British Prime Minister met Weizmann very briefly in January 1905, an encounter evidently omitted from the latter's recollection when he wrote his memoirs *Trial and Error*. Their second meeting was in January 1906. Balfour's government was dissolved and the Conservative leader was fighting a General Election that resulted in a Liberal landslide and cost him his seat in Parliament. Balfour was not then popular with the Jewish community, as it was during his administration that an Aliens Act reducing East European immigration was passed in 1905.

No contemporary record exists of what transpired at that meeting, and many years were to elapse before Weizmann described it in the terms which have come down to us as including the statement 'we had Jerusalem when London was a marsh'. Balfour must have retained a vivid recollection of that encounter, as is evidenced by his readiness to talk to Weizmann again in December 1914, when the Zionist, having embarked on his plan for an alliance with Britain, requested an interview. It was at this meeting that Weizmann brought the other abreast with all that had transpired in Zionism since their earlier talk, and Balfour confessed to sharing many of the anti-semitic views of Cosima Wagner, widow of the composer.

In May 1915 Balfour became First Lord of the Admiralty in the Coalition Government of Herbert Asquith, and although he had had another discussion with Weizmann the previous March, he did not concern himself with the Zionist question until he was appointed Foreign Secretary in the Lloyd George Cabinet – late in 1916. At their meeting on 22 March 1917 Weizmann perceived that Balfour, while sympathetic towards a Jewish return to Palestine, was not at all anxious for British participation in the endeavour. He spoke repeatedly that year of difficulties with the French and the Italians, and was reaching the view that these two Powers could be assuaged only if the Americans joined the British in assuming responsibility for Palestine.

Only with the issuance of the Declaration which bears his name did the Foreign Secretary realize the purport which the Jews, and the Arabs, would attach to it. He had by now developed great personal regard for Weizmann, who kept in close contact with him until the San Remo Conference of April 1920, which awarded the Mandate to Britain. When Balfour visited Palestine formally to open the Hebrew University in 1925 he was greeted rapturously by the Jews, though to the Arabs his name was anathema.

Weizmann's relations with Balfour brought an unexpected dividend for Zionism in the devotion he won from Mrs Blanche (Baffy) Dugdale, the British statesman's niece and biographer. She gave Weizmann shrewd advice as his confidential counsellor. She advanced his cause powerfully through her family ties, which were numerous in the British ruling class, and through her political influence, which permeated all three political parties. She recorded that Weizmann was her uncle's last visitor outside his nearest circle at his death-bed in 1930.

David Lloyd George
Lloyd George's connection with Zionism dated from Herzl's day. A Liberal MP and solicitor, he was commissioned by Leopold Greenberg in May 1903 to draft a charter for the proposed Jewish settlement in

East Africa (the 'Uganda Scheme'). His first meeting with Weizmann, in January 1915, was initiated by C. P. Scott of the *Manchester Guardian*. Lloyd George realized the significance Zionism could have for British interests in the Middle East when this was first put to him some months earlier by his Cabinet colleague Herbert Samuel.

As Minister of Munitions, Lloyd George discussed Britain's shortage of explosives with Weizmann in June 1915. He decided to implement the latter's acetone process and brought the chemist down to London from Manchester to supervise manufacture. Weizmann later took pains to deny that the Balfour Declaration was a reward for his scientific work (see p. 185). In fact he was granted a substantial royalty for this work after the war, and there is no evidence that his success in the one endeavour had any bearing on the other.

Nevertheless, Weizmann's scientific responsibilities opened doors for him in Whitehall and facilitated his approaches to Lloyd George, who became Prime Minister in December 1916 and was able to overrule the opposition of some members of his Cabinet to specific British identification with Zionism. He also had the will to disregard the French contention that Palestine's destiny was already settled by the Sykes-Picot Agreement.

Weizmann pressed Lloyd George for a public statement of support, both in personal discussions early in 1917 and through various intermediaries in addition to Scott. On 3 April 1917 the war leader emphasized to Weizmann his determination that Palestine should become British, and that Jewish soldiers should be employed in a swift campaign to capture Jerusalem, rather than be sent to the Western Front.

The Jew was now on the firmest ground. He saw Lloyd George again on his return from Gibraltar, where he had been the official British representative delegated to frustrate the Morgenthau mission for a separate Turkish peace. He was finally able, by a personal appeal to the Prime Minister, to have the protracted Cabinet debate on Palestine concluded, and despatch by Balfour of his Declaration was approved on 31 October 1917.

Critical days still lay ahead, but at San Remo in April 1920 Lloyd George sealed an arrangement previously made with Clemenceau that Palestine would become a British Mandate, and it was in part through Weizmann's representations that Samuel was appointed High Commissioner.

Lloyd George lost the General Election of October 1922 and never held office again, although his prestige remained undiminished. His spell-binding oratory was turned to the benefit of Zionism for many years afterwards, in America as well as England. He spoke out in Parliament to describe British policy in Palestine as a betrayal of the Balfour Declaration, specifying Weizmann's contribution to British victory in the Great War. He signed an appeal in support of the Palestine Fund for German Jewry in May 1933.

Speaking to a brief prepared by Weizmann, Lloyd George testified *in camera* to the Royal (Peel) Commission in April 1937, though he opposed the partition scheme advanced in its report. His final tribute to Weizmann appears as a Foreword to a book commemorating the Zionist leader's seventieth birthday, edited by Paul Goodman and published in London in 1945.

Prince Faisal of Hedjaz

As field commander of Arab troops in revolt against Turkey on behalf of his father the Shereef of Mecca, Faisal was the first Arab of true authority with whom Weizmann negotiated. The Jewish leader travelled in June 1918 to the Arab headquarters at Waheida, near Ma'an (see p. 209) and there discussed general lines of future co-operation with Faisal. To the relief of the British authorities in Cairo, the meeting went off well, although Faisal refrained from expressing views on the Palestine question. He wrote to Brigadier Sir Gilbert Clayton, Chief Political Officer of the Egyptian Expeditionary Force, on 2 August 1918: 'As to the good reception we showed Dr Weizmann, we consider that we have done nothing but our duty towards him. Moreover, courtesy imposes upon us the duty of welcoming such an illustrious man when he comes into our midst.'

The Balfour Declaration had been a rude shock to the Arabs, and Weizmann endeavoured to strengthen relations with Faisal through a formal agreement. The two had three meetings in London, at the last of which, on 3 January 1919, they signed a document which recognized the Balfour Declaration and foreshadowed definite boundaries between Faisal's contemplated Arab State and Palestine (see Appendix D). However, this agreement contained a reservation, in Arabic in Faisal's hand and translated by T. E. Lawrence, to the effect that its fulfilment depended on the achievement of Arab aspirations as had been conveyed to the British. Faisal abstained from demanding all Asia Minor when he appeared before the Supreme Allied Council at the Peace Conference on 6 February 1919.

Faisal perceived that Anglo-French plans for a division of the Turkish Empire did not conform to his ambitions for a great independent Arabia, and in an interview with *Le Matin*, on 1 March 1919, he opposed sovereign rights for the Jews in Palestine. The same day Weizmann, with Felix Frankfurter, won a partial retraction. Faisal signed a letter to Frankfurter, published in the *New York Times* of 5 March 1919, stating that both the Jewish and Arab movements were not imperialist but nationalist, and 'there is room in Syria for us both'. It was not his last word. He gave an interview to the London *Jewish Chronicle* on 3 October 1919 asserting that Palestine belonged to the Arabs and would be an inseparable part of their kingdom.

Faisal took steps to make himself ruler of such a kingdom, which British officials in Cairo and Jerusalem wished to have recognized, even though this would bring Britain into conflict with France. Weizmann exerted every effort to prevent recognition of Faisal as king of a united Syria, and in a letter of 31 March 1920 he described the Arab leader to Sir Louis Bols, head of the military administration in Palestine, as follows: 'Two years ago he was a Bedouin sheikh, a capable but modest soldier; at present he is attempting to play the role of a Near Eastern Napoleon and to set up an Arab Empire from the Euphrates to the Nile.'

France drove Faisal out of Damascus in July 1920 and the following year Britain compensated her Arab ally with the kingdom of Iraq.

Jan C. Smuts

Joining the Imperial War Cabinet in June 1917, the South African soldier-statesman at once embraced the principle of a Jewish National Home. In this he required no persuasion from Weizmann, whom he met in September 1917; he was that rare phenomenon among Boer leaders, a dedicated British imperialist. Smuts believed that the Jews' return to Palestine would strengthen a vital artery of empire, and for this reason he also favoured Vladimir Jabotinsky's plan for a Jewish Legion.

As one of those responsible for the Balfour Declaration Smuts ever after remained its faithful adherent. He visited Palestine early in 1918 and from then his association with Weizmann ripened into close friendship. This was reinforced over the years by frequent correspondence, his regular trips to England, and by Weizmann's own visit to South Africa in 1932.

This privileged relationship gave the Zionist powerful leverage in his conflicts with successive British governments, and was used with effect also at the League of Nations and the United Nations. Smuts was recognized internationally as a moral force. His voice was heard in 1929 and 1930 when he intervened at Weizmann's behest in the crisis with Britain over the riots in Palestine and the subsequent Passfield White Paper, returning to the fray when Weizmann charged the British with betrayal of the Mandate in the MacDonald White Paper of 1939. Smuts was exceptionally well-informed on the Palestine problem, and recognized his responsibilities as a friend both of the British and the Jews.

His position on the ultimate destiny of Palestine wavered. He opposed the Peel Commission's recommendation of partition, but accepted this solution, as did Churchill, when he joined the latter's War Cabinet late in 1943. Official Zionist policy (the 'Biltmore Programme') was then for a Jewish Commonwealth in the whole of Palestine, but in 1945, following a stay in the Middle East, Smuts, to Weizmann's dismay, told the Jew that he favoured continuance of the Mandate, possibly with American participation so that the two Powers could together control immigration. Then in July 1947 he wrote to Weizmann, in a letter which the latter included in his testimony to the UN Special Committee, that

> we cannot undo the past, and can only try to find a better way to the future. As I told you in London last year I see now, at this sad stage, no escape except by way of partition. I was long for an undivided Palestine, but after all these failures and missed opportunities I see no other way out of the present impasse. Only yesterday, speaking in our Parliament, I expressed myself publicly in favour of this solution – if solution it is. Palestine never was undivided in the great past, and perhaps a fair share of it for Jewry may once more be the nucleus of a National Home and a Holy Land. . . . It must be a heartbreaking misery for you to live amid all that scene of frustration and suffering, of lawlessness and counter-lawlessness – you who have laboured so hard and so long to enter upon the Promised Land.
>
> I blame no one, I praise no one. I only pray that the Great Mercy will once more come, and wash out even the memory of these years.

Smuts probably felt a personal guilt. He had never opposed the policy of his own country in almost totally barring entry to Jewish refugees. The point was not lost on Ernest Bevin when Smuts came to him to plead the Zionist cause, and the British Foreign Secretary spoke bitterly of it during a House of Commons debate on 25 February 1947.

During the UN deliberations on Palestine in 1947 Smuts particularly requested Weizmann, then out of office, to be on hand in New York and be available for consultation by the South African delegation. Two years later the South African elder statesman, now seventy-nine and in failing health, flew to London to be principal speaker at a banquet to launch the campaign for a Weizmann Forest in Israel.

Winston Churchill
Contesting a Manchester seat in the General Election of December

1905, Churchill took pains to cultivate the Jewish voters there. He addressed a protest meeting against the Russian pogroms, sharing the platform with Moses Gaster and a young foreigner who spoke in Yiddish. That foreigner was Weizmann, Churchill's contemporary in age. Shortly afterwards Churchill sent a request to the chemist enlisting his influence among the Jewish electorate. A discussion on Zionism ensued.

Churchill is on record during the next few years as a Zionist supporter, but to no significant extent. Following the Russian Revolution he was as War Minister concerned with Britain's interventionist policy there, and he publicly criticized Jews who demonstrated Bolshevist sympathies. His period as Colonial Secretary, February 1921 to October 1922, was a time of considerable Arab unrest in Palestine, to which he reacted with a 'neutralism' towards Zionism. Churchill recognized the validity of Zionist aspirations and emphasized Britain's loyalty to the Balfour Declaration, but his attitude was strongly qualified by the need to allay Arab fears. At his meetings with Weizmann he impressed upon the Zionist leader the urgency of a Jewish-Arab rapprochement.

Weizmann reluctantly accepted the Churchill White Paper of June 1922. This document was designed to retain faith with the Jews and simultaneously give assurances to the Arabs by promising the beginnings of Palestinian self-government. The Jews opposed such a step for it would condemn them to permanent minority status, but a more severe blow was the removal of Transjordan from the area commonly accepted as Palestine in September of that year. This denied them access to the major part of the Holy Land.

Weizmann was convinced that Churchill, who was in the political wilderness in the decade 1929–39, could become a valuable friend. In 1936 the two men were fellow-passengers on an aeroplane, and this gave Weizmann an opportunity to renew their acquaintance. His verdict was that Churchill 'is quite sound'. The following year Churchill gave evidence to the Peel Commission and affirmed that his White Paper contained nothing to prohibit the ultimate establishment of a Jewish State.

Churchill's great esteem for the Zionist leader dates from a briefing given him by Weizmann on 23 May 1939, during the House of Commons debate on the 1939 (MacDonald) White Paper. Churchill's speech that day was a *tour de force*, raising his standing in British public life. It rallied the opponents of the policy (many of them, like Churchill himself, Conservatives) and sent the Chamberlain Government into confusion.

The inclusion of Churchill in the Cabinet on the outbreak of war in 1939 gave Weizmann a powerful ally at the centre of authority, and he promptly submitted the Zionists' demands to the new First Lord of the Admiralty. These were: the formation of a Jewish Army under its own flag to fight the common enemy; the utilization of Palestine's industrial resources, particularly in pharmaceuticals; and the abandonment or postponement of the MacDonald White Paper so as to increase immigration and buy land unrestricted in Palestine at a time of great peril to European Jewry. Churchill nominated Brendan Bracken, his adviser and close friend, to be his liaison with the Zionist Organization. He notified the War Office that he supported the Jewish Army plan and opposed the White Paper. But all to no avail.

Though he himself became Prime Minister in May 1940 to enjoy a prestige vouchsafed no national leader in Britain since Lloyd George, Churchill proved powerless to change the situation in Palestine or help the Jews in their European torment. He told Weizmann at their meeting on 12 March 1941 that whenever they met it gave him 'a twist in his heart'. But he made a pledge that 'he would see Weizmann through', and he further advised the Zionist leader to come to an agreement with King Ibn Saud, who after the war would be made 'boss of the bosses' in the Arab world. Weizmann was then nursing a similar idea, and he left the Prime Minister in elated mood. However, Churchill and Roosevelt separately discussed Zionism with Ibn Saud following the Yalta Conference of February 1945, but could not move the Arab king.

Throughout the war Churchill remained deeply aware of his commitment to Weizmann, and more particularly so after the Zionist's younger son, an RAF pilot, was lost on a mission in February 1942. He would describe himself as one of the 'authors' of Zionist policy. In a cable to Roosevelt in August 1942, when the American President was giving strong indication of a pro-Arab stance in the post-war Middle East, he stated that he was 'strongly wedded' to Zionist policy.

In August 1944 Churchill finally overcame his colleagues' objections and acceded to Weizmann's representations for a Jewish military formation. Three months later he gave Weizmann good reason to believe that a solution by partition would be found for the Palestine question. Unhappily, two days after this hopeful meeting, 6 November 1944, Churchill's close friend Lord Moyne was assassinated by Jewish terrorists in Cairo. He then refused to consider the problem further, and left it as a tragic legacy to the Attlee Government.

Woodrow Wilson
Despite the efforts of Louis D. Brandeis and Stephen Wise, the

American Jewish leaders closest to him, President Wilson withheld public endorsement of the Jewish National Home policy, both before and after the Balfour Declaration was issued. His inhibition stemmed from a reluctance to alienate the Turks and a distrust of Anglo-French intentions regarding the Ottoman Empire. This situation, which also prevented Americans from joining Weizmann's Zionist Commission to Palestine in 1918, continued until the end of the war, though on 31 August 1918 Wilson complied with a request from Wise to give him a letter praising the work of Weizmann and the Commission.

Arrangements for a Zionist delegation to appear at the Paris Peace Conference were well advanced, but a Presidential statement recognizing the Zionist desire to return to Palestine under British trusteeship was still lacking. This caused acute anxiety both to Weizmann and the British statesmen.

A change at last occurred when Weizmann had a meeting with Wilson in Paris on 14 January 1919. Interviewed by the *Jewish Chronicle* on 17 January, Weizmann stated that the US President had given him 'assurances of cordial support for the British Declaration', and that Wilson had promised support also for a Jewish Palestine, 'full and unhampered'. This by no means constituted a commitment to British trusteeship, though a diary note by Lawrence (in *The Letters of T. E. Lawrence*, ed. David Garnett) indicated a move in this direction. Lawrence wrote: 'Weizmann was asked by Wilson how he got on with the British – he said so well that he wanted them as his trustee. Then how he got on with the French. He said he knew French perfectly, but he could not understand, or make himself understood by, the French politicians. "Exactly what I find," said Wilson.'

Two days after that meeting Wilson wrote to Felix Frankfurter declaring absolutely that he supported the British Government regarding Palestine. Late in February 1919 the Jews were given, in Wilson's phrase to Weizmann, 'their day in court'. Neither Lloyd George nor Wilson was present at this sitting of the Supreme Allied Council (the 'Council of Ten') and Clemenceau left soon after it began. But at the instance of Robert Lansing, US Secretary of State, Weizmann was given ample opportunity to develop his ideas for the National Home.

Wilson's attitude gave rise to further anxiety. An American Commission (on which both Britain and France refused to be represented) was sent out to investigate the desires of the people of Syria and Palestine regarding their future. It brought back a strongly anti-Zionist report and was hostile also to Britain and France, who were about to proceed with the dismemberment of the Empire under the Mandatory cover for which they desired Wilson's consent. Weizmann was marshalling all available influence for a frontier in northern Palestine that embraced the rich waters there. He could not rely on Britain to resist French intentions in this regard.

Wilson had by now assumed a position of detachment from those Near Eastern arrangements, though Brandeis cabled Weizmann on 16 February 1920, just before the San Remo Conference, that the President had instructed his ambassador in Paris to make 'oral representations' to the French concerning Zionist frontier desiderata. In the event, the ultimate boundary between Palestine and her northern neighbours resulted from an Anglo-French compromise, and the life-giving waters of that region were denied to the Jews.

Léon Blum

Between the wars the policy of France regarding Zionism was guided principally by anxieties regarding the Moslem mood in her North African possessions, and by the difficulties she experienced with her Mandates for Lebanon and Syria. Also, the French Jewish community evinced only the weakest sentiment for Zionism. It thus happened that Palestine ceased to be a question of acute interest to the French. But from the early 1920s Léon Blum maintained a close friendship with Weizmann and actively helped the cause, joining the enlarged Jewish Agency on its establishment in 1929.

He strongly supported Weizmann when, contrary to the impression given in *Trial and Error*, the Zionist leader took up with alacrity a suggestion by the High Commissioner for Syria and Lebanon, Henri de Jouvenel, that the Jews establish colonies on land under his jurisdiction. This was in 1926, but Weizmann would do so only in locations close to Palestine. Understandably, the French were reluctant, fearing a Zionist irredentist movement. They desired the colonies to be situated in remote regions near the Euphrates.

With Blum's intercession Weizmann discussed the subject repeatedly with the leading statesmen of France, always receiving the same response. In 1936, when Blum was himself Premier, Jewish need was growing increasingly urgent, because of Hitler and the restrictions about to be placed on Jewish immigration to Palestine. Moreover, no other country would open its gates to substantial numbers of refugees. Pressed by Weizmann, Blum took the view that the Zionists might come to a direct arrangement with the Lebanese, then being given a degree of self-government under an amenable Christian President. It was now too late: the Middle East as a whole was seething with unrest and the Arab rebellion in Palestine was having its repercussions on all neighbouring states.

Weizmann invoked Blum's aid, not always with effect, in successive conflicts with the British, and most particularly in his desperate efforts to prevent implementation of the MacDonald White Paper of 1939. When the French statesman was imprisoned by the Vichy regime in September 1940, Weizmann sought to help him by despatching an urgent plea to Stephen Wise, who was close to Roosevelt, to ensure Blum's protection.

The attitude of France during the UN deliberations on the partition proposals of 1947 was crucial to the outcome, for France could influence a large following of Catholic states. She temporized, again for fear of Moslem reaction, and her abstention from the vote seemed likely. Weizmann secured Blum's intervention with the Premier, Paul Ramadier, and the Foreign Minister, Georges Bidault, and this helped to produce a positive vote from France.

Benito Mussolini

To the Italian dictator went the distinction of being the first national leader to suggest the creation of a Jewish State. This is omitted from Weizmann's acount of three meetings with Mussolini given in *Trial and Error*. It occurred at their second meeting, on 26 April 1933 (wrongly dated in *Trial and Error* as the eve of *Yom Kippur*) when Weizmann came to enlist the other's intercession with Hitler on behalf of the Jews of Germany. Mussolini spoke of the possible transfer of 50,000 German Jews to Palestine.

Weizmann had first met the Italian shortly after Mussolini's accession to power, and used the occasion to improve Zionist standing with the Permanent Mandates Commission of the League of Nations, for the Italian representative on that body, Count Theodoli, was hostile to Zionism. At their third meeting on 17 February 1934 Mussolini returned to the benefits of partitioning Palestine, stating his conviction that only then would the Jews lose their vulnerability.

Mussolini revealed that he had broached the idea with the Arabs. Provided difficulties regarding Jerusalem could be surmounted, an entente might be reached. The Arab position, he said, was that the Jews would have to place their capital in Tel Aviv. Weizmann thereupon asserted that if Jerusalem could not be the Jewish capital, equally the Christian world would not allow it to be the Arab capital. He also intimated that if Italy were to give the Jews her support at the stage of practicability, there would be economic advantages for Italy in the existence of a strong and friendly Jewish community in Palestine.

Franklin D. Roosevelt

Weizmann's first meeting with Roosevelt, on 8 February 1940, left the Zionist leader with the impression that his movement had a reliable friend in the American President: the partnership of Roosevelt and Churchill would silence all Arab opposition to the establishment of a Jewish State. He clung to this view, which was reinforced by periodic reports from Stephen Wise, until it was shown to be false by Roosevelt himself in 1945.

Thus Weizmann ascribed Roosevelt's failure to pronounce favourably for a Jewish State, or condemn the MacDonald White Paper, to the pro-Arab orientation of the State Department's Near Eastern Division, which seemed a mirror image of the British Colonial Office. Roosevelt refrained from exerting influence on Palestine's affairs despite the strong Zionist sentiment of such members of his inner circle as Justice Brandeis (who died in 1941), Felix Frankfurter and Benjamin V. Cohen. These men, Anglophile in all else, had long condemned the London government on grounds of partiality towards the Arabs. It is noteworthy that American Jews, in their reverence for Roosevelt, forebore to apply any pressure on the White House although they maintained an active propaganda arm on Capitol Hill.

Weizmann himself believed he might gain more concrete assistance from the President through the scientific back door. He brought a process to America for the production of synthetic rubber, previously rejected by the British. In the course of a meeting with Roosevelt on 7 July 1942 he indicated that America was not being well served in this matter and that an enquiry should be instituted. Simultaneously, he raised the question of Palestine, and spoke of his frustration at lack of headway in forming a Jewish Division. Roosevelt expressed support for a Jewish formation but defended British hesitation which, he said, sprang from fear lest the move incite the Egyptians, to the detriment of the Middle East campaign. Weizmann told Roosevelt that this was merely an excuse.

In the event, Roosevelt acted on Weizmann's advice regarding rubber, and a committee was set up under Bernard Baruch to investigate the processes available. This exposed a hornets' nest of competing interests among the oil and agricultural industries. Weizmann's process failed to find a champion, except in the person of Vice-President Henry Wallace (see p. 187).

Weizmann remained in America for an extended period during the war in order to consolidate American Jewish strength behind Zionism and to organize his Washington lobby, for which he found useful friends in the Secretary of the Treasury, Henry Morgenthau Jr, and Under-Secretary of State Sumner Welles. But the President himself was subordinating the Jewish problem to what he considered a larger American interest. He was engaged upon a policy of converting Saudi Arabia into his client-state so as to place the kingdom's oil resources under his country's unrivalled control.

Welles brought Weizmann to the President again on 11 June 1943. Roosevelt told the Jewish leader that he had discussed Palestine with Churchill, and they had decided on a joint effort to persuade the Arabs, 'who were purchaseable', to accept a Jewish homeland. No commitment was given, but an American envoy was sent out to test Ibn Saud's reaction. Six weeks later Wise had a discussion with Roosevelt about the desperate Jewish situation in Europe and Palestine's role in its solution. Wise hoped a change was presaged in White House attitudes when the President said: 'I like Weizmann very much – he is very able man.'

As it happened, 1944 was an election year in America, and Wise, unfailingly loyal to Roosevelt, was no longer the unquestioned leader of American Zionism. Abba Hillel Silver, a Republican, was now the most aggressive Zionist figure in the United States, and was enrolling allies among Roosevelt's enemies with a success that alarmed the Democratic Party machine. Roosevelt felt constrained to issue a statement saying 'the American Government has never given its approval to the White Paper'. He reinforced this with a specific commitment on Jewish independence by making the Biltmore Programme of 1942 (which demanded Palestine as a Jewish Commonwealth) a plank of his election platform.

It was a move of cynical opportunism. Following his meeting with Ibn Saud after the Yalta Conference Roosevelt, in an address to Congress, stated: 'Of the problems of Arabia, I learnt more about the whole problem, the Moslem problem, the Jewish problem, by talking with Ibn Saud for five minutes than I could have learned in an exchange of two or three dozen letters.' Weizmann and the Jews of America were shocked. Within a month Roosevelt was dead.

King Ibn Saud

Weizmann's faith in a possible arrangement with Ibn Saud may have been based in part on wishful thinking, to repeat his earlier success with the Hashemite Prince Faisal. But there were also solid grounds for such a hope.

At a meeting in London with Ibn Saud's British adviser and confidant, Harry St John Philby, in October 1939, Weizmann was informed that the king might be amenable to the whole of Western Palestine being handed over to the Jews, except for a 'Vatican City' in the old city of Jerusalem. Ibn Saud would require in return Jewish support for a united, independent Arabia under his rule. Weizmann would make no commitment of a political nature that might conflict with British and French interests. He nevertheless told Philby that any agreement with the Arab leader which would help the Zionists to solve the Jewish problem was bound to evoke international goodwill after the war.

Philby referred to Ibn Saud's financial difficulties, and intimated that a subsidy of £20 millions be made to Ibn Saud, partly in the form of weapons. Little more was heard of the proposal until 1943, though Churchill's personal advice to Weizmann that he come to an agreement with the man who was to be 'boss of the bosses' (see p. 224) encouraged Weizmann to believe it was realistic. He informed State Department officials accordingly in January 1943.

Roosevelt's special envoy, Harold B. Hoskins, arrived in Saudi Arabia in July 1943. He reported that Ibn Saud delivered an angry rebuttal to the idea. This acutely embarrassed Weizmann, who had been urged by Philby to retain the strictest confidentiality. According to Hoskins, Ibn Saud was particularly distressed by the suggestion that he would stoop to a 'bribe', and this now placed Philby in the royal disgrace. This construction of the king's attitude to him was fiercely repudiated by Philby, who was later a guest at the palace and received a friendly letter from Ibn Saud.

Weizmann's subsequent position was that the solution of the Jewish problem could not await the concurrence of any Arab leader, but depended on the determination of the victorious allies alone.

Harry S. Truman

The government of Clement Attlee and Ernest Bevin, which followed Churchill's defeat of July 1945 in Britain, shocked the Zionists because it would not fulfil its policy, repeatedly affirmed at Labour Party conferences, of rescinding the White Paper and establishing a Jewish State. The Jews were demanding the immediate immigration of 100,000 European survivors, but were given equivocal replies. As a result the Jews of Palestine, despite Weizmann's opposition, undertook armed resistance against the British.

The United States was now the all-powerful leader of the West, and American Zionism was influential as never before. President Truman had already requested Churchill to allow the 100,000 into Palestine, though his first public statement, made on 16 August 1945, that 'I have no desire to send half a million American soldiers there to make peace', filled Weizmann with disgust.

How to turn Truman's undeniable goodwill into positive intervention on behalf of the Jews? Weizmann appealed to his friends in Washington, notably Henry Morgenthau Jr, and soon Truman was persuaded to send Earl Harrison to investigate the plight of Displaced Persons in Europe. When this envoy returned with a strong recommendation for action to evacuate the 100,000 to Palestine, the President placed all his authority behind it, though he would not say, in so many words, that he was in favour of a Jewish State. Attlee's response was to invite the Americans to share in a new enquiry. Thus the Anglo-American Committee began its work in January 1946. Weizmann meanwhile had had his first interview with Truman, on 4 December 1945, and had furnished the President with the entire Zionist argument.

Britain, resentful of Zionist agitation in New York (the Jews there were clamouring for the opening of the gates of Palestine while America herself kept her gates virtually closed against Jewish refugees), had thus ensnared America into a degree of responsibility for Palestine. The Anglo-American Committee, in its unanimous report of April 1946, asked for the immediate immigration of the 100,000 though not for a Jewish State – rather, continuation of the British Mandate. Attlee stated on 1 May 1946 that the report as a whole could be adopted only if the Americans shared the military and financial burdens entailed, and if the Jews would disband their 'private armies' and surrender their arms.

Manifestly, Truman would not send soldiers to the Middle East, but he was under great pressure to make Britain more amenable to Zionist demands. This was a Congressional election year and the Democratic Party feared a mass defection of supporters in reaction to the long Roosevelt era. Truman went so far as to send another special envoy, Henry F. Grady, to work with the British on a solution to the Palestine problem acceptable to Arabs and Jews. Out of this collaboration was born the [Herbert] Morrison–Grady Plan for a form of cantonization under British trusteeship, and it was rejected by both sides in the conflict. Anxious to please the Jews, Truman then issued a statement (4 October 1946) in which he thought a compromise could be reached between the Morrison–Grady Plan and a Jewish State.

Weizmann wished to make this the basis for further negotiations with Britain, but he was overruled by the Zionist Congress of December 1946, with the consequence that he ceased to be Jewish Agency President. David Ben-Gurion continued the talks unofficially nevertheless. These terminated without agreement, and relations between British and Jews in Palestine deteriorated still further. Bevin therefore submitted the problem to the United Nations. Events now began to move more swiftly. In August 1947 the UN Special Committee (Unscop) decided by majority verdict that Britain should depart from Palestine and the country be partitioned into Arab and Jewish States, with Jerusalem internationalized as a *corpus separatum*.

Weizmann, it seemed, would have no part in the outcome of the debates at the United Nations. There, Abba Hillel Silver, perhaps the man most responsible for the dismissal of the Jewish leader, was in command of the Zionist case. But new forces had come into play which necessitated the presence of Jewry's elder (some would say only) statesman for the victorious conclusion of the struggle, and it was by no means certain that a resolution in favour of partition would secure the required two-thirds majority in the General Assembly. Moreover, there was a danger that, even if statehood were approved, the map would be drawn so as to place the Negev, with its outlet to the Red Sea, within the Arab area. Such a revision of the Unscop recommendations was strongly canvassed by the British, who hoped thereby to secure a continuous link with Egypt and the Suez Canal; they intended the incorporation of the Arab area within their puppet kingdom of Jordan. The US State Department supported this British scheme, and believed that only by the transfer of the Negev would the Palestine Arabs accept partition. The Jews needed Truman's intervention to abort the plan, but the President had grown resentful of the Zionist lobby in Washington and was not accessible to it.

Weizmann therefore complied with an invitation from the Jewish Agency to aid their efforts. His painstaking activities in Washington during the war years, which had largely been wasted in the case of Roosevelt, now bore fruit. He had the confidence of three men particularly close to Truman: David Niles, who was the President's adviser on American minority interests, Samuel Rosenman, the White House counsel, and Clark Clifford, the special counsel who realized how desperately Truman needed Jewish support if he was to win the Presidency in 1948. The United States and Russia were both represented on the UN sub-committee concerned with fixing the actual boundaries to separate the two states in Palestine.

Truman received Weizmann, albeit reluctantly, on 19 November 1947. The mission was especially delicate because the unexpected Soviet support of partition had thrown not only the State Department, but also the US War Department, into disarray. It was in their strategic interest to keep the British in a strong position in the Middle

East, and to deter Russian intervention in the region's affairs. The American UN delegation protested innocence, maintaining that the Negev might be equitably given to the Arab area by way of an exchange – that is, by enlarging the area of Galilee allocated to the Jews in the Unscop report.

Weizmann brought a map of the Negev and demonstrated to the US President the magnitude of the area the Jewish State was expected to concede. It was at that time an expanse of sparsely-inhabited desert but vital to the future state's communications with Africa and the East in the event of the Arab world's hostility towards its establishment. The mission proved entirely successful. On the following day Truman by-passed the State Department by personally telephoning the head of the American delegation at Lake Success that, whatever his existing instructions, the frontier was to be drawn so as to safeguard the Jews' outlet to the Red Sea. In return, the Jews would transfer Beersheba, then a wholly Arab town, to the Arabs, and accept also a small revision of their frontier along the Egyptian border and on the Mediterranean. It was to be a victory of far-reaching importance for the future of Israel.

An ancillary effect of the meeting was to restore in some measure the reputation of Zionism in the estimation of the President. Weizmann did not correspond to his conception of a Zionist leader as an American Jew ever threatening to use his 'clout' at the ballot box in order to get his way. He had also been distressed by reports of unparliamentary methods being employed by the Zionists to convert the delegations of wavering nations to support partition. Weizmann denied this allegation of illegitimate tactics (the unuttered charge was blackmail by big business) in a letter to the President on 25 November 1947. But this was an anxious month indeed for Jewish hopes, and the aging Jewish spokesman had himself wired the President, three days earlier, imploring his assistance with doubtful nations. In the event, the resolution in favour of Jewish and Arab States was passed on 29 November 1947 by the requisite two-thirds majority.

Celebrations of victory, however, proved to be premature. In the face of Arab guerilla action against the contemplated Jewish State, following the resolution, Britain largely abdicated her policing role in Palestine. Inter-racial warfare had begun, and it became apparent that a UN pacifying force might well be required to impose the UN decision. Such a force was bound to include Soviet or other East European troops, a prospect America viewed with increasing alarm as Russia became partition's most determined champion.

In the new year an anxious State Department initiated moves to shelve partition and have Palestine placed under UN trusteeship for an unspecified period after Britain's declared date of departure, 15 May 1948. Weizmann had returned to England, and Truman, who alone could overrule the State Department, was unreceptive alike to Zionist entreaties and criticism by Silver's Republican following in Congress. So Weizmann was once again summoned to America. Truman at first refused to receive him, but a meeting was engineered on 18 March, through a circuitous route involving the President's former Jewish business partner, Eddie Jacobson. Weizmann entered the White House incognito, by a side door.

He spoke of Palestine going through an extended period of uncertainty and bloodshed if the partition resolution were not implemented. He asked also for the lifting of the arms embargo – it was imposed on both sides though its effect was to penalize the Jews alone, for the Arabs could smuggle arms across the frontiers of neighbouring countries. Finally, he demanded free Jewish immigration during the transition period. Weizmann left the President in the belief that Truman had been won over, but the next day the Americans called for the summoning of the General Assembly to establish temporary trusteeship in Palestine. All seemed lost. Truman, whose account of the episode is given fully in Volume II of his memoirs, *Years of Trial and Hope*, nevertheless sent word through Rosenman to Weizmann that he would keep his promise.

The military situation in Palestine was now changing radically, with the tide turning in favour of the Jews. The country was, in effect, being partitioned by armed confrontation. Trusteeship was facing growing opposition by many delegations while indecisive discussion on the American resolution was proceeding. The Jews announced their determination to proclaim their state on the day of Britain's departure. On 13 May Weizmann wrote to Truman requesting American recognition of the Jewish government in formation. The letter was delivered by hand the same day. The following evening, 14 May, at 6 p.m. Washington time, with discussion of trusteeship still in progress, the United States announced *de facto* recognition of Israel. And when Weizmann next visited Truman, on 24 May 1948, he came as his country's President and as official guest.

There would be many more occasions when Weizmann needed to invoke Truman's support. Fresh proposals arose to give the Negev to the Arabs, anxiety developed over the security and status of Jerusalem, and Israel suffered invasion by all the Arab States of the region. But the two men now exchanged correspondence as Heads of Government, and according to the rules of diplomatic protocol.

Weizmann's relationship with Truman ripened to the extent that when the Israeli President wrote to the American President to congratulate him on his remarkable election victory in November 1948, Truman's reply, dated 29 November, read in part:

> As I read your letter, I was struck by the common experience you and I have recently shared. We had both been abandoned by the so-called realistic experts to our supposedly forlorn lost cause. Yet we both kept pressing for what we were sure was right – and we were both proven to be right. My feeling of elation on the morning of November 3rd must have approximated your own feelings one year ago today, and on May 14th and on several occasions since then.... I remember well our conversations about the Negeb, to which you referred in your letter. I agree fully with your estimate of the importance of the area to Israel, and I deplore any attempt to take it away from Israel.... We have announced in the General Assembly our firm intention to oppose any territorial changes in the November 29th Resolution which are not acceptable to the State of Israel.

The letter concluded with a promise of *de jure* recognition following the Israel General Election, then forthcoming.

7
Weizmann and the Zionist Congresses

The Zionist Congress was the only international Jewish assembly based upon a democratic procedure, that is apart from the inaugural Congress of 1897, where representation was largely by personal invitation from Theodor Herzl. There were twenty-two full Congresses prior to Israel's statehood. Following the appearance at the 1901 Congress of Weizmann's compact though shortlived Democratic Fraction, a party structure formed. This was partly ideological, partly religious. It survives to this day in Israel's parliament, the *Knesset*, though with different nomenclature.

The Congresses varied in duration, the longest remaining in session for two weeks. Delegates were mandated by the national Zionist federations, and by special interest groups directly affiliated to the world organization. A delegate would frequently represent several constituencies, many of which were too remote or too impoverished to send spokesmen of their own. The final Congress of 1946 represented over two million voters, each paying a modest membership subscription. Due to a revision of electoral rules this produced only 386 delegates, whereas some earlier Congresses, with a much smaller electorate, had over 500.

While the Congress was the ultimate policy-making body, it nominated from its ranks the Greater Actions Committee (or Zionist General Council) to meet more frequently. An Executive, which until 1921 was also known as the Smaller (Inner) Actions Committee, ran the day-to-day affairs of the movement under the President of the Zionist Organization. An annual conference was convened in alternate years beginning with 1902, for by then the Congresses had become biennial. It brought together the Greater and Smaller Actions Committees with representatives of the various commissions (political, cultural, colonization, etc.) elected by the Congress.

Even at its best the Zionist Congress could only be an imperfect parliament. The Jewish national resurgence was a volunteer movement of widely contrasting interests, and the intensity of commitment varied. Several languages were used, none of them universally understood. Important issues often became obscured by extended and ill-regulated debate, with decisions postponed to the next Congress, or rendered irrelevant by the tide of history.

First Congress
Basle, 29–31 August 1897. This adopted the organizational forms, and agreed on Zionism's objectives (the 'Basle Programme'). Weizmann did not attend, being in Russia at the time.

Second Congress
Basle, 27–31 August 1898. Weizmann is elected to the Steering (Standing) Committee. He speaks on the need for Congress to retain financial control over their affairs. This is in the debate on the formation of the Jewish Colonial Trust, due to be the main Zionist banking institution.

Third Congress
Basle, 15–18 August 1899. Weizmann is again on the Steering Committee. He expresses dissatisfaction at the lack of consultation between the leadership and constituent bodies. Herzl is mostly concerned with the political objectives of the movement, but Weizmann joins in the demand now being expressed for more cultural activities, and practical work in Palestine. He is elected to the Cultural Commission.

Fourth Congress
London, 13–16 August 1900. Weizmann, ranged with the majority of Russian delegates, who are displeased with Herzl's autocratic style and his concentration on political issues, again condemns the general neglect of cultural work. He reproaches Herzl for his reliance in Eastern Europe on the rabbis, whom Weizmann considers an obscurantist force.

Fifth Congress
Basle, 26–30 December 1901. Herzl reports on his meeting that year with the Sultan. Weizmann and his friends have been occupied in forming the Democratic Fraction, and it enters the Congress as a force of thirty-seven young delegates. He and Martin Buber introduce a motion, which is carried, that the movement actively study the practicability of establishing a Jewish University.

Sixth Congress

Basle, 23–28 August 1903. Herzl reveals the British offer of a Jewish settlement project in East Africa. Weizmann, heavily engaged behind the scenes with the Russian delegation, makes no substantial speech but votes with the 'Nay-Sayers', for whom Palestine is the only settlement area. He is nevertheless elected to the East Africa Commission, which is entrusted with supervision of arrangements for sending a survey team to the region. He is now an influential opponent of Herzl, working particularly with Menahem Ussishkin of Odessa. His Democratic Fraction has all but collapsed, and with it the Jewish University project.

Seventh Congress

Basle, 27 July–2 August 1905. Following the death of Herzl the previous year, David Wolffsohn of Cologne is elected leader. The survey on East Africa proves unfavourable, and the proposal is rejected. The movement suffers its first serious breakaway with the departure of Israel Zangwill and his 'Ugandists'. Weizmann is elected a representative of Britain on the Greater Actions Committee.

Eighth Congress

The Hague, 14–21 August 1907. While there is continued resistance by 'political' Zionists to embarking on large-scale projects in Palestine without a formal charter from the Turkish authorities, Weizmann makes his mark with a strong speech urging a synthesis of the 'political' and 'practical' schools in the movement. He has decided that Wolffsohn, who maintains the headquarters under his direct control in his home city, is an obstruction to progress in Palestine.

Ninth Congress

Hamburg, 26–30 December 1909. Congress debate is carefully guarded as to the Zionist stance towards Constantinople, which has experienced revolution and counter-revolution. Weizmann is elected chairman of the Steering Committee and seeks, through his key role in the Congress proceedings, to dislodge Wolffsohn, a consistent 'political'. The move is frustrated by the Congress voting by acclaim for Wolffsohn's continued stewardship of the movement. Weizmann is castigated as an intriguer, and consequently loses ground.

Tenth Congress

Basle, 9–15 August 1911. Weizmann is again chairman of the Steering Committee. He has used the interim between Congresses to strengthen the opposition to Wolffsohn, and the latter now resigns. A Smaller Actions Committee is formed entirely of 'practicals', all of them allies of Weizmann. It is led by Otto Warburg, a German botanist and colonization expert. Headquarters are transferred from Cologne to Berlin.

Eleventh Congress
Vienna, 2–9 September 1913. Weizmann's third appointment as chairman of the Steering Committee. He delivers a major address on the need to expand Jewish settlement in Palestine without awaiting Turkish recognition of the Zionist Organization's status. Together with Ussishkin he revives the project for a University, to be established in Jerusalem and for which funds are now forthcoming.

Post-War Conference
London, 7–11 July 1920. This, the first fully international Zionist gathering since the war, acknowledges Weizmann's unequalled authority by electing him President of the Zionist Organization. He is in conflict with Justice Louis D. Brandeis over the future functions of the movement, and in consequence no American joins the Executive. London is now the official headquarters of the movement.

Twelfth Congress
Carlsbad, 1–14 September 1921. For the first time, a Zionist Congress must concern itself with Arab unrest in Palestine. Weizmann defends Herbert Samuel, the High Commissioner, and makes a plea for reconciliation with the Arabs 'in our common homeland'. The Zionist Commission in Palestine is transformed into a branch of the Executive.

Thirteenth Congress
Carlsbad, 6–18 August 1923. The British Mandate having been ratified by the League of Nations, Weizmann now submits to Congress his proposal that the Jewish Agency be expanded by the inclusion of non-Zionists, for they are not strong enough alone to foster Jewish settlement in Palestine successfully. The proposal encounters strong opposition, as many Zionists fear that such an enlarged Jewish Agency will result in a dilution of the ideal.

Fourteenth Congress
Vienna, 18–31 August 1925. Weizmann faces hostility from various quarters, but notably Vladimir Jabotinsky and his newly-formed Revisionist Party, on the grounds that too much finance is invested in

(mainly left-wing) agricultural colonization; masses of immigrants from Poland, settling mostly in Tel Aviv, are given no aid. The endorsement by leading American non-Zionists of a Soviet farming programme for Russian Jews in the Crimea, utilizing American funds, slows down negotiations for an expanded Jewish Agency. Weizmann declares that lack of confidence in the Executive prevents him from continuing in office. But he is re-elected nevertheless, by an overwhelming majority.

Fifteenth Congress
Basle, 30 August–11 September 1927. Morale in the movement is at a low ebb, with an economic crisis in Palestine bringing unemployment and emigration. Weizmann defends the Labour ranks from mounting criticism, for in his view they provide the bulk of Zionism's pioneering material. A well-planned campaign by American delegates to unseat Weizmann is defeated. An Anglo-American triumvirate under his friend Harry Sacher is given plenary powers to reduce expenditure in Palestine and revive the Jewish economy there.

Sixteenth Congress
Zurich, 28 July–11 August 1929. Despite a last-ditch stand by, among others, Jabotinsky's Revisionists to prevent the creation of the expanded Jewish Agency, the Congress approves Weizmann's agreement with the non-Zionists. It is his greatest triumph since the Balfour Declaration. As president of the Zionist Organization he is also *ex officio* President of the Jewish Agency, with which are associated, *inter alia*, Albert Einstein, Léon Blum, Herbert Samuel, Louis Marshall and Lord Melchett, with Baron Edmond de Rothschild as Honorary President. But within days violent Arab attacks are perpetrated against Jews in Palestine, causing much bloodshed and opening an era of heightened tension between the two communities.

Seventeenth Congress
Basle, 30 June–15 July 1931. The Congress is disenchanted with the Weizmann policy, which it condemns as excessively identified with Britain. He himself hints that the chastisement he has received from Zionist leaders on both sides of the Atlantic will prompt his resignation. In his defence he speaks of the necessity to reassure the Arabs and remove their fear of Jewish domination. In restive mood, delegates seize upon a Press interview in which Weizmann has voiced anxiety that a Jewish demand for a majority in Palestine would be construed by the world as a wish to drive the Arabs from the country. As a

consequence he is not re-elected President, the office going to Nahum Sokolow.

Eighteenth Congress
Prague, 21 August–4 September 1933. This meets under the shadow of the assassination of the Labour leader Chaim Arlosoroff (of which crime many delegates accuse the Revisionists) and the new Hitler regime in Germany. Weizmann refuses to attend. Pressed by the Labour group together with some Americans to offer himself for re-election, he makes this conditional on freedom to choose his own Executive and exclusion of the Revisionists from the organization. These terms are unacceptable. Weizmann's absence hovers over the Congress like the ghost in *Hamlet*, and he is nominated to head the Jewish Agency's bureau for the resettlement of German Jews in Palestine. He makes this into an activity virtually independent of the Executive's authority.

Nineteenth Congress
Lucerne, 20 August–4 September 1935. The Revisionists having seceded, Weizmann is returned unanimously as President. This is largely due to the efforts of David Ben-Gurion, who is now the second most powerful figure in the movement. Stephen Wise of New York, hitherto a relentless critic of Weizmann, now pledges the Americans' whole-hearted support. Boom conditions result from greatly increased immigration into Palestine.

Twentieth Congress
Zurich, 3–17 August 1937. The Peel Commission, investigating the causes of the Arab rebellion of 1936, has recommended partition of Palestine. This dramatic and controversial proposal dominates the Congress (though Weizmann and Ben-Gurion have privately accepted the principle). Much of the discussion is held *in camera*, with Wise and Ussishkin the leading opponents of partition. Eventually Weizmann is empowered to negotiate a partition scheme more favourable to the Jews, and bring this to the next Congress.

Twenty-First Congress
Geneva, 16–25 August 1939. The British have abandoned partition as a policy, replacing it with the 1939 White Paper, which is denounced by Congress as illegal. Bitterness against England is compounded by anxiety for the safety of European Jewry in the darkening international situation, and gives rise to another Congress preoccupation: birth of a

Jewish terrorist movement confronting Arab terrorism in Palestine. Weizmann pleads that condemnation of the White Paper policy should not bring them to break off relations with Great Britain. The Hitler–Stalin pact is announced during the Congress sessions, and delegates hurry through the agenda so as to return to their homes before the anticipated European war.

Biltmore Conference
New York, 9–11 May 1942. An Extraordinary Conference of American Zionists at the Biltmore Hotel, meeting against the background of America's entry in the war as the dominant Allied Power. Britain is under fierce attack for her refusal to create a Jewish Fighting Force, and for her strict adherence to the White Paper. In a speech of moderation, Weizmann discusses post-war Zionist policy as being based upon mass immigration into Palestine. But he is overshadowed by Ben-Gurion, who demands the 're-establishment of Palestine as a Jewish Commonwealth'. A resolution to this effect (the Biltmore Programme) becomes the official Zionist platform. Weizmann regards it as irresponsible and dangerous, because impossible of fulfilment.

World Conference
London, 1–13 August 1945. The Jews are counting their losses, but there is no sign that Britain will grant the Zionist demand for the immediate entry of 100,000 survivors and control of Jewish immigration. Weizmann counsels patience while the new Labour Government, elected on 26 July, settles in. But Ben-Gurion and other officers of the Executive, who have the support of Abba Hillel Silver of Cleveland, decide on armed resistance in Palestine, with heightened agitation in the USA, to press Britain to concede a Jewish State.

Twenty-Second Congress
Basle 9–24 December 1946. The final Congress before statehood. Weizmann's position as leader is now much weakened, mainly due to the failure to persuade the British to give the Jews full and immediate independence. Zionist policy has now been modified to Weizmann's original demand for a partitioned Palestine. He is isolated among his principal colleagues by his outright condemnation of Zionist activism and his insistence upon maintaining relations with Britain. To the consternation of many delegates, his re-election as President is foiled by a Ben-Gurion–Silver alliance. Nevertheless talks with the British continue. These fail to produce agreement, and the Palestine problem is referred to the United Nations.

8
The Scientist

It was Chaim Weizmann's good fortune as an organic chemist that he began his career at the turn of the century in Germany, where the interconnection between industry and the academic world of pure science had reached a stage unknown elsewhere in Europe. In England, for example, pure research was still a Cinderella struggling with meagre resources and inadequate equipment.

He first attracted notice as an innovative scientist with his investigation of the phenomenon of colour. In partnership with a young German chemist, Christian Deichler, he discovered new methods of synthesizing dyestuffs from naphthalene and anthracene, significant both for industry and physiology. Besides their contributions to the scientific literature of the day, Weizmann and Deichler patented various processes between 1900 and 1904, so that already from this period the aspiring Zionist leader knew that freedom from financial cares lay within his grasp. He had no wish to be among those who looked to the Jewish national movement for their livelihood.

Primarily he was a teacher, and he refused to allow industry to swallow him up. At Manchester University he joined a circle of brilliant men – William H. Perkin, Samuel Alexander, Robert Robinson, Arthur Schuster, Ernest Rutherford, among others – and the ease with which he, a Jew and a foreigner, was accepted in this alien though stimulating environment gave him that profound affinity with British intellectual society which was to influence his political philosophy ever afterwards.

The next few years were prodigious of effort and ideas. He developed a synthesis for camphor and discovered many new applications for the ketone group. Mostly this research was conducted under his supervision with chosen students, some of whom were themselves to achieve international reputations. In 1909 Weizmann decided to spread his interests over to microbiology. He began spending part of the vacations at the Pasteur Institute in Paris, where he undertook a study of proteins. This continued almost to the outbreak of the First World War and led him into many byways. His expectation that his scientific reputation would be acknowledged with a professorship at Manchester was reasonable. But it was not to be; in 1913 he was appointed Reader in Biochemistry. Another disappointment was his failure to secure election to the Royal Society.

He was now concerned with problems as diverse as artificial rubber, synthetic foods, and the application of carbohydrates to alcohol production. They were subjects to which he was to return again and again. It all hinged upon the correct fermentation chemistry and the isolation of bacteria capable of breaking down a host of complex substances. Out of the fermentation of maize he obtained a bacterium given the systematic name *Clostridium acetobutylicum Weizmann*. He had found a method for producing acetone as a wartime substitute when all the usual sources of supply were being denied Britain by the German blockade. The method also yielded butyl alcohol, for which there was at that time no useful application.

Acetone was the missing ingredient required to blend the three constituents of cordite and render the gunpowder smokeless (essential to conceal the positions of heavy guns, particularly on warships). Later in the war the Weizmann process was transferred first to Canada and then to the USA. It was the first time a biological process, rather than a chemical reagent, was employed on an industrial scale. Subsequently the by-product butyl alcohol, in the form of butyl acetate, gained enormously in importance as the volatile solvent used in varnish for the motorcar.

At the end of the war Weizmann was compelled to divorce himself from chemistry and concentrate on his Zionist activities. This situation endured until 1931. In the interim almost every one of his utterances relating to Palestine revealed the scientist's approach to nation-building. He saw the new Palestine as a laboratory, a place to test out Jewish capacities under the stimulus of the ancestral environment. To him, Palestine's healthy growth demanded not spectacular, dramatic gestures but instead a slow, organic development. He refused to surrender to defeatism when times were bad. Conversely he would not romanticize over achievements, or glorify individual heroics, often to the disappointment of his Jewish audiences. He was especially concerned that the Hebrew University refrain from introducing 'glamorous' scientific studies except when these could be justified on the highest academic standards.

In 1934 Weizmann had the opportunity, through a generous endowment from the Marks-Sieff-Sacher family, to inaugurate the Daniel Sieff Research Institute at Rehovot and thus direct a scientific centre that would satisfy his own exacting requirements. He wished it to be a beacon attracting outstanding scientists rendered homeless in Germany by the Hitler regime, and in this he received valuable guidance from the eminent chemist Richard Willstaetter, himself a victim of German antisemitism. His earliest capture for the Rehovot establishment was Ernest D. Bergmann, already a distinguished biochemist, who became Weizmann's disciple and alter ego in all matters scientific, carrying experimentation forward when other responsibilities called Weizmann away. Their collaboration continued throughout the Second World War and into the expansion of the Sieff Institute as the Weizmann Institute of Science, a major research centre that Weizmann to his dying day hoped would come to serve the entire Middle East.

It was small-scale work to begin with, but an institute under Weizmann's personal control enabled a new generation of scientists to extend his own earlier work on polycyclic structures. Palestine had no prime materials of its own, and if vitamins, synthetic foods and pharmaceuticals were to be made available in times of emergency, they had first to reveal their properties in the test-tube.

At this time his mind was being exercised by the unequal distribution on our planet of fossil fuels: when those we have are exhausted what would replace them? Surely the earth abounded in organic matter from which energy sources might be recovered? During the Second World War this problem struck him as particularly relevant to Britain in her geographical situation as an island remote from her traditional sources of supply. Weizmann foretold as early as 1944 that cheap petroleum and natural rubber in the Middle and Far East were slipping from Britain's hold. He saw that Latin America's immense mineral wealth would, in the post-war world, fall under American domination. He visualized a new era in which plastics would replace many metals for the manufacturing industries.

Of course, Weizmann was not alone in recognizing the portents. However, he felt he had a special responsibility in his wartime appointment as honorary chemical adviser to the British Ministry of Supply to speak of them. His own recommended solution was to turn first to Africa, where he was convinced that the rich vegetation of the jungle, constantly renewing itself, could be converted by fermentation into almost any substance needed both for industry and human nourishment. He did not foresee the loss of Africa to the British Empire (no one did) though even such an eventuality would not diminish the argument. What he wrote in those days is now the commonly accepted view of the interdependence between the developed nations and the

Third World.

The pressure of public work naturally prevented Weizmann from giving himself wholly to the proper consideration of these global issues. Neither did he survive in good health, once he had assumed the honorific office of State President, to become a living inspiration to those who followed him in the realm of science. But he will be remembered as a thinker of the widest vision, endowed with a penetrating understanding of the role which those who gather knowledge must perform in the service of humankind.

Appendices

Appendices

Appendix A

The Weizmann Family

Chaim Weizmann was the third of twelve surviving children of Ozer Weizmann (?1850–1911) and Rachel-Leah Tschmerinsky (?1852–1939). He married Vera Khatzman (1881–1966). She practised medicine during their residence in Manchester. There were two sons. Benjamin (1907–81) had a son David (b. 1941) by his first wife, Maidie Pomeranz, also a medical practitioner. David joined the BBC. Following divorce, Benjamin farmed in Ireland and the Channel Islands with his second wife, Maisie Gains. The Weizmanns' younger son Michael (1916–42) was lost in action in the Bay of Biscay on an RAF mission.

The other members of the family were:

Miriam (Mariya, 1871–1950). She married Chaim Lubzhinsky, and in widowhood settled in London.

Feivel (?1872–1941). He married Lubzhinsky's sister Fanya and remained in the family timber business. After its closure he settled with his mother in Haifa, 1920.

Haya (1878–1959). She married Abraham Lichtenstein. A teacher in Haifa and Tel Aviv, she wrote the family memoirs, published in Hebrew.

Moses (1879–1957). He married Zinaida Rivlin, and became head of the Organic Chemistry Department at the Hebrew University, Jerusalem.

Fruma (?1880–1947), married to Zelig Weicman. A dental surgeon, she settled in Palestine in 1913.

Samuel (1882–?), married to Bazia Rubin. An engineer and Russian Communist Party official, he was involved with Jewish colonization in the Crimea. Died in a Soviet penal camp after the Second World War.

Gita (?1884–1975). She married Tuvia Dounie, who was killed in 1938 during the Arab riots. She was a musician, with her own Conservatoire in Haifa.

Anna (?1886–1963). A biochemist in Moscow, she joined her brother's scientific institute at Rehovot in 1933.

Masha (b. 1888). She married Vassily Savitzky and practised medicine in Moscow. Both succeeded in reaching Israel in 1956.

Minna (1888–1925). Married to Noel Law, an Englishman in government service. She practised medicine in Jerusalem.

Mikhail (Yehiel, 1892–1957). Married Yehudit Krishevsky. An agriculturalist, serving in various capacities in Palestine. His son Ezer, an RAF pilot, became Commander of Israel's Air Force and Minister of Defence in the Begin Government, 1977–80.

Appendix B

The Basle Programme – 31 August 1897

The aim of Zionism is to create for the Jewish people a home in Palestine secured by public law.

The Congress contemplates the following means to the attainment of this end:

1. The promotion, on suitable lines, of the colonization of Palestine by Jewish agricultural and industrial workers.
2. The organization and binding together of the whole of Jewry by means of appropriate institutions, local and international, in accordance with the laws of each country.
3. The strengthening and fostering of Jewish national sentiment and consciousness.
4. Preparatory steps towards obtaining government consent, where necessary, to the attainment of the aim of Zionism.

Appendix C

The Balfour Declaration – 2 November 1917

Dear Lord Rothschild,

I have much pleasure in conveying to you, on behalf of His Majesty's Government, the following declaration of sympathy with Jewish Zionist aspirations which has been submitted to, and approved by, the Cabinet.

'His Majesty's Government view with favour the establishment in Palestine of a national home for the Jewish people, and will use their best endeavours to facilitate the achievement of this object, it being clearly understood that nothing shall be done which may prejudice the civil and religious rights of existing non-Jewish communities in Palestine, or the rights and political status enjoyed by Jews in any other country.'

I should be grateful if you would bring this declaration to the knowledge of the Zionist Federation.

Signed: Arthur James Balfour

Appendix D

The Faisal*–Weizmann Agreement – 3 January 1919

His Royal Highness the Emir Faisal, representing and acting on behalf of the Arab Kingdom of Hedjaz, and Dr Chaim Weizmann, representing and acting on behalf of the Zionist Organization, mindful of the racial kinship and ancient bonds existing between the Arabs and the Jewish people, and realizing that the surest means of working out the consummation of their national aspirations is through the closest possible collaboration in the development of the Arab State and Palestine, and being desirous further of confirming the good understanding which exists between them, have agreed upon the following Articles:

Article I

The Arab State and Palestine in all their relations and undertakings shall be controlled by the most cordial goodwill and understanding, and to this end Arab and Jewish duly accredited agents shall be established and maintained in the respective territories.

Article II

Immediately following the completion of the deliberations of the Peace Conference, the definite boundaries between the Arab State and Palestine shall be determined by a Commission to be agreed upon by the parties hereto.

Article III

In the establishment of the Constitution and Administration of Palestine all such measures shall be adopted as will afford the fullest guarantees for carrying into effect the British Government's Declaration of the 2nd of November 1917.

Article IV

All necessary measures shall be taken to encourage and stimulate immigration of Jews into Palestine on a large scale, and as quickly as possible to settle Jewish immigrants upon the land through closer settlement and intensive cultivation of the soil. In taking such measures the Arab peasant and tenant

* Spelt Feisal throughout the original.

farmers shall be protected in their rights, and shall be assisted in forwarding their economic development.

Article V

No regulation nor law shall be made prohibiting or interfering in any way with the free exercise of religion; and further the free exercise and enjoyment of religious profession and worship without discrimination or preference shall forever be allowed. No religious test shall ever be required for the exercise of civil or political rights.

Article VI

The Mohammedan Holy Places shall be under Mohammedan control.

Article VII

The Zionist Organization proposes to send to Palestine a Commission of experts to make a survey of the economic possibilities of the country, and to report upon the best means for its development. The Zionist Organization will place the aforementioned Commission at the disposal of the Arab State for the purpose of a survey of the economic possibilities of the Arab State and to report upon the best means for its development. The Zionist Organization will use its best efforts to assist the Arab State in providing the means for developing the natural resources and economic possibilities thereof.

Article VIII

The parties hereto agree to act in complete accord and harmony on all matters embraced herein before the Peace Congress.

Article IX

Any matters of dispute which may arise between the contracting parties shall be referred to the British Government for arbitration.

Given under our hand at London, England, the third day of January, one thousand nine hundred and nineteen.

Faisal Ibn-Hussein
Chaim Weizmann

Reservation by the Emir Faisal

If the Arabs are established as I have asked in my manifesto of January 4th addressed to the British Secretary of State for Foreign Affairs, I will carry out what is written in this agreement. If changes are made, I cannot be answerable for failing to carry out this agreement.

Faisal Ibn-Hussein

Appendix E

The League of Nations Mandate for Palestine, 24 June 1922, with Note on Trans-Jordan by the Secretary-General, 23 September 1922

The Council of the League of Nations:

Whereas the Principal Allied Powers have agreed, for the purpose of giving effect to the provisions of Article 22 of the Covenant of the League of Nations, to entrust to a Mandatory selected by the said Powers the administration of the territory of Palestine, which formerly belonged to the Turkish Empire, within such boundaries as may be fixed by them; and

Whereas the Principal Allied Powers have also agreed that the Mandatory should be responsible for putting into effect the declaration originally made on November 2nd, 1917, by the Government of His Britannic Majesty, and adopted by the said Powers, in favour of the establishment in Palestine of a national home for the Jewish people, it being clearly understood that nothing should be done which might prejudice the civil and religious rights of existing non-Jewish communities in Palestine, or the rights and political status enjoyed by Jews in any other country; and

Whereas recognition has thereby been given to the historical connection of the Jewish people with Palestine and to the grounds for reconstituting their national home in that country; and

Whereas the Principal Allied Powers have selected His Britannic Majesty as the Mandatory for Palestine; and

Whereas the mandate in respect of Palestine has been formulated in the following terms and submitted to the Council of the League for approval; and

Whereas His Britannic Majesty has accepted the mandate in respect of Palestine and undertaken to exercise it on behalf of the League of Nations in conformity with the following provisions; and

Whereas by the afore-mentioned Article 22 (paragraph 8), it is provided that the degree of authority, control or administration to be exercised by the Mandatory, not having been previously agreed upon by the Members of the League, shall be explicitly defined by the Council of the League of Nations;

Confirming the said mandate, defines its terms as follows:

Article 1

The Mandatory shall have full powers of legislation and of administration, save as they may be limited by the terms of this mandate.

Article 2

The Mandatory shall be responsible for placing the country under such political, administrative and economic conditions as will secure the establishment of the Jewish national home, as laid down in the preamble, and the development of self-governing institutions, and also for safeguarding the civil and religious rights of all the inhabitants of Palestine, irrespective of race and religion.

Article 3

The Mandatory shall, so far as circumstances permit, encourage local autonomy.

Article 4

An appropriate Jewish agency shall be recognized as a public body for the purpose of advising and co-operating with the Administration of Palestine in such economic, social and other matters as may affect the establishment of the Jewish national home and the interests of the Jewish population in Palestine, and, subject always to the control of the Administration, to assist and take part in the development of the country.

The Zionist organization, so long as its organization and constitution are in the opinion of the Mandatory appropriate, shall be recognized as such agency. It shall take steps in consultation with His Britannic Majesty's Government to secure the co-operation of all Jews who are willing to assist in the establishment of the Jewish national home.

Article 5

The Mandatory shall be responsible for seeing that no Palestine territory shall be ceded or leased to, or in any way placed under the control of, the Government of any foreign Power.

Article 6

The Administration of Palestine, while ensuring that the rights and position of other sections of the population are not prejudiced, shall facilitate Jewish immigration under suitable conditions and shall encourage, in co-operation with the Jewish agency referred to in Article 4, close settlement by Jews on the land, including State lands and waste lands not required for public purposes.

Article 7

The Administration of Palestine shall be responsible for enacting a nationality law. There shall be included in this law provisions framed so as to facilitate the acquisition of Palestinian citizenship by Jews who take up their permanent residence in Palestine.

Article 8

The privileges and immunities of foreigners, including the benefits of consular jurisdiction and protection as formerly enjoyed by Capitulation or usage in the Ottoman Empire, shall not be applicable in Palestine.

Unless the Powers whose nationals enjoyed the afore-mentioned privileges and immunities on August 1st 1914, shall have previously renounced the right to their re-establishment, or shall have agreed to their non-application for a specific period, these privileges and immunities shall, at the expiration of the mandate, be immediately re-established in their entirety or with such modifications as may have been agreed upon between the Powers concerned.

Article 9

The Mandatory shall be responsible for seeing that the judicial system established in Palestine shall assure to foreigners, as well as to natives, a complete guarantee of their rights.

Respect for the personal status of the various peoples and communities and for their religious interests shall be fully guaranteed. In particular, the control and administration of Wakfs shall be exercised in accordance with religious law and the dispositions of the founders.

Article 10

Pending the making of special extradition agreements relating to Palestine, the extradition treaties in force between the Mandatory and other foreign Powers shall apply to Palestine.

Article 11

The Administration of Palestine shall take all necessary measures to safeguard the interests of the community in connection with the development of the country, and, subject to any international obligations accepted by the Mandatory, shall have full power to provide for public ownership or control of any of the natural resources of the country or of the public works, services and utilities established or to be established therein. It shall introduce a land system appropriate to the needs of the country, having regard, among other things, to the desirability of promoting the close settlement and intensive cultivation of the land.

The Administration may arrange with the Jewish agency mentioned in Article 4 to construct or operate, upon fair and equitable terms, any public works, services and utilities, and to develop any of the natural resources of the country, in so far as these matters are not directly undertaken by the Administration. Any such arrangements shall provide that no profits distributed by such agency, directly or indirectly, shall exceed a reasonable rate of interest on the capital, and any further profits shall be utilized by it for the benefit of the country in a manner approved by the Administration.

Article 12

The Mandatory shall be entrusted with the control of the foreign relations of Palestine and the right to issue exequaturs to consuls appointed by foreign

Powers. He shall also be entitled to afford diplomatic and consular protection to citizens of Palestine when outside its territorial limits.

Article 13

All responsibility in connection with the Holy Places and religious buildings or sites in Palestine, including that of preserving existing rights and of securing free access to the Holy Places, religious buildings and sites and the free exercise of worship, while ensuring the requirements of public order and decorum, is assumed by the Mandatory, who shall be responsible solely to the League of Nations in all matters connected herewith, provided that nothing in this article shall prevent the Mandatory from entering into such arrangements as he may deem reasonable with the Administration for the purpose of carrying the provisions of this article into effect; and provided also that nothing in this mandate shall be construed as conferring upon the Mandatory authority to interfere with the fabric or the management of purely Moslem sacred shrines, the immunities of which are guaranteed.

Article 14

A special Commission shall be appointed by the Mandatory to study, define and determine the rights and claims in connection with the Holy Places and the rights and claims relating to the different religious communities in Palestine. The method of nomination, the composition and the functions of this Commission shall be submitted to the Council of the League for its approval, and the Commission shall not be appointed or enter upon its functions without the approval of the Council.

Article 15

The Mandatory shall see that complete freedom of conscience and the free exercise of all forms of worship, subject only to the maintenance of public order and morals, are ensured to all. No discrimination of any kind shall be made between the inhabitants of Palestine on the ground of race, religion or language. No person shall be excluded from Palestine on the sole ground of his religious belief.

The right of each community to maintain its own schools for the education of its own members in its own language, while conforming to such educational requirements of a general nature as the Administration may impose, shall not be denied or impaired.

Article 16

The Mandatory shall be responsible for exercising such supervision over religious or eleemosynary bodies of all faiths in Palestine as may be required for the maintenance of public order and good government. Subject to such supervision, no measures shall be taken in Palestine to obstruct or interfere with the enterprise of such bodies or to discriminate against any representative or member of them on the ground of his religion or nationality.

Article 17

The Administration of Palestine may organize on a voluntary basis the forces necessary for the preservation of peace and order, and also for the defence of the country, subject, however, to the supervision of the Mandatory, but shall not use them for purposes other than those above specified save with the consent of the Mandatory. Except for such purposes, no military, naval or air forces shall be raised or maintained by the Administration of Palestine.

Nothing in this article shall preclude the Administration of Palestine from contributing to the cost of the maintenance of the forces of the Mandatory in Palestine.

The Mandatory shall be entitled at all times to use the roads, railways and ports of Palestine for the movement of armed forces and the carriage of fuel and supplies.

Article 18

The Mandatory shall see that there is no discrimination in Palestine against the nationals of any State Member of the League of Nations (including companies incorporated under its laws) as compared with those of the Mandatory or of any foreign State in matters concerning taxation, commerce or navigation, the exercise of industries or professions, or in the treatment of merchant vessels or civil aircraft. Similarly, there shall be no discrimination in Palestine against goods originating in or destined for any of the said States, and there shall be freedom of transit under equitable conditions across the mandated area.

Subject as aforesaid and to the other provisions of this mandate, the Administration of Palestine may, on the advice of the Mandatory, impose such taxes and customs duties as it may consider necessary, and take such steps as it may think best to promote the development of the natural resources of the country and to safeguard the interests of the population. It may also, on the advice of the Mandatory, conclude a special customs agreement with any State the territory of which in 1914 was wholly included in Asiatic Turkey or Arabia.

Article 19

The Mandatory shall adhere on behalf of the Administration of Palestine to any general international conventions already existing, or which may be concluded hereafter with the approval of the League of Nations, respecting the slave traffic, the traffic in arms and ammunition, or the traffic in drugs, or relating to commercial equality, freedom of transit and navigation, aerial navigation and postal, telegraphic and wireless communication or literary, artistic or industrial property.

Article 20

The Mandatory shall co-operate on behalf of the Administration of Palestine,

APPENDIX E

so far as religious, social and other conditions may permit, in the execution of any common policy adopted by the League of Nations for preventing and combating disease, including diseases of plants and animals.

Article 21

The Mandatory shall secure the enactment within twelve months from this date, and shall ensure the execution of a Law of Antiquities based on the following rules. This law shall ensure equality of treatment in the matter of excavations and archaeological research to the nations of all States Members of the League of Nations.

(1)

'Antiquity' means any construction or any product of human activity earlier than the year AD 1700.

(2)

The law for the protection of antiquities shall proceed by encouragement rather than by threat.

Any person who, having discovered an antiquity without being furnished with the authorization referred to in paragraph 5, reports the same to an official of the competent Department, shall be rewarded according to the value of the discovery.

(3)

No antiquity may be disposed of except to the competent Department, unless this Department renounces the acquisition of any such antiquity.

No antiquity may leave the country without an export licence from the said Department.

(4)

Any person who maliciously or negligently destroys or damages an antiquity shall be liable to a penalty to be fixed.

(5)

No clearing of ground or digging with the object of finding antiquities shall be permitted, under penalty of fine, except to persons authorized by the competent Department.

(6)

Equitable terms shall be fixed for expropriation, temporary or permanent, of lands which might be of historical or archaeological interest.

(7)

Authorization to excavate shall only be granted to persons who show sufficient guarantees of archaeological experience. The Administration of Palestine shall not, in granting these authorizations, act in such a way as to exclude scholars of any nation without good grounds.

(8)

The proceeds of excavations may be divided between the excavator and the competent Department in a proportion fixed by that Department. If division seems impossible for scientific reasons, the excavator shall receive fair indemnity in lieu of a part of the find.

Article 22

English, Arabic and Hebrew shall be the official languages of Palestine. Any statement or inscription in Arabic on stamps or money in Palestine shall be repeated in Hebrew, and any statement or inscription in Hebrew shall be repeated in Arabic.

Article 23

The Administration of Palestine shall recognize the holy days of the respective communities in Palestine as legal days of rest for the members of such communities.

Article 24

The Mandatory shall make to the Council of the League of Nations an annual report to the satisfaction of the Council as to the measures taken during the year to carry out the provisions of the mandate. Copies of all laws and regulations promulgated or issued during the year shall be communicated with the report.

Article 25

In the territories lying between the Jordan and the eastern boundary of Palestine as ultimately determined, the Mandatory shall be entitled, with the consent of the Council of the League of Nations, to postpone or withhold application of such provisions of this mandate as he may consider inapplicable to the existing local conditions, and to make such provision for the administration of the territories as he may consider suitable to those conditions, provided that no action shall be taken which is inconsistent with the provisions of Articles 15, 16 and 18.

Article 26

The Mandatory agrees that, if any dispute whatever should arise between the Mandatory and another Member of the League of Nations relating to the interpretation or the application of the provisions of the mandate, such dispute, if it cannot be settled by negotiation, shall be submitted to the Permanent Court of International Justice provided for by Article 14 of the Covenant of the League of Nations.

Article 27

The consent of the Council of the League of Nations is required for any modification of the terms of this mandate.

Article 28

In the event of the termination of the mandate hereby conferred upon the Mandatory, the Council of the League of Nations shall make such arrangements as may be deemed necessary for safeguarding in perpetuity, under guarantee of the League, the rights secured by Articles 13 and 14, and shall use its influence for securing, under the guarantee of the League, that the Government of Palestine will fully honour the financial obligations legitimately incurred by the Administration of Palestine during the period of the mandate, including the rights of public servants to pensions or gratuities.

The present instrument shall be deposited in original in the archives of the League of Nations and certified copies shall be forwarded by the Secretary-General of the League of Nations to all Members of the League.

Done at London the twenty-fourth day of July, one thousand nine hundred and twenty-two.

For the Secretary-General, Rappard, Director of the Mandates Section

NOTE

Geneva,
September 23rd, 1922

ARTICLE 25 OF THE PALESTINE MANDATE
Territory Known as Trans-Jordan
Note by the Secretary-General

The Secretary-General has the honour to communicate for the information of the Members of the League, a memorandum relating to Article 25 of the Palestine Mandate presented by the British Government to the Council of the League on September 16th, 1922.

The memorandum was approved by the Council subject to the decision taken at its meeting in London on July 24th, 1922, with regard to the coming into force of the Palestine and Syrian mandates.

Memorandum by the British Representative

1. Article 25 of the Mandate for Palestine provides as follows:
   'In the territories lying between the Jordan and the eastern boundary of Palestine as ultimately determined, the Mandatory shall be entitled, with the consent of the Council of the League of Nations, to postpone or withhold application of such provisions of this Mandate as he may consider inapplicable to the existing local conditions, and to make such provision for the administration of the territories as he may consider suitable to those conditions, provided no action shall be taken which is inconsistent with the provisions of Articles 15, 16 and 18.'
2. In pursuance of the provisions of this Article, His Majesty's Government invite the Council to pass the following resolution:
'The following provisions of the Mandate for Palestine are not applicable to

the territory known as Trans-Jordan, which comprises all territory lying to the east of a line drawn from a point two miles west of the town of Akaba on the Gulf of that name up to the centre of the Wady Araba, Dead Sea and River Jordan to its junction with the River Yarmuk; thence up the centre of that river to the Syrian Frontier.'

Preamble – Recitals 2 and 3.

Article 2 – The words 'placing the country under such political administration and economic conditions as will secure the establishment of the Jewish national home, as laid down in the preamble, and'

Article 4.

Article 6.

Article 7 – The sentence 'There shall be included in this law provisions framed so as to facilitate the acquisition of Palestinian citizenship by Jews who take up their permanent residence in Palestine.'

Article 11 – The second sentence of the first paragraph and the second paragraph.

Article 13.

Article 14.

Article 22.

Article 23.

In the application of the Mandate to Trans-Jordan, the action which, in Palestine, is taken by the Administration of the latter country, will be taken by the Administration of Trans-Jordan under the general supervision of the Mandatory.

3. His Majesty's Government accept full responsibility as Mandatory for Trans-Jordan, and undertake that such provision as may be made for the administration of that territory in accordance with Article 25 of the Mandate shall be in no way inconsistent with those provisions of the Mandate which are not by this resolution declared inapplicable.

Appendix F

The MacDonald White Paper: British Statement of Policy, May 1939 (Cmd. 6019)

In the Statement on Palestine, issued on 9th November 1938* His Majesty's Government announced their intention to invite representatives of the Arabs of Palestine, of certain neighbouring countries and of the Jewish Agency to confer with them in London regarding future policy. It was their sincere hope that, as a result of full, free and frank discussion, some understanding might be reached. Conferences recently took place with Arab and Jewish delegations, lasting for a period of several weeks, and served the purpose of a complete exchange of views between British Ministers and the Arab and Jewish representatives. In the light of the discussions as well as of the situation in Palestine and of the Reports of the Royal Commission† and the Partition Commission,‡ certain proposals were formulated by His Majesty's Government and were laid before the Arab and Jewish delegations as the basis of an agreed settlement. Neither the Arab nor the Jewish delegations felt able to accept these proposals, and the conference therefore did not result in an agreement. Accordingly His Majesty's Government are free to formulate their own policy, and after careful consideration they have decided to adhere generally to the proposals which were finally submitted to, and discussed with, the Arab and Jewish delegations.

2. The Mandate for Palestine, the terms of which were confirmed by the Council of the League of Nations in 1922, has governed the policy of successive British Governments for nearly twenty years. It embodies the Balfour Declaration and imposes on the Mandatory four main obligations. These obligations are set out in Articles 2, 6 and 13 of the Mandate. There is no dispute regarding the interpretation of one of these obligations, that touching the protection of and access to the Holy Places and religious buildings or sites. The other three main obligations are generally as follows:

(i) To place the country under such political, administrative and economic conditions as will secure the establishment in Palestine of a national home for the Jewish people, to facilitate Jewish immigration under suitable conditions, and to encourage, in co-operation with the Jewish Agency, close settlement by Jews on the land.

(ii) To safeguard the civil and religious rights of all the inhabitants of

---

* Cmd. 5893   † Cmd. 5479   ‡ Cmd. 5854

Palestine irrespective of race and religion, and, whilst facilitating Jewish immigration and settlement, to ensure that the rights and position of other sections of the population are not prejudiced.

(iii) To place the country under such political, administrative and economic conditions as will secure the development of self-governing institutions.

3. The Royal Commission and previous Commissions of Enquiry have drawn attention to the ambiguity of certain expressions in the Mandate, such as the expression 'a national home for the Jewish people', and they have found in this ambiguity and the resulting uncertainty as to the objectives of policy a fundamental cause of unrest and hostility between Arabs and Jews. His Majesty's Government are convinced that in the interests of the peace and well-being of the whole people of Palestine a clear definition of policy and objectives is essential. The proposal of partition recommended by the Royal Commission would have afforded such clarity, but the establishment of self-supporting Arab and Jewish States within Palestine has been found to be impracticable. It has therefore been necessary for His Majesty's Government to devise an alternative policy which will, consistently with their obligations to Arabs and Jews, meet the needs of the situation in Palestine. Their views and proposals are set forth below under the three heads, (I) The Constitution, (II) Immigration, and (III) Land.

I. The Constitution

4. It has been urged that the expression 'a national home for the Jewish people' offered a prospect that Palestine might in due course become a Jewish State or Commonwealth. His Majesty's Government do not wish to contest the view, which was expressed by the Royal Commission, that the Zionist leaders at the time of the issue of the Balfour Declaration recognized that an ultimate Jewish State was not precluded by the terms of the Declaration. But, with the Royal Commission, His Majesty's Government believes that the framers of the Mandate in which the Balfour Declaration was embodied could not have intended that Palestine should be converted into a Jewish State against the will of the Arab population of the country. That Palestine was not to be converted into a Jewish State might be held to be implied in the passage from the Command Paper of 1922* which reads as follows:

'Unauthorized statements have been made to the effect that the purpose in view is to create a wholly Jewish Palestine. Phrases have been used such as that "Palestine is to become as Jewish as England is English". His Majesty's Government regard any such expectation as impracticable and have no such aim in view. Nor have they at any time contemplated . . . the disappearance or the subordination of the Arabic population, language or culture in Palestine. They would draw attention to the fact that the terms of the (Balfour) Declaration referred to do not contemplate that Palestine as a whole should be converted into a Jewish National Home, but that such a Home should be founded *in Palestine.*'

But this statement has not removed doubts, and His Majesty's Government

* Cmd. 1700

APPENDIX F

therefore now declare unequivocally that it is not part of their policy that Palestine should become a Jewish State. They would indeed regard it as contrary to their obligations to the Arabs under the Mandate, as well as to the assurances which have been given to the Arab people in the past, that the Arab population of Palestine should be made the subjects of a Jewish State against their will.

5. The nature of the Jewish National Home in Palestine was further described in the Command Paper of 1922 as follows:

> 'During the last two or three generations the Jews have recreated in Palestine a community, now numbering 80,000, of whom about one-fourth are farmers or workers upon the land. This community has its own political organs; an elected assembly for the direction of its domestic concerns; elected councils in the towns; and an organization for the control of its schools. It has its elected Chief Rabbinate and Rabbinical Council for the direction of its religious affairs. Its business is conducted in Hebrew as a vernacular language, and a Hebrew press serves its needs. It has its distinctive intellectual life and displays considerable economic activity. This community, then, with its town and country population, its political, religious and social organizations, its own language, its own customs, its own life, has in fact "national" characteristics. When it is asked what is meant by the development of the Jewish National Home in Palestine, it may be answered that it is not the imposition of a Jewish nationality upon the inhabitants of Palestine as a whole, but the further development of the existing Jewish community, with the assistance of Jews in other parts of the world, in order that it may become a centre in which the Jewish people as a whole may take, on grounds of religion and race, an interest and a pride. But in order that this community should have the best prospect of free development and provide a full opportunity for the Jewish people to display its capacities, it is essential that it should know that it is in Palestine as of right and not on sufferance. That is the reason why it is necessary that the existence of a Jewish National Home in Palestine should be internationally guaranteed, and that it should be formally recognized to rest upon ancient historic connection.'

6. His Majesty's Government adhere to this interpretation of the Declaration of 1917 and regard it as an authoritative and comprehensive description of the character of the Jewish National Home in Palestine. It envisaged the further development of the existing Jewish community with the assistance of Jews in other parts of the world. Evidence that His Majesty's Government have been carrying out their obligation in this respect is to be found in the facts that, since the statement of 1922 was published, more than 300,000 Jews have immigrated to Palestine, and that the population of the National Home has risen to some 450,000, or approaching a third of the entire population of the country. Nor has the Jewish community failed to take full advantage of the opportunities given to it. The growth of the Jewish National Home and its achievements in many fields are a remarkable constructive effort which must command the

admiration of the world and must be, in particular, a source of pride to the Jewish people.

7. In the recent discussions the Arab delegations have repeated the contention that Palestine was included within the area in which Sir Henry McMahon, on behalf of the British Government, in October 1915, undertook to recognize and support Arab independence. The validity of this claim, based on the terms of the correspondence which passed between Sir Henry McMahon and the Sharif of Mecca, was thoroughly and carefully investigated by British and Arab representatives during the recent conferences in London. Their Report, which has been published,* states that both the Arab and British representatives endeavoured to understand the point of view of the other party but that they were unable to reach agreement upon an interpretation of the correspondence. There is no need to summarize here the arguments presented by each side. His Majesty's Government regret the misunderstandings which have arisen as regards some of the phrases used. For their part they can only adhere, for the reasons given by their representatives in the Report, to the view that the whole of Palestine west of Jordan was excluded from Sir Henry McMahon's pledge, and they therefore cannot agree that the McMahon correspondence forms a just basis for the claim that Palestine should be converted into an Arab State.

8. His Majesty's Government are charged as the Mandatory authority 'to secure the development of self-governing institutions' in Palestine. Apart from this specific obligation, they would regard it as contrary to the whole spirit of the Mandate system that the population of Palestine should remain for ever under Mandatory tutelage. It is proper that the people of the country should as early as possible enjoy the rights of self-government which are exercised by the people of neighbouring countries. His Majesty's Government are unable at present to foresee the exact constitutional forms which government in Palestine will eventually take, but their objective is self-government, and they desire to see established ultimately an independent Palestine State. It should be a State in which the two peoples in Palestine, Arabs and Jews, share authority in government in such a way that the essential interests of each are secured.

9. The establishment of an independent State and the complete relinquishment of Mandatory control in Palestine would require such relations between the Arabs and the Jews as would make good government possible. Moreover, the growth of self-governing institutions in Palestine, as in other countries, must be an evolutionary process. A transitional period will be required before independence is achieved, throughout which ultimate responsibility for the government of the country will be retained by His Majesty's Government as the Mandatory authority, while the people of the country are taking an increasing share in the government, and understanding and co-operation amongst them are growing. It will be the constant endeavour of His Majesty's Government to promote good relations between the Arabs and the Jews.

* Cmd. 5974

APPENDIX F

10. In the light of these considerations His Majesty's Government make the following declaration of their intentions regarding the future government of Palestine:

(1) The objective of His Majesty's Government is the establishment within ten years of an independent Palestine State in such treaty relations with the United Kingdom as will provide satisfactorily for the commercial and strategic requirements of both countries in the future. This proposal for the establishment of the independent State would involve consultation with the Council of the League of Nations with a view to the termination of the Mandate.

(2) The independent State should be one in which Arabs and Jews share in government in such a way as to ensure that the essential interests of each community are safeguarded.

(3) The establishment of the independent State will be preceded by a transitional period throughout which His Majesty's Government will retain responsibility for the government of the country. During the transitional period the people of Palestine will be given an increasing part in the government of their country. Both sections of the population will have an opportunity to participate in the machinery of government, and the process will be carried on whether or not they both avail themselves of it.

(4) As soon as peace and order have been sufficiently restored in Palestine steps will be taken to carry out this policy of giving the people of Palestine an increasing part in the government of their country, the objective being to place Palestinians in charge of all the Departments of Government, with the assistance of British advisers and subject to the control of the High Commissioner. With this object in view His Majesty's Government will be prepared immediately to arrange that Palestinians shall be placed in charge of certain Departments, with British advisers. The Palestinian heads of Departments will sit on the Executive Council, which advises the High Commissioner. Arab and Jewish representatives will be invited to serve as heads of Departments approximately in proportion to their respective populations. The number of Palestinians in charge of Departments will be increased as circumstances permit until all heads of Departments are Palestinians, exercising the administrative and advisory functions which are at present performed by British officials. When that stage is reached consideration will be given to the question of converting the Executive Council into a Council of Ministers with a consequential change in the status and functions of the Palestinian heads of Departments.

(5) His Majesty's Government make no proposals at this stage regarding the establishment of an elective legislature. Nevertheless they would regard this as an appropriate constitutional development, and, should public opinion in Palestine hereafter show itself in favour of such a development, they will be prepared, provided that local conditions permit, to establish the necessary machinery.

(6) At the end of five years from the restoration of peace and order, an appropriate body representative of the people of Palestine and of His

Majesty's Government will be set up to review the working of the constitutional arrangements during the transitional period and to consider and make recommendations regarding the constitution of the independent Palestine State.

(7) His Majesty's Government will require to be satisfied that in the treaty contemplated by sub-paragraph (1) or in the constitution contemplated by sub-paragraph (6) adequate provision has been made for:

(a) The security of, and freedom of access to, the Holy Places, and the protection of the interests and property of the various religious bodies.

(b) the protection of the different communities in Palestine in accordance with the obligations of His Majesty's Government to both Arabs and Jews for the special position in Palestine of the Jewish National Home.

(c) such requirements to meet the strategic situation as may be regarded as necessary by His Majesty's Government in the light of the circumstances then existing.

His Majesty's Government will also require to be satisfied that the interests of certain foreign countries in Palestine, for the preservation of which they are at present responsible, are adequately safeguarded.

(8) His Majesty's Government will do everything in their power to create conditions which will enable the independent Palestine State to come into being within ten years. If, at the end of ten years, it appears to His Majesty's Government that, contrary to their hope, circumstances require the postponement of the establishment of the independent State, they will consult with representatives of the people of Palestine, the Council of the League of Nations and the neighbouring Arab States before deciding on such a postponement. If His Majesty's Government come to the conclusion that postponement is unavoidable, they will invite the co-operation of these parties in framing plans for the future with a view to achieving the desired objective at the earliest possible date.

11. During the transitional period steps will be taken to increase the powers and responsibilities of municipal corporations and local councils.

II. Immigration

12. Under Article 6 of the Mandate, the Administration of Palestine, 'while ensuring that the rights and position of other sections of the population are not prejudiced', is required to 'facilitate Jewish immigration under suitable conditions'. Beyond this, the extent to which Jewish immigration into Palestine is to be permitted is nowhere defined in the Mandate. But in the Command Paper of 1922 it was laid down that for the fulfilment of the policy of establishing a Jewish National Home

'it is necessary that the Jewish community in Palestine should be able to increase its numbers by immigration. This immigration cannot be so great in volume as to exceed whatever may be the economic capacity of the country at the time to absorb new arrivals. It is essential to ensure that the immigrants should not be a burden upon the people of Palestine as a whole, and that they should not deprive any section of the present population of their employment.'

In practice, from that date onwards until recent times, the economic absorptive capacity of the country has been treated as the sole limiting factor, and in the letter which Mr Ramsay MacDonald, as Prime Minister, sent to Dr Weizmann in February 1931* it was laid down as a matter of policy that economic absorptive capacity was the sole criterion. This interpretation has been supported by resolutions of the Permanent Mandates Commission. But His Majesty's Government do not read either the Statement of Policy of 1922 or the letter of 1931 as implying that the Mandate requires them, for all time and in all circumstances, to facilitate the immigration of Jews into Palestine subject only to consideration of the country's economic absorptive capacity. Nor do they find anything in the Mandate or in subsequent Statements of Policy to support the view that the establishment of a Jewish National Home in Palestine cannot be effected unless immigration is allowed to continue indefinitely. If immigration has an adverse effect on the economic position in the country, it should clearly be restricted; and equally, if it has a seriously damaging effect on the political position in the country, that is a factor that should not be ignored. Although it is not difficult to contend that the large number of Jewish immigrants who have been admitted so far have been absorbed economically, the fear of the Arabs that this influx will continue indefinitely until the Jewish population is in a position to dominate them has produced consequences which are extremely grave for Jews and Arabs alike and for the peace and prosperity of Palestine. The lamentable disturbances of the past three years are only the latest and most sustained manifestation of this intense Arab apprehension. The methods employed by Arab terrorists against fellow-Arabs and Jews alike must receive unqualified condemnation. But it cannot be denied that fear of indefinite Jewish immigration is widespread amongst the Arab population and that this fear has made possible disturbances which have given a serious setback to economic progress, depleted the Palestine exchequer, rendered life and property insecure, and produced a bitterness between the Arab and Jewish populations which is deplorable between citizens of the same country. If in these circumstances immigration is continued up to the economic absorptive capacity of the country, regardless of all other considerations, a fatal enmity between the two peoples will be perpetuated, and the situation in Palestine may become a permanent source of friction amongst all peoples in the Near and Middle East. His Majesty's Government cannot take the view that either their obligation under the Mandate, or consideration of common sense and justice, require that they should ignore these circumstances in framing immigration policy.

13. In the view of the Royal Commission, the association of the policy of the Balfour Declaration with the Mandate system implied the belief that Arab hostility to the former would sooner or later be overcome. It has been the hope of British governments ever since the Balfour Declaration was issued that in time the Arab population, recognizing the advantages to be derived from

* *Hansard*, vol. 248, 13/2/31, cols. 751–7

Jewish settlement and development in Palestine, would become reconciled to the further growth of the Jewish National Home. This hope has not been fulfilled. The alternatives before His Majesty's Government are either (i) to seek to expand the Jewish National Home indefinitely by immigration, against the strongly expressed will of the Arab people of the country; or (ii) to permit further expansion of the Jewish National Home by immigration only if the Arabs are prepared to acquiesce in it. The former policy means rule by force. Apart from other considerations, such a policy seems to His Majesty's Government to be contrary to the whole spirit of Article 22 of the Covenant of the League of Nations, as well as to their specific obligations to the Arabs in the Palestine Mandate. Moreover, the relations between the Arabs and the Jews in Palestine must be based sooner or later on mutual tolerance and goodwill; the peace, security and progress of the Jewish National Home itself require this. Therefore His Majesty's Government, after earnest consideration, and taking into account the extent to which the growth of the Jewish National Home has been facilitated over the last twenty years, have decided that the time has come to adopt in principle the second of the alternatives referred to above.

14. It has been urged that all further Jewish immigration into Palestine should be stopped forthwith. His Majesty's Government cannot accept such a proposal. It would damage the whole of the financial and economic system of Palestine and thus affect adversely the interests of Arabs and Jews alike. Moreover, in the view of His Majesty's Government, abruptly to stop further immigration would be unjust to the Jewish National Home. But, above all, His Majesty's Government are conscious of the present unhappy plight of large numbers of Jews who seek a refuge from certain European countries, and they believe that Palestine can and should make a further contribution to the solution of this pressing world problem. In all these circumstances, they believe that they will be acting consistently with their Mandatory obligations to both Arabs and Jews, and in the manner best calculated to serve the interests of the whole people of Palestine, by adopting the following proposals regarding immigration:

(1) Jewish immigration during the next five years will be at a rate which, if economic absorptive capacity permits, will bring the Jewish population up to approximately one-third of the total population of the country. Taking into account the expected natural increase of the Arab and Jewish populations, and the number of illegal Jewish immigrants now in the country, this would allow of the admission, as from the beginning of April this year, of some 75,000 immigrants over the next five years. These immigrants would, subject to the criterion of economic absorptive capacity, be admitted as follows:

(a) For each of the next five years a quota of 10,000 Jewish immigrants will be allowed, on the understanding that a shortage in any one year may be added to the quotas for subsequent years, within the five-year period, if economic absorptive capacity permits.

(b) In addition, as a contribution towards the solution of the Jewish refugee problem, 25,000 refugees will be admitted as soon as the High Commissioner is satisfied that adequate provision for their maintenance is ensured, special consideration being given to refugee children and dependents.

(2) The existing machinery for ascertaining economic absorptive capacity will be retained, and the High Commissioner will have the ultimate responsibility for deciding the limits of economic capacity. Before each periodic decision is taken, Jewish and Arab representatives will be consulted.

(3) After the period of five years no further Jewish immigration will be permitted unless the Arabs of Palestine are prepared to acquiesce in it.

(4) His Majesty's Government are determined to check illegal immigration, and further preventive measures are being adopted. The numbers of any Jewish illegal immigrants who, despite these measures, may succeed in coming into the country and cannot be deported will be deducted from the yearly quotas.

15. His Majesty's Government are satisfied that, when the immigration over five years which is now contemplated has taken place, they will not be justified in facilitating, nor will they be under any obligation to facilitate, the further development of the Jewish National Home by immigration regardless of the wishes of the Arab population.

III. Land

16. The Administration of Palestine is required, under Article 6 of the Mandate, 'while ensuring that the rights and position of other sections of the population are not prejudiced', to encourage 'close settlement by Jews on the land', and no restriction has been imposed hitherto on the transfer of land from Arabs to Jews. The Reports of several expert Commissions have indicated that, owing to the natural growth of the Arab population and the steady sale in recent years of Arab land to Jews, there is now in certain areas no room for further transfers of Arab land, whilst in some other areas such transfers of land must be restricted if Arab cultivators are to maintain their existing standard of life and a considerable landless Arab population is not soon to be created. In these circumstances, the High Commissioner will be given general powers to prohibit and regulate transfers of land. These powers will date from the publication of this statement of policy and the High Commissioner will retain them throughout the transitional period.

17. The policy of the Government will be directed towards the development of the land and the improvement, where possible, of methods of cultivation. In the light of such development it will be open to the High Commissioner, should he be satisfied that the 'rights and position' of the Arab population will be duly preserved, to review and modify any orders passed relating to the prohibition or restriction of the transfer of land.

---

18. In framing these proposals His Majesty's Government have sincerely

endeavoured to act in strict accordance with their obligations under the Mandate to both the Arabs and the Jews. The vagueness of the phrases employed in some instances to describe these obligations has led to controversy and has made the task of interpretation difficult. His Majesty's Government cannot hope to satisfy the partisans of one party or the other in such controversy as the Mandate has aroused. Their purpose is to be just as between the two peoples in Palestine whose destinies in that country have been affected by the great events of recent years, and who, since they live side by side, must learn to practise mutual tolerance, goodwill and co-operation. In looking to the future, His Majesty's Government are not blind to the fact that some events of the past make the task of creating these relations difficult; but they are encouraged by the knowledge that at many times and in many places in Palestine during recent years the Arab and Jewish inhabitants have lived in friendship together. Each community has much to contribute to the welfare of their common land, and each must earnestly desire peace in which to assist in increasing the well-being of the whole people of the country. The responsibility which falls on them, no less than upon His Majesty's Government, to co-operate together to ensure peace is all the more solemn because their country is revered by many millions of Moslems, Jews and Christians throughout the world who pray for peace in Palestine and for the happiness of her people.

Appendix G

The Proclamation of Israel's Independence: Tel Aviv, 14 May 1948

The Land of Israel was the birthplace of the Jewish people. Here their spiritual, religious and national identity was formed. Here they achieved independence and created a culture of national and universal significance. Here they wrote and gave the Bible to the world.

Exiled from the Land of Israel, the Jewish people remained faithful to it in all the countries of their dispersion, never ceasing to pray and hope for their return and the restoration of their national freedom.

Impelled by this historic association Jews strove throughout the centuries to go back to the land of their fathers and regain their statehood. In recent decades they returned in their masses. They reclaimed the wilderness, revived their language, built cities and villages, and established a vigorous and ever-growing community, with its own economic and cultural life. They sought peace yet were prepared to defend themselves. They brought the blessings of progress to all inhabitants of the country and looked forward to sovereign independence.

In the year 1897 the First Zionist Congress, inspired by Theodor Herzl's vision of the Jewish State, proclaimed the right of the Jewish people to national revival in their own country.

This right was acknowledged by the Balfour Declaration of November 2, 1917, and re-affirmed by the Mandate of the League of Nations, which gave explicit international recognition to the historic connection of the Jewish people with Palestine and their right to reconstitute their National Home.

The recent holocaust, which engulfed millions of Jews in Europe, proved anew the need to solve the problem of the homelessness and lack of independence of the Jewish people by means of the re-establishment of the Jewish State, which would open the gates to all Jews and endow the Jewish people with equality of status among the family of nations.

The survivors of the disastrous slaughter in Europe, and also Jews from other lands, have not desisted from their efforts to reach *Eretz Israel*, in face of difficulties, obstacles and perils; and have not ceased to urge their right to a life of dignity, freedom and honest toil in their ancestral land.

In the Second World War the Jewish people in Palestine made their full contribution to the struggle of the freedom-loving nations against the Nazi evil. The sacrifices of their soldiers and their war effort gained them the right to rank with the nations which founded the United Nations.

On November 29, 1947, the General Assembly of the United Nations adopted a Resolution requiring the establishment of a Jewish State in Palestine. The General Assembly called upon the inhabitants of the country to take all the necessary steps on their part to put the plan into effect. This recognition by the United Nations of the right of the Jewish people to establish their independent State is unassailable.

It is the natural right of the Jewish people to lead, as do all other nations, an independent existence in its sovereign State.

ACCORDINGLY WE, the members of the National Council, representing the Jewish people in Palestine, and the World Zionist Movement, are met together in solemn assembly today, the day of termination of the British Mandate for Palestine; and by virtue of the natural and historic right of the Jewish people and of the Resolution of the General Assembly of the United Nations.

WE HEREBY PROCLAIM the establishment of the Jewish State in Palestine, to be called '*Medinat Israel*' (The State of Israel).

WE HEREBY DECLARE that, as from the termination of the Mandate at midnight, the 14th–15th May, 1948, and pending the setting up of the duly elected bodies of the State in accordance with a Constitution, to be drawn up by the Constituent Assembly not later than the 1st October, 1948, the National Council shall act as the Provisional State Council, and that the National Administration shall constitute the Provisional Government of the Jewish State, which shall be known as Israel.

THE STATE OF ISRAEL will be open to the immigration of Jews from all countries of their dispersion; will promote the development of the country for the benefit of all its inhabitants; will be based on the principles of liberty, justice and peace as conceived by the Prophets of Israel, will uphold the full social and political equality of all its citizens, without distinction of religion, race or sex; will guarantee freedom of religion, conscience, education and culture; will safeguard the Holy Places of all religions; and will loyally uphold the principles of the United Nations Charter.

THE STATE OF ISRAEL will be ready to co-operate with the organs and representatives of the United Nations in the implementation of the Resolution of the Assembly of November 29, 1947, and will take steps to bring about the Economic Union over the whole of Palestine.

We appeal to the United Nations to assist the Jewish people in the building of its State and to admit Israel into the family of nations.

In the midst of wanton aggression, we yet call upon the Arab inhabitants of the State of Israel to preserve the ways of peace and play their part in the development of the State, on the basis of full and equal citizenship and due representation in all its bodies and institutions – provisional and permanent.

We extend our hand in peace and neighbourliness to all the neighbouring states and their peoples, and invite them to co-operate with the independent Jewish nation for the common good of all. The State of Israel is prepared to

APPENDIX G

make its contribution to the progress of the Middle East as a whole.

Our call goes out to the Jewish people all over the world to rally to our side in the task of immigration and development and to stand by us in the great struggle for the fulfilment of the dream of generations for the redemption of Israel.

With trust in Almighty God, we set our hand to this Declaration, at this Session of the Provisional State Council, on the soil of the Homeland, in the city of Tel Aviv, on this Sabbath eve, the fifth of Iyar, 5708, the fourteenth day of May, 1948.

The signatories   David Ben-Gurion, Daniel Auster, Mordechai Bentov, Isaac Ben-Zvi, Eliyahu Berligne, Fritz (Peretz) Bernstein, Rabbi Wolf Gold, Meir Grabovsky, Isaac Gruenbaum, Dr Abraham Granovsky (Granott), Eliyahu Dobkin, Meir Wilner-Kovner, Zerach Wahrhaftig, Herzl Vardi, Rachel Cohen, Rabbi Kalman Kahana, Saadia Kobashi, Rabbi Isaac Meir Levin, Meir David Loewenstein, Zvi Luria, Golda Myerson (Meir), Nachum Nir, Zvi Segal, Rabbi Yehuda Leib Fishman (Maimon), David Zvi Pinkas, Aharon Zisling, Moshe Kolodny (Kol), Eliezer Kaplan, Abraham Katznelson, Felix Rosenblueth (Rosen), David Remez, Berl Repetur, Mordechai Shattner, Ben Zion Sternberg, Bechor Shitreet, Moshe Shapira, Moshe Shertok (Sharett).

Glossary

Agudath Harabbonim   Association of Rabbis
Agudath Israel   Non-Zionist Orthodox movement founded 1912
Aliyah   Immigration to the Land of Israel
Bnai Brith   Jewish service organization founded in New York 1843
Bund   Socialist organization devoted to secular Jewish nationalism and opposed to Zionism. Founded in Russia 1897
Chalukah (Halukah)   Distribution of alms among Orthodox poor of Jerusalem
Chalutz   Pioneer agricultural labourer in Palestine
Cheder (Heder)   Elementary school for religious instruction
Dunam   A quarter-acre
Eretz Israel   Land of Israel
Fellah (pl. *Fellaheen*)   Arab peasant
Galut   Exile, diaspora
Goy   Gentile
Hadassah   American Women's Zionist Organization, founded 1912 for hospital and welfare work in Palestine
Haganah   Organization of Jewish armed defence
Hatikvah   'The Hope', Zionist anthem
Herut   Lit., 'Freedom'. Political party founded 1948, subsequently absorbed in right-wing bloc
Hora   Folk dance of the pioneers in Palestine
ICA   Jewish Colonization Association, founded 1891 to promote emigration and resettlement of needy Jews, mainly to North and South America.
Irgun Zvai Leumi   Underground military organization formed 1931 as breakaway from *Haganah*
Keren Hayesod (KH)   Foundation Fund. The main fund-raising organization of Zionism
Kvutza (pl. *Kvutzot*)   Agricultural commune, as *kibbutz*
Lohamei Herut Israel   Stern Group which in 1941 broke away from *Irgun*
Machlul (Arab.)   Turkish law bringing land uncultivated for three years into government hands
Meshuggener (Yidd.)   crazy
Mizrachi   Religious Zionist party founded 1902
Moshav (pl. *Moshavim*)   Co-operative smallholders' village
Poalei Zion   Socialist Zionist party founded 1906
Poritz (Yidd.)   Man achieving status through his wealth
Sechel   Understanding, intelligence

GLOSSARY

Shabbas   Sabbath
Talmud Torah   Hebrew elementary school for poor children
Va'ad Leumi   National Council of Jews in Palestine, which gave way in May 1948 to Provisional State Council
Wakf   Moslem religious endowment
Yeshiva (pl. *Yeshivot*)   Talmud students' seminary
Yishuv   Jewish community within Israel, as opposed to *Galut*

Bibliography

Adams, Michael (ed.), *The Middle East* (London 1971)
Adler, Frank J., *Roots in a Moving Stream* (Kansas City 1972)
Antonius, George, *The Arab Awakening* (London 1938, Philadelphia 1939)
Barbour, Nevill, *Nisi Dominus* (London 1946)
Bein, Alex, *Theodor Herzl* (Philadelphia 1956, London 1957)
Ben-Gurion, David, *Letters to Paula* (London 1971, Pittsburgh 1972)
Ben-Gurion, David, and Pearlman, Moshe, *Ben-Gurion Looks Back* (London 1965)
Bentwich, Norman, *For Zion's Sake* (Biography of Judah L. Magnes), (Philadelphia 1954)
Berlin, Isaiah, *Zionist Politics in Wartime Washington* (Lecture), (Jerusalem 1972)
Berlin, Isaiah, and Kolatt, Israel, *Chaim Weizmann as Leader* (Lectures), (Jerusalem 1970)
Blumberg, Harold M., *Weizmann, His Life and Times* (London, New York 1975)
Brodetsky, Selig, *Memoirs* (London 1960)
Cattan, Henry, *Palestine, the Arabs and Israel* (London 1967)
Churchill, Winston, *The Second World War* (London 1948–54)
Clark, Ronald W., *Einstein* (London 1973)
Cohen, Israel, *A Short History of Zionism* (London 1951)
Cohen, Michael J., *Palestine: Retreat from the Mandate* (London 1978)
Crossman, Richard H. S., *Palestine Mission* (London, New York 1947)
Crum, Bartley, *Behind the Silken Curtain* (New York 1947)
Dugdale, Blanche, *Arthur James Balfour* (London 1936)
Eban, Abba, *Chaim Weizmann* (Lecture), (London 1962)
Eban, Abba, *Chaim Weizmann* (in *Encyclopaedia Judaica*), (Jerusalem 1971)
Elath, Eliahu, *Israel and Elath* (Lecture), (London 1966)
Esco Foundation, *Palestine: A Study of Jewish, Arab and British Politics* (New Haven 1947)
Friedman, Isaiah, *Germany, Turkey and Zionism* (Oxford 1977)
Garnett, David (ed.), *The Letters of T. E. Lawrence* (London 1938, New York 1939)
Goldmann, Nahum, *Memories* (New York 1969, London 1970)
Goodman, Paul (ed.), *The Jewish National Home 1917–1942* (London 1943)
Goodman, Paul (ed.), *Chaim Weizmann, A Tribute on his Seventieth Birthday* (London 1945)
Haas, Jacob de, *Louis D. Brandeis* (New York 1929)

BIBLIOGRAPHY

Herzl, Theodor, *The Complete Diaries* (London, New York 1960)
Jabotinsky, Vladimir, *The Story of the Jewish Legion* (New York 1945)
Kimche, Jon, *The Unromantics* (London 1968)
Kisch, Fred H., *Palestine Diary* (London 1938)
Knightley, Philip, and Simpson, Colin, *The Secret Lives of Lawrence of Arabia* (London 1969)
Krojanker, Gustav (ed.), *Reden und Aufsätze* (Weizmann speeches), (Tel Aviv 1937)
Laqueur, Walter, *A History of Zionism* (London 1972)
Lawrence, Arnold W. (ed.), *T. E. Lawrence by his Friends* (London 1937)
Leftwich, Joseph, *Israel Zangwill* (London, New York 1957)
Lipsky, Louis, *A Gallery of Zionist Profiles* (New York 1956)
Litvinoff, Barnet, *Weizmann, Last of the Patriarchs* (London, New York 1976)
Lloyd George, David, *War Memoirs* (London 1933-6)
Manuel, Frank E., *The Realities of American-Palestine Relations* (Washington 1949)
Meinertzhagen, Richard, *Middle East Diary 1917-1956* (London 1959)
Millin, Sarah G., *General Smuts* (London 1936)
Nordau, Anna and Maxa, *Max Nordau* (New York 1943)
Rabinowitz, Oskar K., *Fifty Years of Zionism* (Critique of *Trial and Error*), (London 1952)
Rose, Norman A. (ed.), *Baffy, The Diaries of Blanche Dugdale 1936-47* (London 1973)
Ruppin, Arthur, *Memoirs, Diaries, Letters* (ed. Alex Bein), (London, New York 1971)
Sacher, Harry (ed.), *Zionism and the Jewish Future* (London 1916)
Sacher, Harry, *Zionist Portraits and Other Essays* (London 1959)
Samuel, Herbert (Viscount), *Memoirs* (London 1945, Indianapolis 1946)
Schechtman, Joseph, *The Jabotinsky Story* (New York 1956, 1961)
Sieff, Israel, *Memoirs* (London 1970)
Silver, Abba Hillel, *Vision and Victory* (Addresses), (New York 1949)
Simon, Julius, *Certain Days* (Jerusalem 1971)
Simon, Leon, *Ahad Ha'am* (London, Philadelphia 1960)
Sokolow, Nahum, *History of Zionism* (London 1919)
Stein, Leonard, *The Balfour Declaration* (London 1961)
Stettinius, Edward R., *Diaries* (New York 1975)
Storrs, Ronald, *Orientations* (London 1937)
Truman, Harry S., *Memoirs* (London, New York 1955-56)
Webster, Charles K., *The Founder of the National Home* (Lecture), (Rehovot 1955)
Weisgal, Meyer W. (ed.), *Chaim Weizmann, Statesman and Scientist* (New York 1944)
Weisgal, Meyer W., *... So Far* (London, New York 1971)
Weisgal, Meyer W., and Carmichael, Joel (eds), *Chaim Weizmann, A Biography by Several Hands* (London, New York 1962)
Weisgal, Meyer W., and Litvinoff, Barnet (gen. eds), *The Letters and Papers*

of Chaim Weizmann (Series A, Letters, 23 vols), (London, Jerusalem, New Brunswick, NJ, 1968–80)
Weizmann, Chaim, *Trial and Error* (London, New York 1949)
Weizmann, Vera, *The Imposssible Takes Longer* (London 1967)
Welles, Sumner, *We Need Not Fail* (Boston 1948)
Wilson, Trevor (ed.), *The Political Diaries of C. P. Scott* (London 1970)
Wischnitzer, Mark, *To Dwell in Safety* (Philadelphia 1948)
Wise, Stephen S., *Challenging Years* (New York 1949)

Other Sources

Documents on British Foreign Policy, 1918–39, vols IV, VII, VIII (London 1952, 1958)
Foreign Relations of the United States. Documents from 1915 (Washington, DC)
Book of Documents. Submitted to UN General Assembly by Jewish Agency for Palestine (New York 1947)
Zionist Organization and Jewish Agency Reports, Statements and Memoranda, including Stenographic Records of Zionist Congresses. In Central Zionist Archives, Jerusalem
Unpublished Correspondence, Speeches and Writings of Chaim Weizmann. In Weizmann Archives, Rehovot
British documents in Crown Copyright. In Public Record Office, London
Weizmann material as State President. In Israel State Archives, Jerusalem
Papers of American Zionists and relevant official US documents (including microfilms) in Zionist Archives and Library, New York
British Government Statements, issued as Command Papers (London, from 1922)
Jewish Chronicle, London; *Zionist Review*, London; *New Judaea*, London; *New Palestine*, New York
Files of European Jewish Newspapers at Jewish National and University Library, Jerusalem, and Central Zionist Archives, Jerusalem

Index

Aaronsohn, Aaron, 4, 77
Abdullah, King Ibn Hussein, 73, 83
Aberson, Zvi, 39
Admiralty, 4, 194–5
Agudath Harabbonim, 135
Agudath Israel, 135
Ahad Ha'am (Asher Z. Ginzberg), 1, 3, 109, 165–6, 192, 201; W. assesses, 155–6
Akaba, and boundaries, 262
Aleppo, Brand–Shertok meeting there, 141
Alexander, David L., 199
Alexander, Samuel, 192, 243
Allenby, Gen. Edmund H., 66–8, 76
Alliance Israélite Universelle, 50, 164
America, W. visits, 5, 8–9, 228; and the Americans, 94–108, 159, 174, 192–3; and Turkey, 94, 194, 200; and Zionism, 95–7, 102, 170, 230; and State of Israel, 107; immigration to, 117, 127–8, 231; and Crimean Scheme, 118, 240; and Brand mission, 140; Provisional Executive Committee for General Zionist Affairs (PEC), 192–4; declares war on Germany, 198; and Palestine, 198–9, 201, 225, 228, 233, 240, 242; its State Department, 228, 232–4; and WWII, 242
American Jewish Committee, 106, 135, 164–5
American Jewish Congress, 135
American Joint Emergency Committee, 136
American Red Cross, 94
American War Refugee Board, 141

American Zionist Emergency Committee, 102
Amery, Leopold S., 77
Angel, Sir Norman, his assessment of W., 177
Anglican Bishop of Jerusalem, 183
Anglo-American Committee of Enquiry, 9, 24, 146–7, 180, 231
Anglo-Jewish Association, 50, 93, 199
Arab Higher Committee, 23
Arabs, Jews' relations with, x, xi, 11–25, 128, 163, 165, 169, 187–9, 197, 201, 211–12, 223, 228, 240, 269–71, 274; Faisal–W. Agreement, 5, 220–21, 252–3; their attacks on Jews, 6–7, 68–9, 149, 174, 227, 233, 240; and Jerusalem, 70; MacDonald White Paper, 91, 263–72; Arab labour, 121–2, 210–11; in WWII, 130; and partition of Palestine, 227, 232–4, 241; and America, 228–9, 231; and Ibn Saud, 230; their invasion of Palestine, 234
Archbishop of Canterbury, *see* Lang, Cosmo
Argentina, colonization there, 128
Arlosoroff, Chaim, 156, 173, 241
Armenian massacres, 14
Asquith, Herbert, 191, 193, 195–6, 218
Athlit Agricultural Experimental Station, 65
Athlit Camp, 145
Attlee, Clement, and his government, 145, 224, 230–31, 242
Auster, Daniel, 275
Austria, Catholics there, 199

INDEX

Baer, Richard, 214
Balfour, Arthur J., 23, 25, 85, 89, 107, 194–6, 200–2; and Hebrew University, 6, 66–7, 110, 218, 251; W.'s meetings with, 2–4, 36, 94, 192, 197, 200, 217–18; wants Anglo-American protectorate for Palestine, 197; in America, 199
Balfour Declaration, x, 22, 45, 55, 76, 84, 88–9, 139, 155, 164, 180, 185, 187, 191–202, 211, 218, 221, 223, 240; its issuance, 4, 219–20, 251, 273; and Wilson, 199, 225; drafting of, 201–2; 'betrayal' of, 220, 222; and Arabs, 268–9
Bar-Kochba Student Society, Prague, 48
Baruch, Bernard, 228
Basle Programme, 22, 166, 250
Beaverbrook, Lord, 131
Beck, Joseph, 124
Beersheba, and partition, 233
Begin, Menahem, 156; his Government, 249
Benedict XV, Pope, 198–9
Ben-Gurion, David, ix–xi, 8–9, 148, 153, 213, 231, 275; W. assesses, 156–8; his assessment of W., 177–8; and Nineteenth Z. C., 241; and partition, 241; and Biltmore Conference, 242; and armed resistance, 242
Bentov, Mordechai, 275
Ben-Zvi, Isaac, 275
Bergmann, Ernst David, 23, 245
Berligne, Bella, 172
Berligne, Eliyahu, 275
Berlin, Sir Isaiah, his assessment of W., 178–9
Bermuda (Refugee) Conference, 8, 135–9
Berne Academic Zionist Society, 33
Bernstein, Fritz (Peretz), 275
Bertie, Sir Francis, 193
Bevin, Ernest, 93, 222, 230, 232
Bialik, Chaim Nachman, 67, 184
Bidault, Georges, 227
Billikopf, Jacob, 99
Biltmore (New York) Conference, 8, 222, 229, 242
Birkenau Camp, 141–2

Blum, Léon, x, 7, 226–7, 240
Bnai Brith, 135
Board of Deputies (of British Jews), 199, 216
Bograchov, Chaim, 50
Bols, Gen. Louis, 221
Bonham-Carter, Lady Violet, 149
Boston, and Jews there, 97
Bracken, Brendan, 126, 131, 224
Brand, Joel, his mission, 8, 140–42
Brandeis, Louis D., x, 5, 60, 76, 94–7, 178, 189, 192, 198, 201–2, 224, 226, 228, 239; W. assesses, 158–9, 161; message to Turkey, 194; meeting with Balfour, 199; meeting with Wilson, 199
British Joint Emergency Committee, 136
British Palestine Committee, 196
Brown, Philip Marshall, 179
Bruening, Heinrich, 120
Brussels Conference (1906), 45
Buber, Martin, 2, 108, 159, 237; his assessment of W., 179
Budapest, and Jews there, 141–2
Bund, The, 41, 52

Cairo Conference (1921), 83
Cambridge University, 206–7, 214
Carlsbad Zionist Conference (1922), 18
Cazalet, Victor A., 129
Cecil, Robert (Viscount Cecil of Chelwood), 23, 76, 88, 195; his assessment of W., 179
Central Powers, 4, 192–3, 200
Chamberlain, Joseph, 25, 29
Chamberlain, Neville, 7, 126, 132–4, 223
Charlottenburg Polytechnic, 1
Chicago World Fair, 7
Churchill White Paper (1922), 5, 83, 223
Churchill, Winston, 3, 7, 9, 17, 83, 92, 127, 131, 134, 142, 158, 195, 217, 222, 228–30; and Moyne assassination, 145; his assessment of W., 179; his White Paper, 223; first meeting with W., 223–4
Clayton Aniline Company, 2
Clayton, Sir Gilbert, 90, 220

INDEX

Clemenceau, Georges, 219, 225
Clerk, Sir George, 116–17
Cleveland Conference (1921), 5
Clifford, Clark, 232
Cohen, Benjamin V., 228
Cohen, Rachel, 275
Commercial Solvents Corporation, 5
Conjoint Foreign Committee, 199
Coolidge, Calvin, 6
Council of Ten, 5, 78, 163, 220, 225
Cowen, Joseph, 3, 193, 195, 197
Cranborne (*later* Marquis of Salisbury), Lord, 135, 164
Creech Jones, Arthur, 93, 148
Cromer, Lord, 30
Crossman, Richard H. S., his assessment of W., 180
Cunningham, Sir Alan (H. C. of Palestine), 148, 159–60
Curzon, George Nathaniel (Lord), 85, 186
Czernowitz, W.'s speech there, 204–5

Daily Chronicle, 59
Daily Express, its attack on W., 181–2
Damascus, 197, 209; and French, 81, 221
Daniel Sieff Research Institute, 6–7, 23, 214, 244–5, 249
Dardanelles campaign, 194–5
Darmstadt Polytechnic, 1
Dawson, Geoffrey, 213
Deedes, Sir Wyndham, 90
Deichler, Christian, 243
Democratic Fraction, 2, 27, 159, 236, 238; its Geneva Bureau, 2; and Jewish University, 2, 237
Diaspora, xi, 31–2, 56, 146, 151, 153, 161
Dill, Sir John, 129
Djemal Pasha, 209
Dobkin, Eliyahu, 275
Dorfman, Catherine, 155
Dounie, Tuvia, 249
Dreyfus, Charles, 2, 217
Dugdale, Blanche ('Baffy'), 125, 156, 218; her assessment of W., 180
Duma, *see under* Russia

East Africa ('Uganda') Scheme, 2–3, 25–36, 162, 175–6, 204, 219; East Africa Commission, 26, 238; as 'overnight shelter', 31–3; and Sixth Z. C., 238
Eban, Abba, his assessment of W., 181
Eden, Anthony, 8, 136, 142; and Jewish Fighting Force, 129–31
Eder, M. David, 66, 99
Egypt, 105, 228, 232; and invasion of Palestine, 93
Egyptian Expeditionary Force, 198
Ehrlich, Paul, 175
Einstein, Albert, x, 5, 22, 240; and Hebrew University, 6, 110, 114–15, 164, 178, 214–15; W. assesses, 160
El Arish, and possible colonization, 30; Palestine boundaries, 83
Eliot, Sir Charles, 29
Elkus, Abraham, 95
English Zionist Federation (EZF), 3, 85, 191, 193–4, 199, 201; Special Conference, 43; W. elected President, 4, 197; Extraordinary Conference, 199
Errera, Jacques, 160
Evening Standard, 190
Evian Inter-Governmental Conference on Refugees, 137
Exile, and Jewish assimilation, 46–9, 52–3

Faisal, Ibn Hussein, 163, 229; W.'s meeting with, 5, 15, 81, 209, 220; Faisal–Weizmann Agreement, 5, 220, 252–3; rights for Jews in Palestine, 220; as king, 221
Feiwel, Berthold, 2, 99, 108, 211
Fischel, Walter J., his article, 115–16
Fishman (Maimon), Yehuda Leib, 275
Foreign Affairs, W.'s article there, 8, 212
Fox, Douglas and Partners, 79
France, and Palestine, 75–6, 193–4, 198, 209, 225–7; Anglo-French Convention, 80; and dual rights, 163; its Jewish community, 167; Jewish Regiment, 195; Sykes–Picot Agreement, 196–7; anti-Zionists in, 208; and Faisal, 221; and American Commission of 1919, 225; Vichy regime, 227
Franck, James, 214

INDEX

Franck, Mrs James, 214–15
Frankfurter, Felix, 94, 103, 143, 162, 200–1, 215, 221, 225, 228; W. assesses, 160–61; his assessment of W., 182
Freeman, John (Ralph), 79
Fribourg University, 1

Galut, see Diaspora
Garnett, David, 225
Gaster, Moses, 3, 30, 33, 41, 151, 175, 192–5, 197, 209, 223; W. assesses, 161
Gaza, British attack on, 198
Geddes, Sir Auckland, 97
George V, King, 5
Georges-Picot, François, 76, 196
Geneva University, 1
Germany, its Jews, 122–4, 173, 227, 245; and Brand mission, 140–42; and Zionist Executive, 191; its Catholics, 199; compared with Britain, 206–7; Jewish learning there, 209; scientific advances there, 243
Getzova, Sophia, 1
Gibraltar, and Morgenthau mission, 4, 200, 219
Ginsburg, C. David, 170
Ginzberg, Asher Z., *see* Ahad Ha'am
Grabovsky, Meir, 275
Granovsky (Granott), Abraham, 217
Great Britain, 86–93, 171, 182, 191, 221; and Balfour Declaration, x, 88, 201–2, 218–21; as Mandatory Power, x, 5, 83, 85, 93, 107, 139, 144–5, 149, 160, 165, 231, 233–4, 239, 242, 253, 254–62; W. naturalized, 3; and Jewish Regiment in wwi, 4, 196; Jewish Commonwealth, 4, 192–200, 231, 240, 242; and partition, 7, 232; its post-war attitude to refugees, 9, 242; East Africa Scheme, 26, 30, 33–5, 204–5, 238; its Jewish intelligentsia, 45, 53–4; Hebrew University, 62–3; Jerusalem, 69–70; Palestine boundaries, 75–6, 226; Anglo-French Convention, 80; and America, 98, 103–5, 225, 228; wwii, 125–6, 130–31, 133–4, 138, 140, 242; and Brand mission, 140–42; Attlee Government, 145–6; Russian immigrants, 196, 200,
217; Sykes–Picot Agreement, 196–7; and Vatican, 199; decline of, 206–7; anti-Zionists in, 208; and *Mein Kampf*, 213; MacDonald White Paper, 223, 227, 230, 241–2, 263–72; and American Commission of 1919, 225; its Labour Party, 230
Greater Actions Committee (GAC), 2, 23, 26, 153, 172, 186, 191, 213, 236, 238
Goering, Hermann, his Magdeburg speech, 123
Gold, Wolf, 275
Goldmann, Nahum, his assessment of W., 182
Goldsmid, Albert, 30
Goodman, Paul, 220
Gort, Viscount (H. C. for Palestine), 161–2
Grady, Henry F., 231
Graham, Sir Ronald, 199–200, 202
Greenberg, Leopold, 35, 218
Grey, Sir Edward, 192–3
Grinblatt, Rosa, 39
Gruenbaum, Isaac, 275

Hacohen, M. Ben-Hillel, 163
Haganah, 9, 67, 143, 145, 174
Hahn-Warburg, Lola, 164
Haifa, Technical College, 3, 65; Conservatoire, 249
Halifax, Lord, 131, 138
Halpern, George, 211
Hansard, 70, 180
Hantke, Arthur, 87
Harding, Warren, 5
Harrison, Earl G., 231
Hatzefirah (Hebrew daily), 162
Hebrew National Library, Jerusalem, 72
Hebrew University, 3–4, 15, 72–3, 108–16, 159, 172, 179, 214–15, 239, 244, 249; site dedicated, 5, 62–5, 110, 216; inauguration of, 6, 66–8, 218; W. refused research facilities there, 6, 114–15; W.'s hon. doctorate, 9, 116; its deficiencies, 111–14; W. appointed Dean, 115; its Executive Council, 116; and Einstein, 160; and Magnes, 164; and Edmond de Rothschild, 167

INDEX

Hebron, Arab attacks, 21, 68
Hedjaz railway, 78–9, 81–3, 197
Hertz, Joseph H., 199
Herut Party, 156
Herzl, Theodor, ix, 1–2, 17, 22, 25–7, 30, 34–5, 38, 86, 150, 161, 166, 175, 178–9, 182, 218, 236, 273; W. assesses, 162; and Third Z. C., 237; and Fourth Z. C., 237; and East Africa Scheme, 204, 238
Hexter, Maurice, 172
Hilfsverein der deutschen Juden, 50
Hill, Sir Clement L., 2, 34–5
Hillel (the Sage), 57
Hitler, Adolf, 6–7, 132, 134, 136, 144, 149, 226–7, 241; Jews' extermination order, 135; his *Mein Kampf*, 212; Stalin pact, 242
Hollywood, 215
Homel pogrom, 38
Hoskins, Harold B., 230
Hull, Cordell, 136
Hull incident (1904), 40
Hungary, and Brand mission, 140–42; Jews' deportation from, 141
Husseini, Hajj Amin al-, 91
Hyamson, Albert M., 199

ICA, *see* Jewish Colonization Association
Immigration, 5, 7, 23, 217; W. heads Jewish Agency Dept., 7; to Palestine, 8–9, 92, 127, 135, 226, 230, 234, 255, 263, 268–9, 274; to America, 117; from Russia (1914), 124; Bermuda Conference, 135–9
Iraq, as Faisal kingdom, 221
Irgun Zvai Leumi, 9, 144–5, 156; and King David Hotel, 146
Israel, 166, 181, 188, 217, 235; and statehood, x–xi, 9; W. as first President, 9–10, 246; and Jerusalem, 70; Proclamation of Independence, 93, 273–5; American support, 107–8, 234; Begin Government, 249
Istanbul, Brand mission, 140–41
Italy, and Palestine boundaries, 76, 227; and Sykes–Picot Agreement, 197; its Catholics, 199

Jabotinsky, Vladimir, 7, 20, 45, 162–3, 178, 195–8, 221, 239; his assessment of W., 183
Jacobson, Edward, 234
Jaffa, riots (1921), 17; Gymnasium, 50; and partition, 69–70; land tenure, 77; W. visits, 207–9
Jarblum, Marc, 158
Jerusalem, 18, 21, 59–74, 76, 219, 230, 234; Holy Places, 15, 59, 68, 72–4, 194, 253, 257, 263, 274; as capital, 59, 227; Wailing Wall, 60–61, 68, 72; defence of, 70–72; partition, 70–74; internationalization, 73–4; its religious life, 15, 18–19, 61–2; Knesset building, 168
Jewish Agency, 5, 21, 24, 56, 72, 90, 119, 123, 141, 143, 148, 156, 158, 171–2, 231; its Executive, x, 171; enlarged Agency, 6, 159, 165, 167, 239–40; its German Refugees Bureau, 7, 241; and MacDonald White Paper, 125–6, 263; Jewish Fighting Force, 133–4; and Bermuda Conference, 135–7; and Jewish terrorism, 9, 146–7; its Political Dept., 169–70; and Léon Blum, 226; and partition, 232
Jewish Chronicle, 221, 225
Jewish Colonial Trust (JCT), 237
Jewish Colonization Association (ICA), 31
Jewish Fighting Force (WWII), 9, 125, 140, 173–4, 224, 228, 242; W. proposes Jewish Division, 8; postponement of, 8; and Eden, 129–31; and British Army, 132–4; its formation, 142
Jewish Labour Committee, 135
Jewish Medical Centre, Jerusalem, 72
Jewish National Fund (JNF), 72, 172
Jewish Regiment, Legion (WWI), 4, 20, 162, 195–7, 221; formation of, 200; and Royal Fusiliers, 201
Jewish Telegraphic Agency, 23
Jewish Territorial Organization, 176
Johnston, Sir Harry, 28–30
Jordan, kingdom of, 232
Jouvenel, Henri de, 226
Joyce, P. C., 16
Jude, Der, 159
Judenstaat, Der, 22, 155, 162

Kahana, Kalman, 275
Kalvarisky, Chaim M., 18
Kaplan, Eliezer, 171, 275
Katznelson, Abraham, 275
Keren Hayesod (KH), 5, 72, 97–8
Kerensky, Alexander, 44, 197
Kerr, Philip, *see* Lothian, Lord
Khatzman, Vera, *see* Weizmann, Vera
King David Hotel, Jerusalem, 146
Kisch, Frederick H., 18, 66
Kishinev pogrom, 2, 25, 37–8; and East Africa Scheme, 204
Kligler, Israel J., 113
Klotz, Henrietta, 105
Knesset, 236
Kobashi, Saadia, 275
Kolodny (Kol), Moshe, 275
Kovno, condition of its Jews, 117
Kuroki, Tamesada, 40

Landman, Samuel, 199
Landsberg, Alfred, 211
Landsberg, Leonie, 162, 211
Lang, Cosmo G. (Archbishop of Canterbury), 7, 70–71, 74
Lansdowne, Lord, 34
Lansing, Robert, 225
Laski, Harold, his assessment of W., 183
Law, Noel, 249
Lawrence, T. E. ('Lawrence of Arabia'), 163, 220, 225; his *Seven Pillars of Wisdom*, 163; his assessment of W., 183
League of Nations, and Mandate for Palestine, 5, 83, 166, 239, 254–62, 273
Lebanon, Mandate for, 226
Legislative Council, 173
Lévi, Sylvain, 163–4
Levin, Isaac Meir, 275
Levin, Shmarya, 167, 184, 191, 193
Lewin-Epstein, Eliahu, 200
Lichtenstein, Abraham, 249
Lindbergh, Charles, 103
Lipsky, Louis, his assessment of W., 183–4
Lister Institute, 4
Litani River, and Palestine boundaries, 78–80

Litvinoff, Barnet, 185
Lloyd, George Ambrose (Lord), 130–31
Lloyd George, David, 16, 80, 192, 194, 196, 201, 224–5; his exchange with W., 184–5; W.'s meetings with, 4, 94, 193, 195, 198, 200–1; Zionism connection, 218–20
Locker, Berl, 157, 171
Loewenstein, Meir D., 275
London, W. visits, 1, 205; makes his home there, 4, 219
London University Zionist Society, 47
Lothian, Lord (Philip Kerr), 127–9, 201
Lourie, Arthur, 214
Luria, Zvi, 275
Lvov, Prince Georgi, 42–3, 197

MacArthur, Douglas, 107
Maccabean, 196
MacDonald Letter, 6
MacDonald, Malcolm, 126, 128, 133–4; relations with W., 185
MacDonald, Ramsay, 6, 21, 269
MacDonald White Paper (1939), x, 7–8, 91, 125, 128, 134, 139–40, 142, 144, 164, 222–4, 227–8, 263–72; and terrorism, 148–9
McMahon, Sir Henry, and pledge to Arabs, 197, 266
MacMichael, Sir Harold (H.C. of Palestine), 91, 144, 164
Magnes, Judah L., 6, 46, 110, 113, 115–16, 189, 193; W. assesses, 164–5
Malcolm, James, 196
Manchester, W. settles there, 2; its University, 2–4, 184, 192, 207, 243–4; its Zionist Association, 2; and election campaign, 3, 217, 222–3; on May Day, 205–6
Manchester Guardian, 4, 184, 192, 195, 219
Marks, Sir Simon, 158, 172, 192, 199; Daniel Sieff Research Institute, 244–5
Marshall, George C., 106
Marshall, James, 22
Marshall, Louis, 5, 99, 118, 240; W. assesses, 165
Massada, 147
Matin, Le, 220
Mauritius, refugees sent to, 145

INDEX

May, Doris, 171
Meinertzhagen, Richard, 186
Melchett, Lord, *see* Mond, Sir Alfred
Menorah Journal, 54, 111
Metcalfe, Sir Charles, 79
Millin, Sarah Gertrude, 160, 187
Ministry of Munitions, 4, 195, 219
Ministry of Supply, 8, 245
Minsk, Conference there, 2; Social Democrats arrested, 38
Mizrachi Party, 28, 120, 135, 150, 152–3
Mond, Sir Alfred, 65, 98, 240
Montagu, Edwin, 200–2
Montefiore, Claude C., 199
Morgenthau, Jr, Henry, 105, 165–6, 229, 231
Morgenthau, Sr, Henry, 4, 94–5, 165, 194, 200, 219
Morning Post, 117
Morrison–Grady Plan, 231
Mossinson, Ben-Zion, 50
Motol, W.'s birthplace, 1, 203
Motzkin, Leo, 174
Moyne, Lord (Walter E. Guiness), 104, 133; assassination, 9, 145, 165, 224
Mufti of Jerusalem, *see* Husseini, Hajj Amin al-
Munich, Zionist youth conference, 1
Munitions of War Committee, 184
Mussolini, Benito, W.'s meetings with, 5, 227
Myerson (Meir), Golda, 275

Namier, Lewis, 156–7, 170, 173
Nation, The, 89
Nebi Moussa festival, 65
Negev, and partition, 232–3, 235
New Judaea, 174
New Palestine, 115, 155
New York Herald Tribune Forum, 58
New York Times, 221
New Zionist Organization, *see* Revisionist Party
Nicholas II, Tzar, 36–7, 42
Niles, David, 232
Nir, Nachum, 275
Nobel's Explosives Company, 4, 194
Nordau, Max, 150, 166, 175, 186

Odessa, revolutionary activity there, 41

Oppenheimer, Franz, 28
Ormsby-Gore, William, 61, 70, 94, 168
Oxford University, 206–7, 214

Palestine, x, 168–9, 171–3, 183, 185, 209, 221; W. visits, 3, 142–3, 207–10, 214–16; Jewish Commonwealth, 4, 8, 22, 192–4, 199, 222, 225, 227–31; and Mandate, 5, 22–3, 218–19, 239, 241–2, 254–62; its Administration, 6, 89–92, 105, 135, 144–6, 149, 170, 186, 211–12, 271; Arab attacks, 6–7, 68–9, 149, 240; partition, 7, 69, 86, 220, 227, 232–3, 241; immigration, 8, 92, 125, 127, 135, 137–40, 144–6, 149, 166, 231, 241–2, 268–71; W.'s 70th birthday, 9; statehood, 9; Hebrew language, 50–51, 64; its achievements, 54–6; its boundaries, 74–86, 226; pioneers there, 121–2, 239–40; WWII, 125, 130–31, 134, 216, 273–4; mobilization of Jews, 132, 134, 138; its Jewish population, 143; Jewish terrorism, 143–9, 224, 230–31, 242; Jewish Resistance Movement, 145–6, 242; and Orthodox Jewry, 151–2; religious politics, 153–4; Council of Ten, 163; Edmond de Rothschild's contribution, 166–8; WWI, 192–3; Sykes–Picot Agreement, 197, 219; and Vatican, 199; lack of Jewish intelligentsia, 214–15; and Smuts, 221; and Churchill, 224; and Wilson, 225–6; American Commission, 225; and France, 226–7; and Ibn Saud, 230; and Truman, 230–35; trusteeship, 233–4; Arab invasion of, 234; MacDonald White Paper, 263–72
Palestine, 196–7
Palestine Fund for German Jewry, 220
Palestine Gazette, 135
Paris, ss., 210–11
Paris Peace Conference, 17, 165, 220, 225; and Council of Ten, 5; boundary proposals, 77–8, 81
Passfield White Paper (1930), 6, 99, 221
Pasteur Institute, 3, 243
Patria, ss, 145
Peel Commission, *see* Royal Commission on Palestine

INDEX

Percy, Earl (Henry), 2, 34–5, 205
Perkin, William H., 40, 243
Permanent Mandates Commission, 139, 227, 269
Petach Tikvah, Arab labourers there, 11; W. visits, 207–8
Petrograd, All-Russian Zionist Conference there, 200; *see also* St Petersburg
Philby, Harry St John, 8, 229–30
Picot, *see* Georges-Picot, François
Pinkas, David Zvi, 275
Pinsk, conditions there, 39, 205; W.'s family there, 1
Placzek, physicist, 214
Plehve, Vyacheslav von, 26–7
Plumer, Herbert, Viscount (H.C. of Palestine), 90
Poalei-Zion Party, 33, 135
Poland, its Jews, 116, 124; emigrants to Palestine, 240
Political Committee, London, 201
Ponsonby, Charles E., 129

Rafah land tenure, 77
Ramadier, Paul, 227
Reclus, Elisée, 28–30
Refugees, 117–18, 123–5, 140, 144, 146, 222, 226, 230–31, 270–71, 273; Bermuda Conference, 135–8; Brand mission, 140–42
Rehovot, W.'s first visit, 207–8
Remez, David, 275
Repetur, Berl, 275
Revisionist Party, 7, 120, 163, 239, 241
Rishon-le-Zion, 207–8
Robinson, Robert, 243
Rokach, Israel, 148
Rome, W. visits, 59
Roosevelt, Franklin D., 102–3, 105–7, 137, 161, 166, 175, 224, 227, 230, 232; W.'s meetings with, 8, 127–9, 228–9; Jewish Commonwealth, 228; and MacDonald White Paper, 229; his statement on Ibn Saud, 229
Rosebery, Lord, 30
Rosenblueth (Rosen), Felix, 275
Rosenman, Samuel, 100, 104–6, 232, 234
Rosov, Israel, 45, 202

Rothschild, Dorothy de, 193
Rothschild, Baron Edmond de, 6, 19, 109, 164, 178, 193, 195, 202; W.'s meetings with, 4, 193; and Zionist Left, 119–22; W. assesses, 166–7; his contribution to Palestine, 166–8; and enlarged Jewish Agency, 240
Rothschild, James de, 49, 167–8, 178, 192–3, 197
Rothschild, (Lionel Walter), Lord, 78, 197, 199–200, 202, 251
Rothschild, Louis de, 125
Royal Asiatic Society, 30
Royal Commission on Palestine (1936), 7, 69, 71, 90–92, 123–5, 129, 152, 220, 222–3, 241, 263–4, 269
Royal Institute of International Affairs, 177
Royal Society, 3, 87, 244
Ruppin, Arthur, 186
Russia, and separate peace, 4, 201; Zionists there, 33, 43–4, 197, 202, 237–8; war against Japan, 36; the Duma, 42; condition of Jews there, 33, 36, 46, 51–2, 109, 118–19; and Bolshevism, 117, 223; and Crimean Scheme, 118, 240, 249; and Brand mission, 140; WWI, 194, 200; and Sykes–Picot Agreement, 197; and Palestine, 194, 198, 200, 232–3; Pale of Settlement, 203
Russian-Jewish Academic Society, 1
Russian Revolution (1905), 36–42
Russian Revolution (1917), 42–5, 197
Russian Zionist Organization, 78
Rutenberg, Pinhas, 65, 99
Rutherford, Ernest, 243

Sacher, Harry, 3, 94, 192, 195–6, 199, 240; his assessment of W., 186–7; and Daniel Sieff Research Institute, 244–5
Sadat, Anwar, 156
Safed, and Arab attacks, 21, 68
Said, Nuri es-, 7
St James's Conference (1939), 7, 153
St Petersburg, and disorders there, 36, 39; *see also* Petrograd
Samuel, Herbert (H. C. of Palestine), x, 4–5, 76, 81, 90, 96, 159, 161, 192–7, 200, 211, 219, 239–40; W.'s exchange

with, 168–9
San Remo Conference (1920), 5, 218–19, 226
Saud, King Ibn, 8, 224, 229–30; Saudi Arabia, 229
Savitzky, Vassily, 249
Scientific activities of W., 4, 6, 8, 115, 185, 187, 194–6, 219, 228, 243–6
Schiff, Jacob, 94
Schocken, S. Salman, 115–16
Schuster, Arthur, 243
Scott, C. P., 4, 45, 184, 192, 194–6, 198, 201, 219
Second Aliyah, 153
Segal, Zvi, 275
Shapira, Moshe, 275
Shattner, Mordechai, 275
Shaw, Sir Walter, and Commission on Palestine Disturbances (1929), 68
Shereef of Mecca, 197, 220, 266
Shertok (*later* Sharett), Moshe, 8, 131, 170, 173, 275; Brand mission, 141–2
Shitreet, Bechor, 275
Shuckburgh, Sir John, 98, 118
Sieff, Israel M., 6, 107, 173, 192, 199; his assessment of W., 187; Daniel Sieff Research Institute, 244–5
Silver, Abba Hillel, 9, 145, 148, 187, 229, 232, 234, 242; W. assesses, 170–71
Simon, Leon, 3, 116, 192, 197, 199
Sinclair, Sir Archibald, 166
Smaller Actions Committee (SAC), *see* Zionist Executive
Smuts, Jan C., 10, 139–40, 145, 187; and Palestine, 221–2
Sneh, Moshe, 149
Sokolow, Nahum, 5–6, 42, 76–8, 89, 95, 163, 172, 184, 186, 193–5, 197–8, 200–1, 211, 241; W. assesses, 171
Soskin, Evgeny (Selig), 28
South Africa, W.'s fund-raising mission, 6, 221; and refugees, 222
Stalin, Joseph, 142, 217; Hitler pact, 242
Stern Group, 9, 144–6
Sternberg, Ben Zion, 175
Storrs, Sir Ronald, 15
Straus, Isaac, 192
Struma, ss, 91–2, 145

Supreme Allied Council, *see* Council of Ten
Sykes, Sir Mark, 4, 161–2, 196–8
Sykes–Picot Agreement, 74, 78, 196–8, 219
Synagogue Council of America, 135
Syria, and Palestine boundaries, 76–7; and France, 194, 209, 226; Faisal as king, 221; American Commission, 225

Tel Aviv, as capital, 227; new immigrants there, 240
Theodoli, Count, 227
Times, The, 199; and *Mein Kampf*, 212–13
Tobruk, fall of, 105
Togo, Heihachiro, 40
Torczyner, Numa, 170
Toscanini, Arturo, 215
Transjordan, 209, 223; and Old City of Jerusalem, 70; and Palestine boundaries, 81–5; and League of Nations Note, 261–2
Trial and Error, 226–7; publication of, 7, 10
Truman, Harry S., 74, 93, 107–8, 146, 154, 230; W.'s meetings with, 9, 231–2, 234; Morrison–Grady Plan, 231; partition, 232–4; trusteeship, 234; his *Years of Trial and Hope*, 234; recognition of Israel, 234; letter to W., 235
Trumpeldor, Joseph, 194–6
Tschlenow, Yehiel, 167, 193–5, 198, 200, 202
Tulin, Abraham, 52
Turkey, and Ottoman Empire, 214–15, 225, 138–9; WWI, 4, 74, 94, 163, 191–2, 194, 209, 220; a separate peace, 4, 165, 198, 200, 219; W.'s mission, 7; Arabs and Jews there, 11–13

United Nations, 24, 59, 107, 221, 227, 232, 235, 242, 274; partition, 9, 70, 74, 140, 233; and Bermuda Conference, 136; its Political Committee, 171; trusteeship, 233–4
United Nations Ad Hoc Committee, 9
United Nations Special Committee on Palestine (UNSCOP), 9, 86, 116, 149,

INDEX

222, 232–3
Ussishkin, Menahem, 2, 28, 30–31, 161, 166, 171–2, 175, 184, 238–9; and partition, 241

Va'ad Leumi, 135
Vardi, Herzl, 275
Vatican, 59, 198–9
Vienna Zionist Conference (1904), 35
Vilna, condition of its Jews, 117

Wagner, Cosima, 218
Waheida, Arab H.Q., 5, 16, 209, 220
Wahrhaftig, Zerach, 275
Wallace, Henry A., 100–1, 187, 228
War Refugee Board, 166
Warburg, Felix M., 99, 115, 159–60, 164, 167, 172, 174
Warburg, Max, 172–3
Warburg, Otto, 28, 239
Washington, W.'s activities there, 8
Wauchope, Sir Arthur (H.C. of Palestine), 173, 187–8
Wavell, Gen. Archibald, 130, 173
Webster, Sir Charles, 188
Weicman, Zelig, 249
Weigener, chemist, 214
Weisgal, Meyer W., 59; and W.'s defeat at Seventeenth Z.C., 188–9
Weizman, Ezer, 249
Weizmann, Anna, 249
Weizmann (*formerly* Rubin), Bazia, 249
Weizmann, Benjamin, 3, 151, 249
Weizmann, David, 249
Weizmann (*formerly* Lubzhinsky), Fanya, 249
Weizmann, Feivel, 249
Weizmann (*later* Weicman), Fruma 249
Weizmann (*later* Dounie), Gita, 249
Weizmann (*later* Lichtenstein), Haya, 249
Weizmann (*formerly* Pomeranz), Maidie, 249
Weizmann (*formerly* Gains), Maisie, 249
Weizmann (*later* Savitzky), Masha, 249
Weizmann, Michael, 4; missing on RAF mission, 8, 224, 249
Weizmann, Mikhail (Yehiel), 249
Weizmann (*later* Law), Minna, 249
Weizmann (*later* Lubzhinsky), Miriam (Mariya), 249
Weizmann, Moses, 249
Weizmann, Ozer, 1, 204, 249
Weizmann, Rachel-Leah, 1, 249
Weizmann, Samuel, 249
Weizmann (*formerly* Khatzman), Vera, 1, 3, 12, 34–6, 39–42, 45, 60, 62, 89, 95, 109, 166–7, 169, 175, 186, 205–6, 208, 210; her marriage, 249
Weizmann (*formerly* Krishevsky), Yehudit, 249
Weizmann (*formerly* Rivlin), Zinaida, 249
Weizmann Forest, 10, 222
Weizmann Institute of Science, xi, 245; inaugurated, 10
Welles, Sumner, 107, 229; his assessment of W., 189
Weltsch, Robert, 98–9, 189
Weyl, Hermann, 214
Wheeler, Burton K., 103
Whitechapel, W. there, 204–5
Willstaetter, Richard, 245
Wilner-Kovner, Meir, 275
Wilson, Woodrow, 16, 95, 174, 199, 201–2, 225–6; meets W., 5
Wingate, Orde, 173–4
Wise, Stephen, 6–7, 135, 147, 224–5, 227, 229; W. assesses, 174; on Twenty-Second Z.C., 190; and Nineteenth Z.C., 241
Wolffsohn, David, 3, 165, 175, 238
World Jewish Congress, 135
World War One, 4, 59–60, 62, 188, 191
World War Two, 7, 69, 92, 125–43, 245, 249, 273–4; and America, 103–6; Jews' extermination order, 135, 140, 144
World Zionist Organization, ix–x, 2–4, 7, 19, 21, 27, 34, 169, 176, 182, 186, 224, 274; W. elected President, 5; W. rejected as President, 6, 9; its first post-war conference, 9, 239; East Africa Scheme, 35; statement to Peace Conference, 78; economic survey, 79; Hebrew University, 109; Revisionists, 163; its Copenhagen Bureau, 191, 194–5; and Congresses, 236, 239–40; its World Conference (1945), 242; and Faisal–W. Agreement, 252–3;

INDEX

and Mandate, 255; *see also* Zionist Executive
Wormser, Gaston, 19

Yalta Conference (1945), 224, 229
Yarmuk River, 82, 262
Yishuv, 148, 157, 170–71

Zagheb, Michel de, 76
Zangwill, Israel, 33, 35–6, 191, 238; W. assesses, 175–6
Zhitomir pogrom, 40
Zichron Ya'acov, and Arab labourers there, 11
Zimmern, Alfred, 207
Zion Mule Corps, 194–6, 198
Zionist Advisory Committee, 17
Zionist Commission in Palestine, 5, 59, 94–5, 164, 167, 225, 253; transformed into Zionist Executive branch, 239
Zionist Congresses, *listed and described*, 236–42
Zionist Executive, 5, 49, 87, 161, 168, 191, 193–4, 211, 236, 239–40; *see also* World Zionist Organization
Zionist General Council, *see* Greater Actions Committee
Zionist Organization, *see* World Zionist Organization
Zionist Organization of America (ZOA), 94, 97, 99, 102, 171; and Cleveland Conference, 5
Zionist Review, 44
Zisling, Aharon, 275
Zoppot, W.'s marriage there, 3
Zurich, and academic refugees there, 214